I0649923

Making Peace with Money

OTHER BOOKS ON MONEY
BY JERROLD MUNDIS

How to Get Out of Debt,
Stay Out of Debt & Live Prosperously

Earn What You Deserve

Making Peace with Money

Jerrold Mundis

**Andrews McMeel
Publishing**

Kansas City

www.andrewsmcmeel.com

99 00 01 02 03 RDC 10 9 8 7 6 5 4 3 2 1

Library of Congress Cataloging-in-Publication Data
Mundis, Jerrold J.
    Making peace with money / Jerold Mundis.
        p.   cm.
    Includes bibliographical references.
    ISBN 0-7407-0040-5 (hardcover)
    1. Finance, Personal.   2. Finance, Personal—Religious aspects.   I. Title.
HG179.M857   1999
332.024—dc21   99–18925
                                                    CIP

Dedication

Every student is someone's teacher;
every teacher is someone's student.

May all of them—us—know a new
freedom and a new happiness.

My thanks are due to people too numerous to name,
some of whom know who they are, others of whom I
encountered only glancingly, but each of whom has my
gratitude and love. I am especially conscious of the
generosity of Karen DeMauro, a storyteller and
careful tender of the heart-donkey—hers and others.

Contents

Making Peace *with* Money

Introduction

....

This is a book about making peace with money—no matter from where you begin. You may be rich, poor, overwhelmed by debt, or looking for a tax shelter; you may be practicing an art, trapped in a job you hate, overworking, or sunk in procrastination. If you are uncomfortable in *any* way with money—with how you feel about it, what you do or don't do with it, or the role it plays in your consciousness and daily life—this is almost certainly a book for you.

I began the process of making peace with money myself from a point of debt, pain, and despair over it. That was fifteen years ago. Today I am at peace with money.

I have written two earlier books on personal money: *How to Get Out of Debt, Stay Out of Debt & Live Prosperously* and *Earn What You Deserve: How to Stop Underearning & Start Thriving*. In them, I shared my own experience and that of many others in doing just what the titles said, and taught readers how they could do the same.

Here in *Making Peace with Money* I offer a program through which *anyone* can do just what this title says, make peace with money. What does it mean to make peace with money? It means to create a relationship with money that is simple, comfortable, and free of stress, worry, or pain; to create a relationship with money that is satisfying, even joyful.

Do you have that kind of relationship with money? Do you know many people who do? I did not, and I knew hardly anyone else who did either. Not many people do, across the entire spectrum of possible finances, from the wealthy to the hard-pressed, and irrespective of where they stand on the social scale.

But you can, if you would like. *You can no matter who you are.* You can regardless of your history with money, regardless of your current situation. There is no one who cannot make peace with money: no one.

This book will teach you how.

Does that mean, then, that everyone who reads this book will, therefore, come to have a peaceful relationship with money? No, they won't. Because while making peace with money is a simple process, it does require effort, and not everyone is willing to make that effort.

But the rewards, if you are willing, are tremendous. How much would you be willing to pay for the ability to live at peace with money for the rest of your life? You can do that. I promise you. The program in this book works. I have lived its principles and techniques; I continue to live them on a daily basis.

I have drawn and created the practices here from my own life and the lives of a great number of others from every kind of background and circumstances imaginable. Over the past decade and a half, I have worked closely with a few hundred of these people, briefly with thousands more in seminars and workshops I have led across the country for institutions as diverse as the United States Customs Service, the U.S. Tobacco Company, Unity Church, and Alabama's Governor's Conference on Addiction and Recovery.

Making Peace with Money has two elements: practices to undertake and insights into the nature of money. The latter are in the form of tales, quotations, and parables. Each part is important. Each complements and strengthens the other. Together, they form the whole of the program.

Undertaking the practices will bring immediate positive financial change into your life and begin to relieve the troubling or difficult emotions you might have about money. Contemplating, considering, reflecting upon the insights will—sometimes quickly, sometimes slowly—revolutionize the way you think and feel about money and about yourself in relationship to it.

I suggest you begin with chapter 1, "Debt," even if the subject of another seems of more immediate appeal, and then take each chapter in order. The tales, parables, and quotations will serve you for a very long time. They can be a reservoir to which you can return again and again. The best way to work with them over an extended period, to extract their greatest value, is to read one or two of them in the morning, then carry it or them around in your mind for the day, pausing now and then to bring them into your consciousness and reflect on them for a minute or two.

Finally, I would ask you to approach this program with an open mind, as free of bias and preconception as you can. Work it gently, but do work it: Undertake the practices, reflect upon the insights.

You can and *will* make peace with money. This program works. I give you my word on that.

May you be physically happy. May you be mentally happy. May you live joyfully and with ease of well-being.

DEBT

One

Debt

......

"There can be no freedom or beauty about a home life that depends on borrowing and debt."

Henrik Ibsen wrote those words in his play *A Doll's House*.

They were true for me. I think they are true for everyone. I have never seen anyone for whom they weren't. There certainly was no freedom or beauty in my life sixteen years ago, as I was still sinking ever deeper into debt or getting money in, paying off big pieces of what I owed, only to begin borrowing again soon after, or holding off paying bills till the last possible moment (and beyond). What there was then was a lot pain, fear, anger, frustration, and despair.

To some degree or another, nearly everyone who is falling steadily deeper into debt, or just managing to keep the creditors at bay, experiences emotions like these. This first chapter, therefore, has to do with freeing yourself from borrowing and debt. Doing that is the very foundation of making peace with money.

The how, in a nutshell, is simple:

**Do not incur
any new unsecured debt.**

The doing isn't always easy, especially in the beginning.

But it *can* be done, and it can be done by you. Hundreds of thousands of people from every kind of background imaginable are doing it right now and have been for years. In ceasing to incur new unsecured debt, one day at a time, you will become wholly self-supporting through your own contributions. This is tremendously liberating. It produces self-esteem, freedom, joy; it gives you a sense of self-sufficiency, of potency.

Note that we're differentiating between *secured* and *unsecured* debt. For our purposes, the former is often reasonable; the latter is almost always not.

With a *secured* loan, such as mortgage or automobile loan, for example, if for any reason you are unable to repay it, you forfeit your security: lose your house, car, or the camera you've given to the lender to hold during the course of the loan. That may be painful, but you walk away clean. You don't owe anyone money. *You are not in debt.* That is not true with *unsecured* debt. You owe the money no matter what happens, and therefore become vulnerable to harassment by creditors and collection agents—to court judgments, seizure of bank accounts, income garnishment, liens against your property, and other painful and unpleasant possibilities.

Far from being an asset, credit in this form (more accurately, unsecured debt) is for millions of people actually a form of poverty, and one of the cruelest. Unsecured debt gives us the *illusion* of having more money. When we use credit cards, department-store charge accounts, overdraft checking privileges, when we let a bill go unpaid or take a salary advance from an employer or a loan from a friend, we *think* we have more money than we actually do, we *think* we're bringing in more of it than we actually are.

So as long as you consider using some form of unsecured debt to be a valid option for meeting your needs, it is unlikely that you will ever truly be able to make peace with money. For the majority of us, going into new unsecured debt is incompatible with working this program successfully.

That isn't true for everyone, of course. If you have never had any trouble with debt or have never felt under pressure from owing money, then it isn't necessary for you to refrain from paying for dinner with a credit card, putting a television set on your department store account, or borrowing $1,000 in cash if you want to succeed in making peace with money. It is desirable, but not necessary. But please don't try to hide from yourself here. For most of us, not incurring any new unsecured debt is essential to making peace with money.

Practice:

In Full

The way I and others like me stay out of debt is to pay in full for everything we buy *when* we buy it, for every service we receive *when* we receive it. This isn't as difficult as it might sound, once you get over the initial shock you may feel. (I'm not saying it will always be easy. It won't. But it can always be done.) You will find few acts as consistently gratifying and pleasurable as you will eventually find this one to be.

Here is the threshold:

> **Just for today, one day at a time,**
> **do not incur any new unsecured debt.**

We're only talking about one day—today. Tomorrow is irrelevant. What you might do tomorrow, next week, next month, next year doesn't matter. They're not here yet. All that is real, ever, is today. And today, one day at a time, you're not going to incur any new debt. (Whenever we use the word debt, we mean unsecured debt, unless otherwise indicated.)

Anyone can avoid debt for a single day. Today, right now, you have everything you need: You have a roof over your head, food to eat, and clothes to wear. There is no reason for you to incur debt before this day ends. You can choose to, but you don't have to.

Here is a simple truth:

> ## You cannot make peace with money by repeatedly borrowing it.
>
> You just can't. It's that simple. Here are a couple of strategies that will help you in this practice:
>
> First, credit cards. There is only one thing you can do with a credit card: go into debt. That's a simple fact, yet few people are willing to face it at first, even among people who have clearly brutalized themselves with credit cards. Therefore—right—take all your plastic, and cut it up. If you don't have the cards, you can't use them. Then notify the supplier that you wish to cancel the account. If you feel you absolutely *must* have a credit card—for business travel, for example—or are rock-sure of your personal discipline, do this: Retain only one card, carry it only on days in which there is a valid reason to use the card, and if you do use it, write out a check that same day in the amount you charged, deduct that amount from your balance, and then ideally send the check out in the mail within twenty-four hours. If you don't have enough money in your account to do this, then don't use the card.
>
> Another helpful strategy is to keep a Spending Record. A Spending Record is *not* a budget, but simply a record of the money you actually *do* spend. Keeping a Spending Record helps you see clearly—perhaps for the first time—where your money is really going, which is an important step in taking control of it. Write down every expenditure, from 75¢ for a pack of gum to $75 for a sweater. At the

end of each week, total up your expenses (including checks you wrote) and enter them into a one-month record, breaking them into categories, such as clothes, entertainment, newspapers, groceries, and the like. Keep in mind that there are only two ways to avoid debt when expenses exceed income: Cut expenses or bring in more money. In the early stages, most people use a combination of these two. Later on, they emphasize the latter.

Finally, write out a list of ways you can avoid debt. Let your imagination run free. Be as wild and improbable as you can. Hurdle old mental barricades, break out into the open. Put down two kinds of ideas: ways you can trim expenses and ways you can bring in extra income. Some of your ideas will be more desirable than others, and not all will be feasible. That's fine—the point is to get down as many as possible.

Practice:

Emancipate Yourself

To emancipate is to set free, to liberate—in this case, to set yourself free, to liberate yourself, from the slavery of unsecured debt. And a form of slavery it certainly is. Anyone who has ever been in debt for any length of time knows that the constant presence of indebtedness in one's mind is like a kind of psychic set of manacles or leg irons. Obviously, you won't be able to pay off all your debts overnight or by end of the month or even, probably, by the end of the year; in fact, doing that may require a good deal of time. In my own case, it took *eleven years* to pay off one particular debt. (I liquidated others much earlier.)

Everyone's circumstances are different. Some people pay off the few thousand dollars they owe, or tens or even hundreds of thousands of dollars, in just a year or two or so, while others spend a decade or more doing it. But whatever the particular situation, the relief begins for everyone when the downward spiral stops and the emancipation process begins.

Liquidating your unsecured debt just also happens, in many cases, to be one of the most profitable investments you will probably ever be able to make. In practical effect, the impact on your life—the cash benefit you will reap—will be the same as if you had *invested* that money, forever, at a guaranteed, tax-free rate of 16 to 20 percent per year (the interest payments you will no longer have to make). And, ah, my foes, and oh, my friends, there isn't a banker alive who wouldn't be thrilled to get that kind of return on his money. As would I. As would you. And it's yours simply by paying off your unsecured debt.

In despair over their debts, some people turn right away to the idea of bankruptcy. But bankruptcy is usually a bad idea: It does nothing to change the beliefs and behavior that caused the debt in the first place; it often leads to a sense of shame and failure, which only intensifies trouble with money; and it plagues your credit record for ten years (even longer in some cases, such as when applying for a mortgage or for a job paying more than $50,000 a year.) Most people who try to solve a debting problem* through bankruptcy end up in the same kind of trouble again, and usually sooner than later. A home equity loan isn't a much better idea, for basically the same reasons, with the additional one that it strips away what equity you might have built up in your house and at the same time places your house in jeopardy; if your combined first and second mortgage payments, along with payment demands of renewed debting, which will almost certainly occur, become too much for you to meet, your house could be forfeit.

How, then, do we go about emancipating ourselves, if we're seriously in debt, without bankruptcy or a home equity loan?†

The amount you can *reasonably* begin to repay each month will almost always be less than you would like it to be. This is true for most people who have been in debt for a while. In fact, some don't make any repayments at all for the first few months. The primary need is to stabilize—to make sure expenses do not exceed income, that new debt does not occur.

---

* "Debt" is a noun. It has never been used as a verb—"to debt." But I coined it that way more than a decade ago in my early writing on this subject; it helps to distinguish such use of money from other types of spending and from secured loans.

† If you have a long history of carrying unsecured debt, are under truly severe pressure from your debts, or have tried before to get yourself out and failed, you might well want to work with my book *How to Get Out of Debt, Stay Out of Debt & Live Prosperously*. It contains a comprehensive program that will guide you step by step through all phases of recovery from debt and indebtedness.

An important element in creating a successful repayment plan is to assign repayment amounts to your creditors on a proportional basis. For example, if you have only $50 a month for repayment, and you owe Creditor A $1,000, Creditor B $500, and Creditors C and D $250 each, then pay Creditor A $25 a month, Creditor B $12.50, and Creditors C and D $6.25 each. Knowing that others are not being favored above them often helps a creditor become more agreeable to your repayment plan.

"But those are chicken-feed numbers," you might say. "I'm seventy-five thousand dollars in debt!"

Some people owe more than you do, some less. The numbers don't matter: The principle remains the same.

"It'll take forever to pay off sixty-four hundred dollars at fifty dollars a month!"

It only seems that way. Payments nearly always start small. They increase as time passes, as you truly begin to make peace with money. The repayment process builds on itself; in the end, it is often rapid and dramatic. At one point, in the very beginning of my own recovery from debt and debting, I was able to pay only $6.17 a month principal against a $17,500 loan; in the end I was paying $800 a month.

What matters, in the beginning, is that we have completely reversed our situation. We are now getting *out* of debt instead of *into* debt. That is a stunning achievement.

In dealing with creditors, take the initiative rather than waiting for them to come to you. Prepare before you make the contact; have all the facts and figures at hand. Explain your situation forthrightly. Tell your creditor you regret this situation, that you are determined to correct it, and that you are committed to repaying him or her in full. Negotiate according to the realities of your spending and repayment plans. Remember, they are real. You cannot repay more than you are capable of repaying; and you know what that figure is.

It helps to write out a loose script for yourself before getting in touch with a creditor. This ensures that you will have all the information you need ready. It also increases your confidence and sense that you really do know what you're doing here.

If, during the course of your repayment, you run into serious, unavoidable trouble—the loss of a job, hurricane damage to your home—and *must* cut down or even suspend your debt repayments, don't simply do so, cross your fingers, and hope for the best. Get in touch with your creditors immediately. Explain the situation clearly and honestly. Most will be willing, and some perhaps even happy, to help you over this rough spot. But if you simply duck and run, and wait for them to come hunting for you, you will only cause them to be frustrated, angry, and less willing even to think about accommodating you. Understandably: If the situation were reversed, you'd feel the same way.

Congratulations. This is a brave and wonderful thing you're doing, getting free of debt. It isn't always easy. In fact, sometimes it can be downright scary, even painful. But it is wonderfully liberating. And you *can* and *will* do it. Hundreds of thousands of people, perhaps even millions by now, have already done so, many starting in situations identical to your own, and many more are doing so at this very moment.

Welcome to your new freedom.

To have just finished repaying all one's debts. Ah, is this not happiness?

—CHIN SHENGT'AN

A man once said to the Master, "Because I failed to pay my bills again, my creditors came to my room and beat me up and threw me out of the window. What would you advise me to do?"

The Master looked straight through the man and said, "If I were you, from now on I would live on the ground floor."

This startled the Master's disciples. "Why didn't you tell him to stop getting into debt?" they demanded.

"Because I knew he wouldn't," was the Master's simple and sagacious explanation.

—AFTER ANTHONY DE MELLO

Each day a bird would shelter in the withered branches of a tree that stood in the middle of a vast deserted plain.

One day a whirlwind uprooted the tree, forcing the poor bird to fly a hundred miles in search of shelter—till finally it came to a forest of fruit-laden trees.

—BUDDHIST

Be not made a beggar by banqueting upon borrowing.

—ECCLESIASTICUS

Things do not change; we change.

—HENRY DAVID THOREAU

Borrowers are nearly always ill-spenders.

—JOHN RUSKIN

Despair is often the first step on the path of spiritual life and many people do not awaken to the Reality of God and the experience of transformation in their lives till they go through the experience of emptiness, disillusion, and despair.

—BEDE GRIFFITHS

Run not into debt, either for wares sold, or money borrowed; be content to want things that are not of absolute necessity, rather than to run up the score: such a man pays, at the latter end, a third part more than the principal, and is in perpetual servitude to his creditors; lives uncomfortably; is necessitated to increase his debts to stop his creditors' mouths; and many times falls into desperate courses.

—MATTHEW HALE

If you want the time to pass quickly, just give your note for ninety days.

—R. B. THOMAS

Whose bread I eat, his song I sing.

—GERMAN

Too many people spend money they haven't earned, to buy things they don't want, to impress people they don't like.

—WILL ROGERS

Debt is to a man what the serpent is to the bird; its eye fascinates, its breath poisons, its coil crushes sinew and bone, its jaw is the pitiless grave.

—EDWARD GEORGE BULWER-LYTTON

Forgetting a debt does not pay it.

—IRISH

The man of virtue makes the difficulty to be overcome his first business, and success only a subsequent consideration.

—CONFUCIUS

It is very evident what mean and sneaking lives many of you live, for my sight has been whetted by experience; always on the limits, trying to get into business and trying to get out of debt, a very ancient slough, called by the Latins *aes alienum*, another's brass, for some of their coins were made of brass; still living, and dying, and buried by this other's brass; always promising to pay, promising to pay, to-morrow, and dying to-day, insolvent; seeking to curry favor, to get custom, by how many modes.

—HENRY DAVID THOREAU

It is better to pay a creditor than to give to a friend.

—ARISTOTLE

Do not accustom yourself to consider debt only as an inconvenience; you will find it a calamity.

—SAMUEL JOHNSON

Pride does not like to owe, and self-love does not like to pay.

—FRANÇOIS LA ROCHEFOUCAULD

> As, pent in an aquarium, the troutlet
> Swims round and round his tank to find an outlet,
> Pressing his nose against the glass that holds him;
> So the poor debtor, seeing naught around him,
> Yet feels the limits pitiless that bound him;
> Grieves at his debt and studies to evade it,
> And finds at last he might as well have paid it.

—AMBROSE BIERCE

A creditor is worse than a master; for where a master owns only your person, a creditor owns your dignity, and can belabor that.

—VICTOR HUGO

He that hath an hundred and one, and owes an hundred and two, the Lord have mercy on him.

—THOMAS FULLER

Debt is a preceptor whose lessons are needed most by those who suffer from it most.

—RALPH WALDO EMERSON

December 24, 1848

Dear Johnston:

Your request for eighty dollars, I do not think it best to comply with now. At the various times when I have helped you a little, you have said to me, "We can get along very well now," but in a very short time I find you in the same difficulty again. Now this can only happen by some defect in your conduct. What that defect is, I think I know. You are not lazy, and still you are an idler. I doubt whether since I saw you, you have done a good whole day's work, in any one day. You do not very much dislike to work, and still you do not work much, merely because it does not seem to you that you could get much for it.

This habit of uselessly wasting time, is the whole difficulty; it is vastly important to you, and still more so to your children, that you should break this habit. It is more important to them, because they have longer to live, and can keep out of an idle habit before they are in it, easier than they can get out after they are in.

You are now in need of some ready money; and what I propose is, that you shall go to work, "tooth and nail," for somebody who will give you money for it.

Let father and your boys take charge of your things at home—prepare for a crop, and make the crop, and you go to work for the best money wages, or in discharge of any debt you owe, that you can get. And to secure you a fair reward for your labor, I now promise you that for every dollar you will, between this and the first of May, get for your own labor either in money or in your own indebtedness, I will then give you one other dollar.

By this, if you hire yourself at ten dollars a month, from me you will get ten more, making twenty dollars a month for your work. In this, I do not mean you shall go off to St. Louis, or the lead mines, or the gold mines, in California, but I mean for you to go at it for the best wages you can get close to home—in Coles County.

Now if you will do this, you will soon be out of debt, and what is better, you will have a habit that will keep you from getting in debt again. But if I should now clear you out, next year you will be just as deep in as ever. You say you would almost give your place in Heaven for $70 or $80. Then you value your place in Heaven very cheaply, for I am sure you can with the offer I make you get the seventy or eighty dollars for four or five months' work. You say if I furnish you the money you will deed me the land, and if you don't pay the money back, you will deliver possession—.

Nonsense! If you can't now live with the land, how will you then live without it? You have always been kind to me, and I do not now mean to be unkind to you. On the contrary, if you will but follow my advice, you will find it worth more than eight times eighty dollars to you.

Affectionately

> Your brother
> A. Lincoln

> —ABRAHAM LINCOLN
> (TO HIS STEPBROTHER)

It is always so pleasant to be generous, though very vexatious to pay debts.

> —RALPH WALDO EMERSON

He that gets out of debt grows rich.

—ENGLISH

Interest works night and day in fair weather and in foul. It gnaws at a man's substance with invisible teeth.

—HENRY WARD BEECHER

My problem lies in reconciling my gross habits with my net income.

—ERROL FLYNN

Think what you do when you run debt; you give to another power over your liberty. If you cannot pay at the time, you will be ashamed to see your creditor; will be in fear when you speak to him; will make poor, pitiful, sneaking excuses, and by degrees come to lose your veracity, and sink into base, downright lying; for the second vice is lying, the first is running in debt.

—BENJAMIN FRANKLIN

A lender does not hate part payment.

—AFRICAN

A debt is extinguished by force of paying, a journey by force of walking.

—TURKISH

There are but two ways of paying debt—increase of industry in raising income, increase of thrift in laying out.

—THOMAS CARLYLE

Whatever you have, spend less.

—SAMUEL JOHNSON

Good morning! Blessed be thy coming! A Jew! Reb Yankel, how are you? How's your wife, and your father-in-law, and your mother-in-law, and how *gesheft*? You've probably come to give me back my money! It's really *takkeh* a long time already! What, no? Not time yet? What do you want of me anyway? Am I, God forbid, asking you for the money? Say yourself—am I pressing you for it? I'm only going to ask you just one plain question: What have you got against me, you robber? You *mamzer*? One of two things—give me back my money!

—SHOLOM ALEICHEM

Owe no man anything.

—ROMANS 12:8

EARNING

Two

Earning

People who are not at peace with money are often earning less of it than they need or than would be beneficial for them. And often they have been doing that chronically, for a long time. That was certainly the case with me.

What do we mean by *need* and *beneficial*? Coming up with a threshold for the amount of money we *need* is simple: enough to provide ourselves with food, shelter, and clothing of decent quality on a regular basis. While owning a co-op on the park, buying a new car every year, or having the money to send your daughter through Stanford Medical School might be pleasurable, and even desirable, they are not needs. An amount that would be *beneficial* is more open to debate. For our purposes, however, we can define it as enough to meet our basic needs, with, in addition, at least some left over to spend on items that exceed those needs, some more to spend on recreation or relaxation, and some to put into savings. That is what we mean by beneficial.

I call this repeated failure to earn what we need, or to earn less than would be beneficial, "underearning." Underearning is not the same as underachieving—indeed, many underearners, particularly in the arts, crafts, trades, and in some professions, have achieved recognition and honor for their abilities while continuing to underearn. What's more, one can achieve less, even a great deal less, than one's potential and still earn more than is needed or basically beneficial. While under-earning sometimes co-exists with underachieving, it is separate and apart from underachieving and needs to be addressed directly itself.

Practice:
The Two Do-Nots

One definition of insanity is to keep doing the same thing over and over again and expect different results. It is helpful, therefore, to establish a threshold of behavior to avoid, one day at a time, if you want to master earning. By avoiding this behavior it will be difficult—indeed nearly impossible—for you to continue underearning, if underearning is part of your history with money.

Now that the debting has stopped, here are what I call the Two Do-Nots. (There are also actions to *take* in making peace with money, but those will be presented in later chapters; here we are still concerned with what *not* to do.)

The First Do-Not:

Do not take work that pays you less than you need.

This would seem obvious, but for underearners, it isn't. Underearners—and I was one myself—nearly *always* take work that pays them less than they need. We don't see that the employment we obtain, the assignments we accept, the contracts we sign, and projects we undertake frequently bring us less money than we need in order to meet our basic expenses, or just barely enough with only a little left over. Or if we do see it, we say to ourselves, "Well, I have to have something, don't I? Even a little is better than nothing." As underearners, we rarely relate the money we accept to the amount we have to spend in order to live.

There are two ways to circumvent this problem. First, become clear about your needs, in the form of expenses. You're already well on the way to that, having begun to keep a Spending Record in the last chapter. Second, remain aware that as underearners we reflexively, routinely, take work that doesn't pay us enough to meet our basic needs or that pays just that and only a bit more. Make awareness of this lethal reflex an integral part of your consciousness, so that it figures into every decision you make about whether to accept a job or project.

There will be times when, because of fear that there's nothing else out there, pressure from creditors, the feeling that you must get at least *some* money in immediately, or other reasons you'll feel that you have to accept an offer even though it won't fully meet your needs. Don't. For one day, this day, turn it down. For one day, this day, one day at a time: *Do not take work that pays you less than you need.*

What do you do if you're already working in a job for money that is less than you need and where asking for more will not change that? You say, "Guess I'll be moseying on now." That's what the hero used to say in old westerns, after the town had been cleaned up, the hostages rescued, or the gold returned—after the job was done.

Moseying on. Yup.

And that's what you'd better do, too: To remain where you are would be to continue underearning. But don't just up and quit. Not unless you can walk out of your job directly into a new and satisfactory one tomorrow morning. If you can't, then stay where you are for now. While you work the other practices in this book, begin searching for a new job or field of work that will pay you enough to meet your needs in a humane way. When you find one that will, and that you like, take it. This transition is not always easy, but each task involved in making it can be completed, each obstacle overcome—if you are committed to making peace with money. Halfway measures are of little use in this.

Time to be moseying on now.

The Second Do-Not:

Do not say no to money.

To suggest that anyone would say no to money—"No thanks, I've got enough," "I appreciate it, but really, you're too kind, no"—might seem irrational. But underearners do it all the time. They evade, avoid, and deflect money like running backs hurtling toward the goal line of poverty. Touchdown!

As underearners, we say no to money by short-circuiting several potentially profitable notions every day. An idea pops into our mind, we grow excited for an instant, then we're overwhelmed by negative chatter. We say no to money by not following up calls from clients or prospective employers. We do it by blinding ourselves to opportunities, underbidding jobs, botching a project, incurring heavy expenses. We do it by failing to raise fees, not capitalizing on skills or abilities. We do it by refusal: "I don't want to work for that company." "I'm not ready to move yet." "I've never done anything like that."

Do not say no to money. Do not evade, avoid, or deflect it. Let it into your life. (We're talking, of course, about money that isn't debt, and money that satisfies the first Do-Not, that meets your needs. If it isn't, and it does, then do not say no to it.)

Early in my own liberation from underearning, the communications director of a large professional association called me from Washington, D.C. She had heard that I broke writer's block for people. (I perked up, sensing income.) That was not the problem she had. (I sagged.) Her staff writers were not blocked. (I sagged further.) Their problem was burnout and staleness, caused by having to write about the same topics over and over. (Why was she calling me?) Could I help? (How? What did I know about burnout in staff writers?) They could pay $1,250 for an afternoon session with their four writers.

I was about to express my regrets, and thank her for the call, and tell her I hoped she could find an answer somewhere when, with the force of a hammer blow, I was struck by the realization that I had a habit, tendency, inclination, compulsion—whatever you want to call it—to underearn, and that I was about to turn down $1,250.

Though I found it difficult, though my throat began to close and I had trouble getting the words out, I forced myself to say: "Yes, I think I can help you with it. I'd like to give it some thought. Is there a time tomorrow afternoon that would be convenient for me to call you back?"

Six weeks later, I led a four-hour workshop for that woman and her writers down in Washington. I called it "Word Renewal." It was designed to rekindle creative vigor and enthusiasm among staff writers, eliminate staleness and burnout, and provide them with everything they needed in the way of concepts and techniques never to fall victim to this kind of problem again. It was a great success.

One day at a time: *Do not say no to money.*

Practice:

Resolve

First, find in yourself a desire—a *true* desire—to bring, or allow, more money into your life. When you have found that, made contact with it, truly felt and experienced it, create the resolve to do so, whatever doing so might mean. Without such resolve, any efforts you might make are likely to be only enthusiasms of the moment, soon abandoned. Here is a way you can create resolve:

Begin by relaxing, clearing your body of tension. Loosen any part of your clothing that is tight. Sit in a chair with your back erect, but not strained, with your feet flat on the floor. Put your hands on your thighs palms up, in a comfortable position. Close your eyes. Take a breath. As you exhale, let your body relax. Breathe in again, and this time, when you breathe out, consciously relax your feet. Repeat the process with your calves: breathe in, breathe out, relax your calves. Then do the same with your thighs, your buttocks, and work your way up the rest of your body thus, relaxing it part by part: belly, chest, back, shoulders, upper arms, forearms (with wrists and hands), and neck, finishing with your face and scalp. When you have done this, take two more breaths, relaxing your entire body on each exhale.

Sit quietly, without tension. Your breathing will probably be a little deeper and slower than usual. Slowly, become aware of it: . . . in . . . out . . . in . . . out. Don't try to change it. Just be aware of it.

Then, very gently, begin to focus on it: . . . in . . . out . . . in . . . out. You'll probably be distracted by fragmentary thoughts or other awarenesses of your body. Don't try to force these out of your mind. When you become aware of one, just let it drift across your consciousness, like a cloud across the sky, and disappear; then gently return your focus to your breathing: . . . in . . . out . . . in . . . out.

After two or three minutes of this easy focus on your breathing, center your attention, your consciousness, deep within your diaphragm. Let it come to feel stable there: natural, comfortable, at home. Be aware of it.

Now let yourself feel in that place—in your consciousness—the desire to bring more money into your life, the willingness to *allow* more to enter your life. Let yourself feel that desire, that willingness, as a clean, bright kind of happiness, something that may swell quickly into joy, causing you to smile. Let this joy fill your diaphragm, let it be your consciousness. Treasure it. Delight in it. See how pure it is.

Now, while it is full and expansive, assent to it. Silently, say *Yes*. Confirm it. Give it your wholehearted support. Say *Yes . . . Yes . . .* Now *resolve* to bring more money into your life, *resolve* to *allow* more to enter your life. *Determine* to do this.

Then breathe, and relax, letting go. Breathe, and relax, letting that joy, that happiness, that resolve, soften and fade away. Breathe, and relax. . . . Sit with your eyes closed a few moments longer, allowing yourself to be still. Then move your hands a little, shift your feet on the floor. Let your eyes open. Stretch, take a couple of good breaths, and stretch again. Now stand up and do a deep, full-body stretch . . . and go about the rest of your day.

Practice this creation of resolve once each day over the next seven days; then once a week during the coming year. You can reconnect with the resolve at any time. Simply get still a minute, close your eyes, breathe in and out (easily, letting your body relax on the exhale), center your awareness in your diaphragm, and then let the desire, the willingness, and finally, the resolve arise. Stay with the resolve a few moments, luxuriating in it, then let it fade, and slowly bring yourself back to your day.

How much money is "more" money? Just that: more. It may be a modest amount, it may be a large amount. Just *more*.*

---

*To some people, recovery from deep-seated or even lifelong underearning seems all but impossible. If it seems so to you, I recommend you work with my book *Earn What You Deserve: How to Stop Underearning & Start Thriving*, which presents a full, detailed program of recovery for this condition.

A man whom fortune had reduced to wandering vagrancy knocked on the Rebbe's door begging food and a night's shelter. Feeding him, the Rebbe told him he knew of an abandoned cottage where, through God's mercy, the man could stay if he wished. Perhaps he could even dig some roots and pick berries to get himself a little food.

The next morning the Rebbe took the man to the cottage. Its walls were so old and weather-worn that rain could blow through in a dozen places. The roof had fallen in. The chimney was cracked and crumbling. Vines and nettle-bushes grew all about in tangled profusion.

"Trust in God to provide what is needed," said the Rebbe, who then took his leave.

The following month the Rebbe happened to pass that way again and saw that the cottage had a new thatched roof. "God and you have certainly found a way to keep the rain off your head," he said.

"Yes, we have," the man answered gratefully.

The next month, the Rebbe saw that all the walls had been chinked and the window-frames set right. "God and you have certainly made a cozy shelter for you," he said.

"Yes, we have," the man answered gratefully.

The following month, the Rebbe saw that the ground had been cleared and the soil turned for a garden. "God and you are certainly making ready a source of sustenance for you," he said.

"Yes, we are," the man answered gratefully.

So it went for a year. The following summer, the Rebbe gazed in marvel at the gleaming cottage with its new chimney and comfortable porch, its fresh-dug well from which sweet water could be drawn, its well-tended garden fruitful with ripening vegetables, and clever hutches stocked with forest rabbits the man had caught. The man himself was busy digging out a root cellar.

"How truly wonderful is all that God and you have done to reclaim this old place!" the Rebbe exclaimed.

The man paused to mop his brow. "Yes," he said. "And you'll remember, how hard a time God was having when he had to do it all by himself."

—Hasidic

Change is not made without inconvenience, even from worse to better.

—Samuel Johnson

Attorney-General Sir John Holker: That labor of two days, then, is that for which you ask two hundred guineas?

Whistler: No—I ask it for the knowledge of a lifetime.

—James McNeill Whistler

A man walking through the forest saw a fox that had lost its legs, and he wondered how it lived. Then he saw a tiger come up with game in its mouth. The tiger ate its fill and left the rest of the meat for the fox.

The next day God fed the fox by means of the same tiger. The man began to wonder at God's greatness and said to himself, "I too shall just rest in a corner with full trust in the Lord and he will provide me with all that I need."

He did this for many days but nothing happened, and he was almost at death's door when he heard a voice say, "O you who are in the path of error, open your eyes to the truth! Stop imitating the disabled fox and follow the example of the tiger."

—SUFI

Money is the seed of money, and the first guinea is sometimes more difficult to acquire than the second million.

—JEAN-JACQUES ROUSSEAU

Fortune is like the market, where many times, if you can stay a little, the price will fall.

—FRANCIS BACON

This is what I want to explain to you young man. People keep coming to me knowing that this is someone who has walked the path from here to Nirvana and so knows it perfectly. They come to me and ask, "What is the path to Nirvana to liberation?" And what is there to hide? I explain it to them clearly: "This is the path." If somebody just nods his head and says, "Well said, well said, a very good path, but I won't take the trouble to walk over it," then how can such a person reach the final goal?

I do not carry anyone on my shoulders to take him to the final goal. Nobody can carry anyone else on his shoulders to the final goal. At most, with love and compassion one can say, "Well, this is the path, and this is how I have walked on it. You also work, you also walk, and you will reach the final goal." But each person has to walk himself, has to take every step on the path himself. He who has taken one step on the path is one step nearer the goal. He who has taken a hundred steps is a hundred steps nearer the goal. He who has taken all the steps on the path has reached the final goal. You have to walk on the path yourself.

—BUDDHA

First earn, then eat.

—HINDU

Thousands of people have talent. I might as well congratulate you for having eyes in your head. The one and only thing that counts is: Do you have staying power?

—NOËL COWARD

Money-getters are the benefactors of our race. To them . . . are we indebted for our institutions of learning, and of art, our academies, colleges and churches.

—P. T. BARNUM

An old cat was in the habit of catching all the mice in the barn.

One day the mice met to talk about the great harm that she was doing them. Each one told of some plan by which to keep out of her way.

"Do as I say," said an old gray mouse that was thought to be very wise. "Do as I say. Hang a bell to the cat's neck. Then, when we hear it ring, we shall know that she is coming, and can scamper out of her way."

"Good! Good!" said all the other mice, and one ran to get the bell.

"Now which of you will hang this bell on the cat's neck?" said the old gray mouse.

"Not I! Not I!" said all the mice together. And they scampered away to their holes.

—AFTER AESOP

Unto everyone that hath shall be given, and he shall have abundance: but from him that hath not shall be taken away even that which he hath.

—JESUS

Life shrinks or expands in proportion to one's courage.

—ANAÏS NIN

Do not wait for the last judgment, it takes place every day.

—ALBERT CAMUS

One finds many companions for food and drink, but in a serious business a man's companions are very few.

—Theognis

Miracles sometimes occur, but one has to work terribly hard for them.

—Chaim Weizmann

We do not quite forgive a giver. The hand that feeds us is in some danger of being bitten.

—Ralph Waldo Emerson

It is a rough road that leads to the heights of greatness.

—Seneca

A tailor and a goldsmith were traveling together, and one evening, after the sun had set behind the mountains, they heard the sound of distant music, which became more and more distinct. The music sounded unusual but so charming that they forgot all about how tired they were and rushed forward. The moon had already risen by the time they reached a hill on which they glimpsed a crowd of little men and women, holding hands and dancing joyfully round and round. As they danced, they sang a lovely tune, and this was the music that the travelers had heard.

In the middle of the circle sat an old man who was somewhat larger than the rest. He wore a brightly colored coat, and a whitish gray beard hung over his chest. The two travelers, who were stunned, stood still and watched the dance. The old man motioned to them to enter the circle, and the little folk willingly let them enter. The goldsmith, who had a hump and, like all hunchbacks, was sassy enough, moved into the ring. At first the tailor was afraid and held himself back. However, when he saw how merry everything was, he mustered up his courage and followed the goldsmith. Just as he did this, the circle closed again, and the little folk continued to sing and dance with the wildest leaps. Meanwhile, the old man took a huge knife, which hung on his belt, whetted it, and when it was sufficiently sharpened, he looked around at the strangers. They were frightened, but they did not have any time to reflect, for the old man grabbed the goldsmith, and, quick as lightning, shaved the hair on his head and his beard clean off. Right after this the same thing happened to the tailor. Yet, their fear vanished when the old man, after his work had been completed, slapped them both on the shoulder in a friendly way, as if he wanted to say that they had conducted themselves well by letting this happen to them willingly and without putting up a struggle. Then he pointed to a heap of coal that lay to one side and indicated to the travelers through gestures that they should fill their pockets with it. Both obeyed, although they did not know what use the coal would be to them. They then continued on their way and sought shelter for the night. By the time they arrived in the valley, the clock of the neighboring cloister was striking twelve. The music from the hill stopped abruptly. Everything vanished, and the hill stood alone in the moonlight.

The two travelers found an inn and covered themselves with their coats on their beds made out of straw. They were so tired, however, that they forgot to take the coal out of their pockets. When they were wakened earlier than usual by a heavy weight on their limbs, they reached into their pockets and could not believe their eyes: the pockets were filled not with coal but with gold. Moreover, much to their happiness, they found the hair on their heads and their beards fully restored. They were now rich people. But the goldsmith had filled his pockets more thoroughly than the tailor, in keeping with his greedy disposition, and possessed twice as much as his companion. Once a greedy man has a great deal, he demands even more. So the goldsmith proposed to the tailor that they spend another day in the region and in the evening go out again to fetch even greater treasures from the old man on the hill. The tailor refused and said, "I have enough and am satisfied. Now I can become a master tailor. I'll marry my darling little thing and be a happy man." Nevertheless, to please the goldsmith, he agreed to remain another day.

In the evening the goldsmith hung a few more bags over his shoulder in order to pack away as much as he could, and set out for the hill. As on the previous night, he found the little folk singing and dancing. Once again the old man shaved him clean and indicated to him to take some coal with him. The goldsmith did not hesitate to stuff his pockets with whatever they could carry. He returned to the inn in seventh heaven and covered himself with his coat. "Even if the gold weighs me down," he said, "I'll gladly bear it." Finally, he fell asleep with a sweet feeling that he would awake the next morning as rich as a king. When he opened his eyes, he stood up quickly to examine his pockets, but he was astonished because he pulled out nothing but pieces of black coal. No matter how often he reached into his pockets, it was always the same.

I still have the gold that I won the night before, he thought, and he went to get it. But he was horrified to see that it had also turned to coal once again. As he hit himself on his forehead with his dusty hand, he felt that his entire head had become smooth and bald and his chin as well. But his distress was not over yet. Just then he became aware of a second hump that had grown on his chest and was much larger than the one on his back. He then recognized that he had been punished for his greed and began to weep loudly. The good tailor, who was wakened by all this, consoled his unhappy companion as best he could and said, "Since you have been my comrade during our travels, I want you to stay with me and share my treasure."

He kept his word, but the poor goldsmith had to carry the two humps for the rest of his life, and he wore a cap to cover his bald head.

—THE BROTHERS GRIMM

I trust a good deal to common fame, as we all must. If a man has good corn, or wood, or boards, or pigs, to sell, or can make better chairs or knives, crucibles or church organs, than anybody else, you will find a broad hard-beaten road to his house, though it be in the woods.

—RALPH WALDO EMERSON

Where there is no labor, there is no profit.

—TAMIL

The law of work does seem utterly unfair—but there it is and nothing can change it: The higher the pay in enjoyment the worker gets out of it, the higher shall be his pay in money also.

—MARK TWAIN

As the labor, so the pay.

—GERMAN

A bad workman never finds a good tool.

—FRENCH

A certain brother came to Abbot Silvanus at Mount Sinai, and seeing the hermits at work he exclaimed: Why do you work for the bread that perisheth? Mary has chosen the best part, namely to sit at the feet of the Lord without working. Then the Abbot said to his disciple Zachary: Give the brother a book and let him read, and put him in an empty cell. At the ninth hour the brother who was reading began to look out to see if the Abbot was not going to call him to dinner, and sometime after the ninth hour he went himself to the Abbot and said, Did the brethren not eat today, Father? Oh yes, certainly, said the abbot, they just had dinner. Well, said the brother, why did you not call me? You are a spiritual man, said the elder, you don't need this food that perisheth. We have to work, but you have chosen the best part. You read all day, and can get along without food. Hearing this the brother said: Forgive me, Father. And the elder said: Martha is necessary to Mary, for it was because Martha worked that Mary was able to be praised.

—DESERT FATHERS

The money you refuse will never do you good.

—ENGLISH

Once the mullah, nagged by his wife, as usual for being out of work, announced, "Taking a job is beneath my dignity. I am in the service of Allah."

"If that is so," replied his wife, "please be so kind as to petition Allah for back wages."

—SUFI

All things are ready, if our minds be so.

—WILLIAM SHAKESPEARE

No athlete is crowned but in the sweat of his brow.

—ST. JEROME

Ask, and it shall be given you; seek, and ye shall find; knock, and it shall be opened unto you.

—JESUS

A teacher observed that one of the little boys in her class was pensive and withdrawn.

"What are you worried about?" she asked.

"My parents," he replied. "Dad works all day to keep me clothed and fed and sent to the best school in town. And so does Mom. And they're both working overtime to be able to send me to college. Not only that, but Dad does the shopping and cleaning and Mom does the cooking and ironing so I have nothing to worry about."

"Why, then, are you worried?"

"I'm afraid they might try to escape."

—ANTHONY DE MELLO

If ye would go up high, then use your own legs! Do not get yourselves *carried* aloft; do not seat yourselves on other people's backs and heads!

—FRIEDRICH WILHELM NIETZSCHE

What recommends commerce to me is its enterprise and bravery. It does not clasp its hands and pray to Jupiter.

—HENRY DAVID THOREAU

Go to the ant, thou sluggard; consider her ways, and be wise:
Which having no guide, overseer, or ruler,
Provideth her meat in the summer, and gathereth her food in harvest.

—PROVERBS

It is not necessary that a man should earn his living by the sweat of his brow unless he sweats easier than I do.

—HENRY DAVID THOREAU

Luck is infatuated with the efficient.

—PERSIAN

If you don't want to resign yourself to poverty, resign yourself to work.

—AFRICAN

A young salesman walked up beside a farmer and began to talk excitedly about a book he was carrying. He thumped it. "This book will tell you everything you need to know about farming," he said enthusiastically. "When to sow, when to reap. All about the weather—what to expect, and even when to expect it. This book tells you all you'll ever need to know."

"Young man," the farmer said, "that's not the problem. I know everything that is in that book. My problem is doing it."

—TRADITIONAL

What wound did ever heal but by degrees?

—WILLIAM SHAKESPEARE

No man needs money so much as he who despises it.

—JEAN PAUL RICHTER

To a disciple who was always at his prayers the Master said, "When will you stop leaning on God and stand on your own two feet?"

The disciple was astonished. "But you are the one who taught us to look on God as Father!"

"When will you learn that a father isn't someone you can lean on but someone who rids you of your tendency to lean?"

—ANTHONY DE MELLO

Unto whomsoever much is given, of him shall much be required.

—JESUS

Everybody lives by selling something.

—ROBERT LOUIS STEVENSON

You must be the change you wish to see in the world.

—MAHATMA GANDHI

VISION

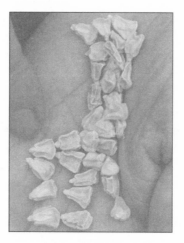

Three

Vision
·················

This chapter deals with vision as the ability to imagine what *could* be
in your life rather than as simply discerning what already *is*.
Recognizing something coiled in the grass as a poisonous snake rather
than a piece of rope—discernment, awareness—might save your life.
Recognizing that an occupation or place of employment is a dead end
might, on a metaphorical level, do the same thing. That kind of vision
is important.

But equally important, even more so at our deepest levels, is vision
in the second sense, seeing what *could* be rather than what *is*. This kind
of vision lies at the heart of all creative activity, and is a prerequisite of
change: Without it, no one would ever compose a song, write a book,
or make a painting; without it, no one would ever so much as paint a
room or change a hairstyle. This kind of vision is also essential to the
realization of joy: Without it, none of us would know fulfillment, bond
with another, be capable of raising healthy children.

It is true that there are limits in life. No matter how hard you flap
your arms, you are not going to soar up into the sky. Most limits orig-
inate in natural law, some from *force majeure* such as an earthquake
that shakes down your house, war, or economic collapse. Still, what

most of us consider to be limits—what we think is possible for us and what is not—are generally limits of vision rather than reality.

If all that can be seen is simply what is, *then what is will never change.*

Everything done by human beings first comes into existence in vision. Only afterward is it translated into the external world. Nothing can be created or accomplished without the idea—a picture, an image, a sense of the thing—first occurring in the mind.

Learning how to work intentionally with vision, rather than simply letting it occur haphazardly in your life, will help you make peace with money. People have used the practices and concepts in this chapter, supported by those in the rest of the book, to get promotions, finish degrees, change careers, start businesses, and support themselves through their art. In one case, an environmental consultant who'd originally had trouble paying his rent each month gained confidence that he was capable enough with money to provide for children, thus feeling free to start the family with his wife they had both longed for. In another, an actress making $50 a week, being supported by her father and by steady debting, went in four years to become the owner of a highly regarded acting school grossing more than $100,000 a year.

I'm not telling you that you will be able to do what these people or any of the others have done. Everyone is different; no one can do exactly what another person does. But I *am* telling that you will be able to realize your particular version of what they, I, and others have done. A great deal of what you have perceived as limits in your life are actually limits you have placed upon yourself—without intending to, and almost always unknowingly, but self-imposed nonetheless. The good news about this is, you have already begun to eliminate them. You began the moment you opened this book. The rest of the chapter will help you address them directly.

Practice:

"Dear Friend"

Sometime this week when you are relaxed, rested, and have some time free of responsibilities, sit down somewhere with a pen and pad. Stretch, take a couple of good deep breaths. Let your mind become clear and still. Turn your thoughts toward people who like you, who care for you, who are well disposed toward you. From among them, pick one who is truly fond of you, who desires nothing for you but your happiness. (It's best to exclude your spouse and any relatives from this process; family dynamics can come into play and interfere with it.)

Now write that person a brief letter—a page or two is enough—which you are *not* going to send. We'll discuss why you won't later. In this letter, describe to your friend how you would be living with money at the end of five years from now if everything were to go well for you over the coming five years. Don't tell her how you would be living if you won the lottery or came into a big inheritance, which are fanciful and unlikely possibilities, but rather how you would be living if your life, starting from right now, were to grow and expand as you would like it to over the next five years, smoothly, without any major difficulty.

Tell her how you would *like* to be living with money if that were to happen. Tell her where you would be living. In an apartment, a house? What kind? Where would it be? What would you be doing to make a living? The same kind of work you're doing now, something else?

What would your evenings and weekends be like? How would you *feel*? Would you have a hobby? What would your relationship with your family be like, your spouse, your parents, your children? Write an overall view, an *honest* view, of how you would truly like your life to be.

The reason we pick someone real to whom to address the letter is because it helps us think more clearly and honestly about the question than we might do otherwise. We stop short of actually mailing the letter because this exercise is strictly for our benefit, meant to inform *us* about ourselves, not anyone else. What's important is for *you* to know—and in some detail—how you would like to be living with money. Knowing this is a great stride forward out of fog into clarity, where you can begin to effect change and where change can begin to take place.

There is no template to follow in writing this letter. Everyone will do it differently. Here, strictly for purposes of illustration, is what Mitch, a thirty-year-old musician and occasional entrepreneur, wrote:

> I'd be living in the country outside the city. Woodstock maybe. Maybe closer in. I'd have a nice white frame house with a big sunny living room, a big bright kitchen. It would have guest bedrooms and a guest cottage. One room would be a gym where I could work out. I'd have a sound studio in a converted barn or garage. There would be a lot of trees. Woods to walk in.

I'd be married and I'd really love my wife and she would really love me. We'd have a kid and another one on the way. My wife would be some kind of artist like a writer or painter.

I wouldn't have any trouble paying the bills. I'd have a couple of albums out. I'd only tour if I wanted to, not because I had to. Other people, like Robert Plant and Paul McCartney, would be doing some of my songs. The _____* business would be netting about $30,000 to $50,000 a year and that would take care of my basic nut. Everything else would be gravy. I'd hire someone else to run the _____ business and anything else like that I got involved in so I could spend most of my time on my music.

I'd take my wife and kids on a trip someplace in the US each year where we'd never been. Once a year my wife and I would go to Europe for week or ten days. When the kids got old enough, we'd bring them, but not for a while.

I'd go back to college and get my degree.

I'd go skiing a lot. My wife would like to ski too.

Your letter can be more detailed or less detailed. Just be sure it includes enough detail to give you truly a clear sense of how you would like to be living with money five years from now if all were to go well for you.

*A particular business Mitch had started, left uncited to protect his anonymity.

Practice:
The Yellow Brick Road

No undertaking can succeed without a plan, nothing from building a dam to going on a vacation to making peace with money. In L. Frank Baum's marvelous fantasy *The Wonderful Wizard of Oz*, following the yellow brick road is what gets Dorothy and her companions to the Emerald City, the place they want to go. Here, in this practice, you'll create your own Yellow Brick Road—and following it is what will get you to where you want to go.

When an architect plans a building, the first thing he does is "see" it in his mind. Then he translates what he sees, his vision, onto paper. This rough sketch is his first look at what he wishes to bring into existence, the beginning of his plan, or Yellow Brick Road. You already have such a sketch for yourself. You created it when you wrote out the letter in "Dear Friend," the first practice in this chapter. After the architect draws his overview, blueprints follow, construction crews go to work, tradesmen are brought in, and finally a building comes into existence. Our own process will be somewhat similar, although in a broader way.

Let's begin with a mission statement. In business, a mission statement is a simple statement of an organization's primary purpose, the strategies it intends to use in serving that purpose, and its values. A mission statement helps employees make sense of the day-to-day activities they're asked to perform and gives meaning to work that otherwise might appear to have little point beyond earning money or reaching an arbitrary goal, such as a sales quota. It helps them be more effective in the choices and tradeoffs they have to make every day. And finally, it promotes commitment, trust, and a spirit of cooperation in them. A personal mission statement can do many of the same things for you: Help clarify your daily activities and infuse them with meaning, help you in making better choices and tradeoffs, and strengthen your confidence in and commitment to what you are doing. A good mission statement is brief and uncomplicated. It contains three elements: purpose, strategy, values.

Purpose. Your purpose is your *raison d'être*, what you ultimately wish to accomplish. It might read, for example, "To be successful, happy, and make money." Or, "To satisfy my basic needs and desires and still put away enough money to buy a house." Or, "To support myself doing something I really enjoy."

Strategy. Your strategy involves a short explanation of how you intend to serve that purpose. For example, "Become good at what I do. Maintain my skills at a high level. Go into therapy. Meditate. Price myself at the top of what's competitive." Or, "Keep my earnings rising. Know how much I'll need for a down payment and the kind of financing I can get. Design an effective monthly savings plan. Pick an area to live and price houses there." Or, "Select which of the activities I enjoy that has the best *real* chance of supporting me. Minimize my expenses.

Develop and implement a plan for gradually shifting into that activity."

Values. Your values are the basic principles that guide or motivate you. For example, "Helping people. Pleasure in mastery. Inner peace. Enjoyment of fine material things." Or, "Cave. Family. Creating security." Or, "Being my own boss. Having a good time. Doing what I think is worthwhile."

To illustrate, here is the mission statement of a small business, a software company, in California.

Purpose: Do good work. Have fun. Make money.

Strategy: Respect each other and ourselves. Treat the customer as king. Promise only what we can follow through with.

Values: Pride in our work. Achievement. Recognition. Helping. Pleasure.

Here is the *personal* mission statement of Wendell, a real estate agent:

Purpose: To give love to and provide for my family.

Strategy: Stay focused on what I think are the unique contributions I am here to make in this life. Share freely ideas and information I have which can benefit others. Charge fairly for the expertise and professional services I provide. Practice yoga, meditation, and physical exercise, which provide me with physical and mental health and awareness of self.

Values: Integrity. Success. Openness. The love and well-being of my wife and children.

Under a heading he called "Principles," Wendell went further and listed some guidelines for himself. Among them were:

- Keep first people first.
- Pay attention, give attention.
- My workday is an earning day.
- I expect to be fairly paid for my work.
- I immediately separate from all I earn a part to keep.
- I grasp opportunity, delegate routine tasks.
- I promote self-discipline.
- I enjoy my successes, but guard against feeling superior or arrogant.
- I work when I'm working, and don't when I'm not.
- I keep business time and money separate from personal time and money.
- I communicate every day with myself, and with God.
- I attempt to live in and remain aware of every moment of the day.
- I reawaken my spirit, refresh my mind, and relax my body on a regular basis.
- I perform charitable acts, strive for social justice.
- I let love and honesty be my guide.

You may not be able to create a mission statement that pleases you, feels right to you, makes you say "Yes! That's it!" on your first try, or even your second or third. Sometimes a mission statement comes to you like lightning, other times it requires days of fiddling. Stay with the process until you have created one that feels good to you, but don't put yourself under any strain doing it.

The next step in creating a Yellow Brick Road is to decide how you're going to carry out your strategy. This means coming up with a tactical plan, a plan for achieving certain objectives that are part of realizing your overall vision. A tactical plan should be simple and straightforward. Here is a good way to create one:

Sit with a pen and pad.

Read your mission statement and fix it in your mind.

Write the heading *Five-Year Goal*. Beneath it, state in one sentence how close you think it would be reasonable for you have come toward fulfilling the purpose in your mission statement by the end of five years from now. Be both realistic *and* confident. Assume you will be effective over the next five years. Keep in mind that it is less important for you actually to realize this goal fully than to have a clear idea of what the goal is. (It's also all right to exceed it. Many people do.)

Next, write the heading *One-Year Actions*. Beneath it, list five actions you would like to have completed by the end of a year from now that would be in the service of your five-year goal, and that seem reasonable to think you can complete in a year's time.

Now write the heading *One-Month Actions*. Beneath this, list four actions you would like to have completed by the end of a month from now that would help you accomplish your one-year actions, and that seem reasonable to think you can complete in the coming month.

Finally, pick one of your one-month actions and execute it this week. Execute the remaining three during the next thirty days.

To illustrate, here is what a tactical plan might look like.

Mission Statement

Purpose: To support myself doing work I truly enjoy.

Strategy: Select which activity among those I enjoy that has the best *real* chance of supporting me. Minimize my expenses. Develop and implement a plan for gradually shifting into that activity.

Values: Being my own boss. Having a good time. Doing what I think is worthwhile.

Five-Year Goal

To be making a decent living doing what I like, either working for myself or for a company where I have a fair degree of autonomy.

One-Year Actions

1. Have decided exactly what activity I plan to do for my profession or work.

2. Have learned what kind of income can be made doing this: on the high side, on the low side, and the average.
3. Know precisely the minimum income I need in order to lead a life that is, if not the kind I ultimately desire, at least acceptable to me for a couple of years.
4. Have contributed each month to a savings fund that will eventually help me make the switch.
5. Have become familiar with how people in this profession or occupation function on a daily basis, the skills and knowledge needed, the way they find clients or get hired.

One-Month Actions

1. Have listed all the activities I enjoy doing.
2. Picked my favorite three.
3. Selected one of these and made a list of three people I could interview or sources I could check to research how feasible it is to make a living at this activity.
4. Decided which interview I'm going to do first and made date to do it. [Or the equivalent, such as having bought a book on the subject and set a date to start reading it.]

You'll note that the larger the timeframe, the larger and more significant the actions you wish to have accomplished. Conversely, the smaller the timeframe, the smaller the actions. By beginning with a vision of what you eventually want, then planning actions to take to achieve that, then reducing the actions into ever smaller and more manageable scale as you approach nearer to today, you ensure that all of your actions—no matter how seemingly insignificant—move you steadily toward your long-term goal, and ultimately, toward achieving your purpose as you set it down in your mission statement. Remember, none of these is something you *must* accomplish. They are simply guidelines, tools, to help you keep moving in the right direction.

Here are a few ways you can continue to work with this practice after you have created your tactical plan. You can: Simply keep your mission statement in mind, letting it inform what you do as you go. Or, four times a year, draw up a new set of one-month actions. Or, each month draw up a set of actions for the coming month. You may want to speed up the time frame or slow it down. You may want to increase or decrease the number of actions.

Once a year, review your mission statement and five-year goal. Either reconfirm them or revise them, whichever seems right. You might want to change them in light of new experiences, new ideas, new desires that have arisen, which is perfectly fine. Rethinking any part of a mission statement or tactical plan is a legitimate part of the process. Finally, have fun with the Yellow Brick Road. Keep it simple. Enjoy it.

There was once an elderly black snake in a certain spot, and his name was Slow-Poison. He considered the situation from this point of view: "How in the world can I get along without overtaxing my energies?" Then he went to a pond containing many frogs, and behaved as if very dejected.

As he waited thus, a frog came to the edge of the water and asked: "Uncle, why don't you bustle about today for food as usual?"

"My dear friend," said Slow-Poison, "I am afflicted. Why should I wish for food? For this evening, as I was bustling about for food, I saw a frog and made ready to catch him. But he saw me and, fearing death, he escaped among some Brahmins intent upon holy recitation, nor did I perceive which way he went. But in the water at the edge of the pond was the great toe of a Brahmin boy, and stupidly deceived by its resemblance to a frog, I bit it, and the boy died immediately. Then the sorrowing father cursed me in these terms: 'Monster! Since you bit my harmless son, you shall for this sin become a vehicle for frogs, and shall subsist on whatever they choose to allow you.' Consequently, I have come here to serve as your vehicle."

Now the frog reported this to all the others. And every last one of them, in extreme delight, went and reported to the frog-king, whose name was Water-Foot. He in turn, accompanied by his counselors, rose hurriedly from the pond—for he thought it an extraordinary occurrence—and climbed upon Slow-Poison's hood. The others also, in order of age, climbed on his back. Yet others, finding no vacant spot, hopped along behind the snake. Now Slow-Poison, with an eye to making his living, showed them fancy turns in great variety. And Water-Foot, enjoying contact with his body, said to him:

> I'd rather ride Slow-Poison than
> The finest horse I've seen,
> Or elephant, or chariot,
> Or man-borne palanquin.

The next day, Slow-Poison was wily enough to move very slowly. So Water-Foot said: "My dear Slow-Poison, why don't you carry us nicely, as you did before?"

And Slow-Poison said: "O King, I have no carrying power today because of lack of food."

"My dear fellow," said the King, "eat the plebeian frogs."

When Slow-Poison heard this, he quivered with joy in every member and made haste to say: "Why, that is a part of the curse laid upon me by the Brahmin. For that reason I am greatly pleased at your command." So he ate frogs uninterruptedly, and in a very few days he grew strong. And with delight and inner laughter he said:

> The trick was good. All sorts of frogs
> Within my power have passed.
> The only question that remains,
> Is: How long will they last?

Water-Foot, for his part, was befooled by Slow-Poison's plausibilities, and did not notice a thing.

—HINDU

Where there is no vision, the people perish.

—PROVERBS

If I am not for myself, who will be? If I am only for myself, what am I? If not now, when?

—HILLEL

Imagination, not invention, is the supreme master of life.

—JOSEPH CONRAD

The greater part of all the mischief in the world arises from the fact that men do not sufficiently understand their own aims.

—JOHANN WOLFGANG VON GOETHE

Suppose, for example, that I am climbing in the Alps, and have had the ill-luck to work myself into a position from which the only escape is by a terrible leap. Being without similar experience, I have no evidence of my ability to perform it successfully; but hope and confidence in myself make me sure I shall not miss my aim, and nerve my feet to execute what without those subjective emotions would perhaps have been impossible.

But suppose that, on the contrary, the emotions of fear and mistrust preponderate; or suppose that, having just read *Ethics of Belief* [by W. K. Clifford], I feel it would be sinful to act upon an assumption unverified by previous experience—why, then I shall hesitate so long that at last, exhausted and trembling, and launching myself in a moment of despair, I miss my foothold and roll into the abyss.

In this case (and it is one of an immense class) the part of wisdom clearly is to believe what one desires; for the belief is one of the indispensable preliminary conditions of the realization of its object. There are then cases where faith creates its own verification. Believe, and you shall be right, for you shall save yourself; doubt, and you shall again be right, for you shall perish. The only difference is that to believe is greatly to your advantage.

—WILLIAM JAMES

All life is a meditation—most of it unintentional.

—JOSEPH CAMPBELL

When I hear of artists or authors making fun of businessmen, I think of a regiment in which the band makes fun of the cooks.

—ANONYMOUS

I tell people to get to know themselves. Some people think this means what beginners observe, and consider it easy to understand. Reflect more carefully, in a more leisurely manner—what do you call your self?

—Zen Master Foyan

Two roads diverged in a yellow wood,
And sorry I could not travel both
And be one traveler, long I stood
And looked down one as far as I could
To where it bent in the undergrowth;

Then took the other, as just as fair,
And having perhaps the better claim,
Because it was grassy and wanted wear;
Though as for that the passing there
Had worn them really about the same,

And both that morning equally lay
In leaves no step had trodden black.
Oh, I kept the first for another day!
Yet knowing how way leads on to way,
I doubted if I should ever come back.

I shall be telling this with a sigh
Somewhere ages and ages hence:
Two roads diverged in a wood, and I —
I took the one less traveled by,
And that has made all the difference.

—ROBERT FROST

Man's main task is to give *birth* to himself.

—ERICH FROMM

A child was born. His father went to a carpenter and asked him to make a cradle for it.

The carpenter agreed. "Come back in a week," he said.

When the man returned, the cradle was not finished.

Nor was it finished a week later, or the week after that.

And so it went, week after week.

Eventually the child grew into a man. The young man married, and, in turn, had a baby boy of his own from his own wife.

The young man's father said, "Go to see the carpenter. Ask him if your cradle is ready yet."

So the young man did. He told the carpenter of his father's order long ago and concluded by saying:

"Here is an opportunity for you to finish the job. I now have a small son of my own, for whom the cradle will be ideal."

"Be off with you," said the carpenter; "I refuse to be rushed in my work just because you and your family are obsessed by your own wants!"

—SUFI

A seeker asked Jalal ad-Din Rumi: "Is the Koran a good book to read?" He replied, "You should rather ask yourself if you are in a state to profit from it."

—SUFI

Without this playing with fantasy no creative work has ever yet come to birth. The debt we owe to the play of imagination is incalculable.

—CARL GUSTAV JUNG

Dare to be naive.

—R. BUCKMINSTER FULLER

A man lay bedridden with a serious illness, and it appeared that his death was near. In her fear, his wife summoned a hakim, the town doctor. The hakim poked and probed the patient and listened for more than a half hour, checked his pulse, put his head on the man's chest, turned him onto his stomach and then his side and back, raised the man's legs and torso, opened his eyes, and looked in his mouth, and then said gravely, "My dear woman, I'm afraid I must give you the sad news that your husband has been dead for two days." At that very moment the ailing man raised his head in shock and whimpered anxiously, "No, my dearest, I'm still alive." His wife gave him a hefty bang on the head with her fist and replied angrily, "Be quiet! The hakim is an expert. He ought to know."

—PERSIAN

Nothing contributes so much to tranquilize the mind as a steady purpose—a point on which the soul may fix its intellectual eye.

—MARY SHELLEY

In the long run men hit only what they aim at.

—HENRY DAVID THOREAU

"There's no use trying," she said: "one can't believe impossible things."

"I daresay you haven't had much practice," said the Queen. "When I was your age, I always did it for half-an-hour a day. Why, sometimes I've believed as many as six impossible things before breakfast."

—LEWIS CARROLL

The things we have to learn before we can do them, we learn by doing them.

—ARISTOTLE

Our destination is never a place, but rather a new way of looking at things.

—HENRY MILLER

A prophet once came to a city to convert its inhabitants. At first the people listened to his sermons, but they gradually drifted away till there was not a single soul to hear the prophet when he spoke.

One day a traveler said to him, "Why do you go on preaching?"

Said the prophet, "In the beginning I hoped to change these people. If I still shout it is only to prevent them from changing me."

—SUFI

You wish to see; Listen. Hearing is a step toward Vision.

—ST. BERNARD

Everything should be made as simple as possible, but not simpler.

—ALBERT EINSTEIN

Effort and work have many different forms. One reason for the institution of a Guide is that he knows when to direct the disciple's effort and work, and when not to direct it. He also knows the kind of effort and work which each individual should do. Only the ignorant mistake any work for useful work, or extra effort at any time they wish for even little effort at a right time.

—PAHLAWAN-I-ZAIF

If ten men want to enter a house, and only nine find their way in, the tenth must not say: "This is what God ordained." He must find out what his own shortcoming was.

—JALAL AD-DIN RUMI

And we have ceased fighting anything or anyone—even [money].

—*ALCOHOLICS ANONYMOUS*[†]

Genius, in truth, means little more than the faculty of perceiving in an unhabitual way.

—WILLIAM JAMES

The goal of practice[‡] is always to keep the beginner's mind. The beginner's mind is always ready for anything; it is open to everything. In the beginner's mind there are many possibilities; in the expert's mind there are few.

—SHUNRYU SUZUKI

[†]Known commonly as the "Big Book."
[‡]*Zazen* meditation

The best way to make your dreams come true is to wake up.

—PAUL VALÉRY

I think the person who takes a job in order to live—that is to say, for the money—has turned himself into a slave.

—JOSEPH CAMPBELL

Faith is the bird that feels the light when the dawn is still dark.

—SRI RABINDRANATH TAGORE

Double your store of life's necessities. You will double life. Don't depend on any single thing, or limit any one resource, no matter how rare and excellent. Double everything, especially the sources of benefit, favor, and taste. The moon is transcendently mutable, setting the limits of permanence, and more mutable still are the things that depend on our frail human will. Store up supplies for frailty. It is a great rule for living to double your sources of happiness and profit. Just as nature doubled the most important and most exposed of our bodily limbs, so should art double the things you depend on.

—BALTASAR GRACIAN

It is a bad plan that admits of no modification.

—PUBILIUS SYRUS

First say to yourself what you would be; and then do what you have to do.

—EPICTETUS

Accomplish the great task
by a series of small acts.

—LAO TZU

One must not cheat anybody, not even the world of one's triumph.

—FRANZ KAFKA

WORK

Four

Work
....

Work is necessary to life. Everything that lives must work—or die. A wolf can't say, "I had a bad cubhood. I can't go out and hunt today." To that, nature replies: Wonderful, farewell.

There is a *getting* necessary to all living things, whether that getting involves sending forth roots, pawing the earth for grubs, migrating to graze lands, nibbling along a coral reef, or soaring the skies in search of prey.

Human beings are not exempt from this getting, from work. We also do it not just for ourselves, but for the young among us, the old, and others who can't get for themselves. We are not unique in this. Other species do this kind of altruistic getting, too, such as porpoises, elephants, others. We simply do it more effectively and on a larger scale than any other species.

Everyone needs a vital, healthy relationship with work. You do. I do. All of us do. And we need it not simply for physical survival, but for our psychological and spiritual health as well. Without some kind of dynamic engagement with work, we sicken and even die psychologically and spiritually. Sigmund Freud called work one of the two most important elements in anyone's life (the other was love). Even the very wealthy among us, who don't *need* to work, usually do, and often much harder and for more hours than other people do.

Yet the fact remains that most of us consider work oppressive. We see it as a necessary evil, a burden. We want to escape it, dream of not having to do it. Meanwhile, we keep our shoulder to the wheel, nose to the grindstone, and work like a dog. We load sixteen tons, and what do we get?—another day older and deeper in debt.

Once upon a time, goes our central Western mythology, our principal religious belief, this was not so. Once upon a time we lived in Edenic ease, where all we needed was given to us, all our desires satisfied without effort. We were free of having to get; we did not have to work. But then came the Fall, goes the story, and we were cast out of the Garden. God said to us, "Cursed is the ground for thy sake; in sorrow shalt thou eat of it all the days of thy life. . . . In the sweat of thy face shalt thou eat bread, till thou return unto the ground."

This is our archetypal belief about work: It is misery.

The story of the Fall can also be read as a metaphor for growing up, for our forced exit from infancy and childhood, where everything was provided for us and all our desires satisfied without effort on our part, into adulthood, where the ground is cursed and where in sorrow we eat of it all our remaining days, in the sweat of our face: where we eat of it through labor, strain—*work*.

Most of us see the time we spend working as dead to us. In a sense, it is; in a sense, we actually die during those hours, waiting for them to end so we can leave and resume our *real* life. This is sad. It steals a large part of our lives from us. It strains our relationship with money—for it is only through this sweat of our face, this daily death, that money comes to us. Therefore, on one level, we hate money. Yet on another we continue to lust for it, unconsciously believing that if only we had enough, we would not have to bring forth this sweat of our face every day, to die each day.

But work is not death. It isn't even the sweat of our face, not in the sense in which we usually conceive of that. It is the sweat of our face as *effort*, not *misery*—as is the sweat of recreational athletics. Effort, yes; misery, no. We experience work as misery mostly because we resist it or object to it. We will continue to experience it thus until we embrace its naturalness.

There is still a Garden, where you do not have to earn your bread by the sweat of your face, by work as misery. It lies within your ability to know work.

Practice:
Knowing It

In *Hamlet*, Polonius, the lord chamberlain, asks: "Do you know me, my Lord?"

"Excellent well," says Hamlet, "you are a fishmonger."

Polonius is not, of course. He is the lord chamberlain. Hamlet may be mad at this point or feigning madness. The audience doesn't know. Hamlet *himself* might not even know.

Most of us miscall work the way Hamlet miscalls Polonius—either because we truly don't recognize it for what it is or because we have accepted society's attitudes toward it without ever having considered those attitudes.

Work—getting—is not something we do so that we can have life afterward at the end of the day, or on weekends, or during vacations, or even, finally, in retirement. Our lives are occurring in full each moment, whether we are conscious of that or not. We are every bit as alive working—getting—as we are when playing, reading, or making love. Potentially, we can be just as happily conscious of life, and engaged with it, while we're working as we can at any of those other times.

Here is something you can do right now to help develop that ability. Read through Part I below, then set the book aside and go through the process it describes.

Part I: Sit back in your chair but don't slump. Keep your spine straight. Relax, close your eyes. Breathe easily. Imagine yourself at work. Picture yourself doing the activities you normally do there. Don't engage in *emotions* about those activities, just see them. What is actually happening as you perform them, as you file papers, give direction to an employee, loosen the tension from a client's back, argue before a judge, or groom an animal? What underlies these activities, whether mental or physical? What permits them, causes them, drives them?

An expenditure of energy. You are expending energy, in a directed way. That is the source of *all* your actions. You can't perform an action without doing so. Expending energy in a directed or focused way is what you do when you perform *any* activity, whether you call that activity work or play.

Clear your mind. Now search among your friends for someone who truly enjoys his work, doesn't look upon it as drudgery or misery. Picture him. See him at work, see what he does: not how he *feels* about what he is doing, but simply *what* he is doing. Keep your own emotions out of this, too. Just watch your friend perform these activities.

What underlies them? What permits them, causes them, drives them? An expenditure of energy. Your friend is expending energy in a directed way in order to perform an activity, just as you do in your own work—just as both of you do when you perform *any* activity, whether either of you calls it work or play.

Sit with this recognition a few moments. Then open your eyes. Breathe. Stretch. Rest a minute or two. Then pick up the book again and go on to Part II. Read through the section, then again set the book aside and go through the process.

Part II: Sit back and relax. Close your eyes. This time, mentally select someone you know who is wealthy or at least very well paid. Bring her to mind. Picture her at work. See what she does. Not what she *feels*, but simply what she is *doing*, her activities. Watch her perform them. And again, keep your own emotions out of this, too. Simply watch her.

Ask yourself: What underlies this woman's actions? What permits them, causes them, drives them? And again, recognize that it is an expenditure of energy. Like you, like your friend who enjoys his work, this person, too, is expending energy in a directed way to perform these activities—exactly as you do, exactly as she does, when you or she perform *any* activity, whether either of you calls the activity work or play.

Go through the exercise once more, this time with someone extraordinarily wealthy: Ted Turner, for example. Ted Turner's money didn't just happen and doesn't just happen. Ted Turner works. Bring him into your mind. Picture him at what you imagine his work activities to be. Watch him do those things. Keep both his emotions and yours about those activities out of the picture. Simply watch him perform them. And again ask: What underlies this man's actions? What permits them, causes them, drives them? And again recognize that the answer is a directed, or focused, expenditure of energy.

Now do the exercise one final time, with someone famous, like Susan Sarandon. Susan Sarandon's fame did not just happen and doesn't just happen. Bring her into your mind. Picture her at what you imagine her working activities to be. Watch her do those things. Keep her emotions and your emotions about these activities out of the picture. Simply watch her perform them. And one last time, ask: What underlies this woman's actions? What permits them, causes them, drives them? And one last time, recognize that the answer is a directed expenditure of energy.

After you have completed Parts I and II, take a break for a minute or two before you pick up the book and continue. Recognize that when you or anyone else is working—Susan Sarandon, Ted Turner, your well-paid acquaintance, your friend who enjoys his work—you are all doing, in essence, precisely the same thing: expending directed, or focused, energy. That is what you do, what *everyone does*, when you perform *any* activity, whether you call that activity work or call it play.

Integrate this new understanding of work into your consciousness. It means nothing less than this: You never have to work—get—by the sweat of your face again; not in the sense of pain or suffering, anyway. In fact, you may even come to work with delight. (And if that happens, you're likely to find that you're receiving more money for what you do than you ever thought possible.) If you begin to lose sight of the real nature of work, take yourself through this exercise again. Do it as often as is helpful.

Practice:
Right Work

This practice is about finding right work—work that is appropriate for you, natural to you, and life-enhancing. The concept behind this practice, in its original form, goes back 2,500 years to the founding of Buddhism.

Buddhism is a system of psychology as well as a religion. In fact, some scholars, Buddhist and non-Buddhist alike, claim it is *strictly* a system of psychology and not a religion at all. Whatever the case, no one has ever denied that Buddhism's insights into the way human beings think, act, and feel are profound, and that the methods it offers people to help them achieve deep, peaceful integration with themselves and the world about them are powerful.

Contemporary religious scholar Huston Smith, in his book *The World's Religions*, says that the Buddha distinguished two ways of living: "One—a random, unreflective way, in which the subject is pushed and pulled by impulse and circumstance like a twig in a storm drain—he called 'wandering about.' The second, the way of intentional living, he called the Path. . . . By long and patient discipline, the Eightfold Path intends nothing less than to pick one up where one is and set one down as a different being, one who has been cured of crippling disabilities." Such a being is one who has come to live in a state of peace, freedom, happiness.

The fifth of the eight principles in the Path is called "Right Livelihood." In the broadest sense, to practice right livelihood means to be engaged in an occupation that promotes life rather than destroys it. Early Buddhism was specific about what occupations to avoid if one wished to master right livelihood: obvious ones such as poison merchant and slave trader, but others not so obvious, too, such as butcher and brewer. Buddhism didn't condemn these occupations (it never condemns anything), but simply says of them—as it does of other actions or behaviors—that to engage in them is not good for oneself or others, will impede one's progress toward integration and happiness, and indeed may even make that impossible.

We're not going to treat Buddhism or the Eightfold Path any further. Since the contribtion of the concept of right livelihood to making peace with money is clear, it is appropriate that we have at least a sense of what that concept is and where it originated. Now we're going to fold it into our own concept of right work.

For our purposes:

> **Right work is work that enhances your experience**
> **of life rather than deadening it.**

Many people, maybe even most, are not involved in what is right work for them. And of those who are, many fail to experience it as such, some because they struggle against the naturalness of work itself, others because they don't know how to engage in it in a conscious or meaningful way.

Below is a simple way to determine where you, personally, stand in relation to right work. Rate each statement according to how closely it describes the way you think or feel about it, from 1 for Rarely to 5 for Most of the Time. Jot your answers on a pad so you can score them afterward:

1=Rarely   2=Occasionally   3=About Half the Time
4=Often   5=Most of the Time

1. I have fun at work.
2. I dread having to leave for work in the morning.
3. I check my watch or glance at the clock in the afternoon to see how much time is left before the workday is over.
4. I believe I *chose* this work instead of falling into it or settling on it as the lesser of several evils.
5. I feel drained at the end of the day.
6. I am angry at my immediate supervisors or with the company as a whole.
7. I respect other people who do what I do for doing it.
8. I would like my children to feel about their work the way I feel about mine.
9. I'm afraid or anxious about losing my job.
10. I'd like someone to marry and support me, or to win the lottery

or receive an inheritance big enough so that I would never have to work again.

11. I enjoy showing the results of the work I do to my family and friends or talking to them about it.

12. I think I'm being exploited.

13. I want to quit, even though I don't have another job or work I could go to.

14. I get opportunities in what I do to say a congratulatory "All right!" to myself or fellow workers on my team.

15. I *long* to be doing something else.

16. I look forward to the day when I can retire and don't have to do this work any longer.

17. After having been away on a vacation or a long holiday, I approach my work with renewed interest or vigor, at least for a while.

18. I perceive "others" as making it difficult for me to get ahead: competitors, supervisors, unskilled employees, the government, and the like.

19. I get drowsy in the mid-afternoon.

20. I enjoy the company of most of my coworkers [or, if you work alone, yourself].

After you've answered the questions, separate them into two groups: In Group A, place questions 1, 4, 7, 8, 11, 14, 17, and 20. In Group B, questions 2, 3, 5, 6, 9, 10, 12, 13, 15, 16, 18, and 19.

To score yourself, add up the total number of points in each group. For Group A, multiply the number by a factor of 1.5, and make the result, the adjusted number of points, the new total. (Example: Group A, 14 points—14 points × 1.5 = 21 adjusted points. New total for Group A, 21.) Using a calculator will make this simple.

Subtract the total for Group B from the total for Group A. (Examples: Group A 57 minus Group B 20 = 37. Or Group A 21 minus Group B 40 = -19 [negative 19].) Whatever the number is, write it down and circle it.

Here is how to interpret your score. (Bear in mind that the test is only a rough indicator of your relationship to right work, not an absolute statement.) If the number is between 20 and 48, you are probably to almost certainly in your right work. If it is between -20 and -48 (negative 20 and negative 48), you are probably to almost certainly *not* in your right work. If it is between 19 and -19 (negative 19), the meaning is less clear; you will need to explore the question further before you can decide it with confidence. If you're in the unclear range, retest yourself after three more months of working this program. The answer will probably be apparent then.

So what do you do if you are *not* in your right work? You will probably want to shift out of that into something that *is* right for you. You won't be able to do that tomorrow, or in a week, a month, or even a year, possibly not even in a few years. But you can begin the process right now, and should.

"Let's be realistic," you might say. "There must be times people have to work at a job or occupation they don't like. And I can't believe it's possible for everyone to do what would be right work for them."

There *are* times we have to work at a job or occupation we don't like. And we're certainly more likely to be in that position before we have consciously begun to make peace with money, or are in the early stages of that. But never able to do your right work? No. Barring war, extended economic depression, early death, and the like, that will be a matter of choice—if you practice *all* of this program—rather than necessity.

What *is* possible is that some people will never discover what is right work for them and thus never become involved with it. But anyone who sensitizes himself or herself to the question and puts real effort into the search probably will be able to discover it and engage with it. Here is an effective way to do that:

On a cheerful weekend morning, sit somewhere bright and comfortable with a cup of fresh coffee, a glass of juice, or whatever else you might want. Have your pad and pen with you. On a clean page, write:

Ten Activities I Truly Enjoy Doing.

Then list ten such activities. True enjoyment, for our purposes, means that three elements must be present in the activity: pleasure, relish, and satisfaction. The emphasis may be greatly on one, but all must be at least present. Don't simply put down the first ten ideas that pop into your mind, but don't spend a lot of time musing over the question either; the process is probably more subtle than you might have first imagined, but shouldn't be something difficult.

One woman, a stock analyst, listed "Sleeping" right off the bat. But after talking with someone else who was working this practice, and some reflection, she deleted that. She *did* sleep a lot, frequently experienced what she thought of as pleasure from it, and *wished* to do it. But it was not an activity she actually enjoyed: she didn't gain any satisfaction from it, didn't relish it, and what she'd first thought was pleasure in it she recognized was actually simply relief at being able to escape her own life, which she experienced as stressful and in many ways unsatisfactory.

After you have written your list, put it away for a few days.

The next step is to link the activities you listed to work for which people are paid. Take your list out, sit with it, and reread it. Reflect on the activities. Begin writing down jobs, occupations, and professions in which these activities are permitted or even required. One man, for example, who was working as a plumber, had listed as one activity he enjoyed, "Making children smile." This might be possible—even likely—in a wide array of occupations, from clown to social worker, from teacher to toy-store owner, from police officer to computer-game designer, from dog trainer to child psychologist, and many others.

Write down as many jobs or occupations as you can, paying special attention to those that would allow you to perform two, three, or more of the activities on your list. Some of the other activities the man who was working as a plumber had listed were being outdoors, performing physical labor, and working in the company of other people. By keeping these in mind, he was able more clearly to see work that was likely to be right for him than he could have if he'd simply focused on the single activity of making children smile.

In the end, this man applied to the fire department, passed the physical and written exams, was accepted, completed his training, and has been working as a firefighter for the last two years. He found his right work, which for him was an important part of making peace with money.

A woman, a corporate writer, enrolled in medical school at age thirty-six. Her own troubled relationship with money had never involved debt. Actually, her fear of spending had caused her to live meanly despite the good income she'd been making. As a result, she had amassed sizable savings. Combining these with a scholarship and the later possibility of student loans (for her, who had no history of trouble with debt, these unsecured loans were perfectly reasonable), she was able to resign from her job and enroll full time. A year from now, she will graduate and move on to her internship.

Some people list as many as fifteen or more possibilities when they create a list of jobs or occupations that might be right work for them. If you have done that, trim your list to the seven you find the most appealing. Others put down only four or five. If that's what you've done, fine, it's enough. Next, narrow the list to the three possibilities you prefer most. Ideally, each will involve at least two of the activities you enjoy. The more the better, but even work that involves only one may be enough, if that activity is of fundamental importance to you.

Now, select the possibility from among these three that most appeals to you and that also seems to offer a chance of actually being possible.

Finished? Congratulations! Compared to where you began, you've come a long way toward seeing your right work. Now you need a way to make a transition into that work (or, as will be the case with some, a way to modify what you're already doing so that it *becomes* right work for you, which we'll discuss next).*

In other words, you need a plan. You already know how to make and implement an effective plan. You did that in the last chapter with the "The Yellow Brick Road." Planning a transition from your present job or occupation into your right work is similar to that, with only a few modifications.

Begin this plan, as you did the last one, with a mission statement. Include your purpose in the statement—in this case, ending up in your right work—and the strategy you intend to use in service of that. Lay out

---

*If neither option seems truly possible, reduce the amount of work you are now doing. Then fill the time you have freed with new work that is right for you. This will at least give you balance.

your tactics, the actions you'll take. Start with your longest time frame: five years, three, two, even one, whatever is appropriate. Be both realistic and confident. Work next with a reduced time frame, say a year. Spell out the actions you would like to have completed by the end of a year which would be in service of your long-term goal. Then repeat the process, this time for a single month. Finally, pick one of your one-month actions—and execute it by the end of the coming week.

Working through this practice once may be enough to enable you to make the transition into your right work, or it may not. If not, work through it again, as many times as is necessary.

Will *everyone* who undertakes this practice move into his or her right work? I would like to say yes; and maybe it's true. But I don't know. What I do believe is that anyone who truly gives himself or herself to it probably will. That has been my observation and experience over the years. The people I have seen fail, and there haven't been many, all went about it in a desultory and halfhearted way. Those who devoted themselves to it succeeded.

Trying to measure success here can be as subjective as trying to measure it in other areas of life. I have watched two persons accomplish the same thing or occupy the same position in life, but one look upon herself as being successful while the other looked upon herself as having failed. It is also possible that someone might discover her right work but be prevented by *force majeure* from entering into it, or discover it only to *choose* not to do it, because she wants the ego gratification of being more noticed by the world, because her parents want something else and she is not willing to give up their support or approval, because she wants the bigger salary she can make doing other work, or for other reasons.

Remember, finding your right work necessarily involves an element of subjectivity. Not God, nor the universe, nor the stars, nor anything else you might believe in has decreed that there is but one single job or occupation that is right for you, and one alone, and that you will be condemned to suffer if you do not find it. For most of us, perhaps *all* of us, there are several jobs or occupations that would constitute right work. This practice, therefore, cannot become a mechanism of potential failure for you. No matter how or on what level you work it, nothing negative can result from it, only benefits.

What do you do if you believe or discover that you are *already* in your right work, but aren't experiencing it as such, as appropriate, natural, life-enhancing? Here is a simple practice that can change that.

First, select a weekday. Let's say you've picked Monday. Each Monday, then, for the coming four weeks, conceive, understand, and perform your work as service—as *giving*, as selflessly benefiting someone else. Do this no matter what your job or profession is. Do it in every part of your work. Help people. *Give* to them. Freely, joyfully, with no thought of getting anything back from them. Give: To make their lives better. To bestow upon them. To gladden their hearts. To better their days.

Give. Let *giving* be your reality through the working day. Let what you are doing be not "work," but rather the act and process of giving. Do this for its own sake, without thought of anything else.

While you are engaged in this, another reality will be taking place. Other people will be also be working, be putting forth a directed flow of energy: thousands of them, hundreds of thousands, millions. They will be doing it all around the globe; and a great deal of what they are doing will—directly and indirectly, to some infinitesimal degree or another—make your life better, bestow something upon you.

And yet a third reality will be occurring, too. While you are giving and while great numbers of others are performing actions around the world that are in some way contributing to your well-being, you and they are being awarded money for this. All *you* are doing is giving. That is how you are spending your day, with no thought other than to give. Yet you are being paid at the same time, *paid* for *giving!* Know and understand that you will be paid either way—for giving, or for laboring, suffering, resisting, and resenting. All that will change is *what* you are being paid for. What you are being paid for is your choice.

This is not an easy concept to absorb. If you want to work with it as a regular practice, you will have to bring your attention back to conceiving, understanding, and performing your work as service—giving, selflessly benefiting someone else—time and time again over your first few tries and perhaps over many tries. But it is worth the effort. The rewards of this practice can be enormous. Also, it becomes easier with experience. If you undertake it regularly, you will find this way of perceiving work happening to you spontaneously and spilling into other days. For some people, the very fortunate, it may become the primary way they experience their work.

Rabbi Elimelekh once set out for home from a city he had visited and all the hasidim accompanied him for a long stretch of the way. When his carriage drove through the gate, he got out, told the coachman to drive on, and walked behind the carriage in the midst of the throng. The astonished hasidim asked him why he had done this. He answered: "When I saw the great devotion with which you were performing the good work of accompanying me, I could not bear to be excluded from it!"

—HASIDIC

Before I was a genius I was a drudge.

—IGNACE PADEREWSKI

Mullah Nasrudin was the village judge. An agitated man in scarcely any clothes and with his hair in disarray, came running into the courtroom one afternoon crying out for justice.

"I have been set upon and robbed," he cried.

"Where?" the mullah asked with concern. "By whom?"

"Just outside the village. It must be someone from here. I demand that you uncover and punish him. He stole my robe, my sword, my books. He even stole my boots!"

The mullah frowned. "I see he did not take your undergarment, which you are still wearing."

"No, he did not."

"Alas. In that case, he was not from this village. Things are done thoroughly here. I'm sorry, I cannot investigate your case."

—SUFI

See the job, do the job, stay out of the misery.

—HINDU

Work keeps us from three great evils, boredom, vice, and poverty.

—VOLTAIRE

Returning from a period of solitary meditation, a disciple rode his camel down from the mountains to the tent of his Master. He dismounted, strode right into the tent, and bowed low before the Master, saying:

"So great is my trust in God that I have left my camel outside untied, convinced that God protects the interests of those who love him."

"Go tie your camel, you fool!" said the Master. "God cannot be bothered doing for you what you are perfectly capable of doing for yourself."

—SUFI

The struggle to reach the top is itself enough to fulfill the heart of man. One must believe that Sisyphus is happy.

—ALBERT CAMUS

When the sun rises, I go to work.
When the sun goes down, I take my rest,
I dig the well from which I drink,

I farm the soil which yields my food,
I share creation, Kings can do no more.

—CHINESE

Everything considered, work is less boring than amusing oneself.

—CHARLES BAUDELAIRE

At daybreak, when you loathe the idea of leaving your bed, have this thought ready in your mind: "I am rising for the work of man." Should I have misgivings about doing that for which I was born, and for the sake of which I came into this world? Is this the grand purpose of my existence: to lie here snug and warm underneath my blankets?— "Certainly it feels more pleasant."—Was it for pleasure that you were made, and not for work, nor for effort? Look at the plants, sparrows, ants, spiders, and bees, all working busily away, each doing its part in welding an orderly Universe. So who are you to go against the bidding of Nature? Who are you to refuse man his share of the work?

—MARCUS AURELIUS

A man must sit in a chair a long time with his mouth open before a duck will fly in.

—ANONYMOUS

He who refuses to embrace a unique opportunity loses the prize as surely as if he tried and failed.

—WILLIAM JAMES

It was told of Abbot John the Dwarf that once he had said to his elder brother: I want to live in the same security as the angels have, doing no work, but serving God without intermission. And casting off everything he had on, he started out into the desert. When a week had gone by he returned to his brother. And while he was knocking on the door, his brother called out before opening, and asked: Who are you? He replied: I am John. Then his brother answered and said: John has become an angel and is no longer among men. But John kept on knocking and said: It is I. Still the brother did not open, but kept him waiting. Finally, opening the door, he said: If you are a man, you are going to have to start working again in order to live. But if you are an angel, why do you want to come into a cell? So John did penance and said: Forgive me, brother, for I have sinned.

—Desert Fathers

To do great work a man must be very idle as well as very industrious.

—Samuel Butler

> The ecstatic meditation ended.
> Dishes of food were brought out.
> The [visiting] sufi remembered his donkey
> that had carried him all day.
>
> He called to the servant there, "Please
> go to the stable and mix the barley generously
> with the straw for the animal. Please."

"Don't worry yourself with such matters.
All things have been attended to."

"But I want to make sure that you wet the barley first.
He's an old donkey, and his teeth are shaky."
"Why are you telling me this?
I have given the appropriate orders."

"But did you remove the saddle gently,
and put salve on the sore he has?"

"I have served thousands of guests
with these difficulties, and all have gone away
satisfied. Here, you are treated as family.
Do not worry. Enjoy yourself."

"But did you warm his water
just a little, and then add only a bit of straw
to the barley?"

           "Sir, I am ashamed for you."

                          "And please,

sweep the stall clean of stones and dung,
and scatter a little dry earth in it."

"For God's sake, sir,
leave my business to *me*!"

"And did you currycomb his back?
He loves that."

"Sir! I am *personally*
responsible for all these chores!"
The servant turned and left at a brisk pace . . .
to join his friends in the street.

The sufi then lay down to sleep
and had terrible dreams about his donkey,
how it was being torn to pieces by a wolf,
or falling helplessly into a ditch.

And his dreaming was right! His donkey
was being totally neglected, weak and gasping,
without food or water all the night long.
The servant had done nothing he said he would.

There are such vicious and empty flatterers
in your life. Do the careful,
donkey-tending work.

Don't trust that to anyone else.
There are hypocrites who will praise you,
but do not care about the health
of your heart-donkey.
Be concentrated and *leonine*
in the hunt for what is your true nourishment.
Don't be distracted by blandishment-noises,
of any sort.

—Jalal ad-Din Rumi

WORK: QUOTATIONS & MEDITATIONS

Choose a job you love, and you will never have to work a day in your life.

—CONFUCIUS

One must not always think so much about what one should do, but rather what one should be. Our works do not ennoble us; but we must ennoble our works.

—MEISTER ECKHART

A man is a worker. If he is not that he is nothing.

—JOSEPH CONRAD

Shun those studies in which the work that results dies with the worker.

—LEONARDO DA VINCI

Work is love made visible. And if you cannot work with love but only with distaste, it is better that you should leave your work and sit at the gate of the temple and take alms of those who work with joy.

—KAHLIL GIBRAN

The philosopher Diogenes was sitting on a curbstone, eating bread and lentils for his supper. He was seen by the philosopher Aristippus, who lived comfortably by flattering the king.

Said Aristippus, "If you would learn to be subservient to the king, you would not have to live on lentils."

Said Diogenes, "Learn to live on lentils, and you will not have to cultivate the king."

—HASIDIC

There comes a time in a man's life when to get where he has to go—if there are no doors or windows he walks through a wall.

—BERNARD MALAMUD

The joy about our work is spoiled when we perform it not because of what we produce but because of the pleasure with which it can provide us, or the pain against which it can protect us.

—PAUL TILLICH

The moment a man can really do his work, he becomes speechless about it; all words are idle to him; all theories. Does a bird need to theorize about building its nest, or boast of it when built? All good work is essentially done that way; without hesitation; without difficulty; without boasting.

—JOHN RUSKIN

The fruitfulness of a gift is the only gratitude for the gift.

—MEISTER ECKHART

Most men would feel insulted if it were proposed to employ them in throwing stones over a wall, and then in throwing them back, merely that they might earn their wages. But many are no more worthily employed now.

—HENRY DAVID THOREAU

God helps those who help themselves.

—BENJAMIN FRANKLIN

> When a friend calls to me from the road
> And slows his horse to a meaning walk,
> I don't stand still and look around
> On all the hills I haven't hoed,
> And shout from where I am, What is it?
> No, not as there is a time to talk.
> I thrust my hoe in the mellow ground,
> Blade-end up and five feet tall,
> And plod: I go up to the stone wall
> For a friendly visit.

—ROBERT FROST

If the building of a bridge does not enrich the awareness of those who work on it, then that bridge ought not to be built.

—FRANTZ FANON

Every man is rich or poor according to the degree in which he can afford to enjoy the necessaries, conveniences, and amusements of human life. But after the division of labor has once thoroughly taken place, it is but a very small part of these with which a man's own labor can supply him. The far greater part of them he must derive from the labor of other people, and he must be rich or poor according to the quantity of that labor which he can command, or which he can afford to purchase. The value of any commodity, therefore, to the person who possesses it, and who means not to use or consume it himself, but to exchange it for other commodities, is equal to the quantity of labor which it enables him to purchase or command. Labor, therefore, is the real measure of the exchangeable value of commodities.

—ADAM SMITH

Not everything that is more difficult is more meritorious.

—ST. THOMAS AQUINAS

For us, there is only the trying. The rest is not our business.

—T. S. ELIOT

A merchant had a hundred and fifty camels to carry his things, and forty servants who did as he ordered. One evening, he invited a friend, Saadi, to join him. The whole night, he couldn't get any rest and talked constantly about his problems, troubles, and the pressures of his profession. He told of his wealth in Turkestan, spoke of his estates in India, and displayed his jewels and the titles to his lands. "O, Saadi," he sighed, "I have another trip coming up. After this trip, I want to settle back and have a hard-won rest. That's what I want more than anything in the world. This trip, I'm going to take Persian sulphur to China, since

I've heard that it is very valuable there. From there I want to transport Chinese vases to Rome. My ship will then carry Roman goods to India, and from there I will take Indian steel to Halab. From Halab, I will export mirrors and glass to Yemen and take velvet into Persia." With a sad expression on his face, he then proclaimed to Saadi, who had been listening in disbelief, "And, after that, my life will belong to peace, reflection, and meditation, the highest goal of my thoughts."

—AFTER SAADI

A man died and woke to find himself in the loveliest environment imaginable, with everything he had ever wished for close at hand. A polite and elegantly dressed man appeared and said to him, "Anything you desire is yours. Any kind of food, pleasure, amusement or entertainment. You need only ask."

The man was thrilled. For weeks he partook of every wonderment and delight he had ever dreamed of and many more that occurred to him only now. But finally he was sated, and he began to grow bored. He summoned his attendant. "Look," he said, "I'm tired of this. I need something to do. What kind of work can you offer me?"

"Work, sir?" the attendant asked sadly. "Oh, sir, I'm very sorry, but that is the one thing we cannot do for you. There is no work here for you."

The man snorted. "That's a fine thing. I might as well be in hell."

"Where, sir," the attendant asked softly, "do you think you are?"

—TRADITIONAL

In work, do what you enjoy.

—Lao Tzu

Know therefore what is work, and also know what is wrong work. And know also of a work that is silence: mysterious is the path of work. The person who in his or her work finds silence and who sees that silence is work, this person in truth sees the Light and in all his or her works finds peace.

—*Bhagavad-Gita*

Work should be in order to live. We don't live in order to work. That shift in awareness is necessary.

—Matthew Fox

It is not by any means certain that a man's business is the most important thing he has to do.

—Robert Louis Stevenson

I go on working for the same reason that a hen goes on laying eggs.

—H. L. Mencken

The growth of bigness has resulted in ruthless sacrifices of human values. . . .When a nation of shopkeepers is transformed into a nation of clerks, enormous spiritual sacrifices are made.

—William O. Douglas

This is a world of action, and not for moping and groaning in.

—CHARLES DICKENS

Now in order that people may be happy in their work, these three things are needed: They must be fit for it: they must not do too much of it: and they must have a sense of success in it—not a doubtful sense, such as needs some testimony of others for its confirmation, but a sure sense, or rather knowledge, that so much work has been done well, and fruitfully done, whatever the world may say or think about it.

—JOHN RUSKIN

Nothing in the world can take the place of persistence. Talent will not; nothing is more common than unsuccessful men with talent. Genius will not; unrewarded genius is almost a proverb. Education will not; the world is full of educated derelicts. Persistence and determination alone are omnipresent.

—CALVIN COOLIDGE

Most men that do thrive in the world do forget to take pleasure during the time that they are getting their estate, but reserve that till they have got one, and then it is too late for them to enjoy it.

—SAMUEL PEPYS

It is not enough to be busy, so are the ants. The question is, what are we busy about?

—HENRY DAVID THOREAU

MONEY

Five

Money
····················

Money isn't real—it isn't a thing like an apple, a mountain, or a piece of coal. It is an idea, a symbol. It exists only in that it represents something *else*, other than itself. The moment it ceases to do that, it ceases to be money.

Once there was no money in human life. Now there is no aspect of our lives it does not color, no crevice into which it does not flow, no activity it does not overarch. No one can avoid money, and its impact. Not unless we cut ourselves off entirely from every other human being, which of course we cannot do.

Books beyond counting have been written about money and its history. But never, notes economist John Kenneth Galbraith, a history of all money during all time. That, he says, is "something with which no historian is likely soon to offend." The subject, in its enormity, is virtually ungraspable. Still, we need at least a sense of money's history if we are ever to make peace with it, so we are going touch upon some of the more significant parts of it here.

In the Beginning

At the dawn of our history, proto-humans and then finally early humans as we now know them lived in tiny groups, akin to the way a pride of lions, a tribe of gorillas, or a pack of wolves do today. Their experience of life was direct and immediate: They spent most of their time seeking food, they found shelter, they rested. Even as human intelligence first rose, then leaped forward, humans still engaged in no activity for which anything like money was required. Each group comprised only a few members, and these cooperated with each other in finding food, arranging shelter, raising young, and eventually, in caring for the less able among them.

There were almost certainly hierarchies of status within each group, which would have meant hierarchies of privilege, too. But since the bands were each small enough to function something like a single organism (in that, basically, it thrived or waned as a unit), there was still no function for anything like money.

But move the evolutionary clock ahead: Now, instead of avoiding each other or driving the other away, these little bands are beginning to interact with each other. Soon the need arises for a tangible basis on which to conduct the interaction. Thus comes exchange, the transfer of some object like a piece of food or stone tool from one band to another. From exchange, trade is born. The concepts of ownership, of value, arise.

Objects are amassed and bargained for. Time passes. Foodstuffs are carried from one place to another, spices, tools, weapons, clothing. The goods are passed from hand to hand. In time, the need for a symbol—something that will allow people to deal and trade with each other without having to haul their herds of cattle and wagons of salt around with them, that will allow individuals and small groups to travel ever farther from their homelands and kinship groups—reaches critical mass. In short, the need for money arises; for that which will represent something else, for that which can be used to equate bushels of grain with pieces of fabric, timber, a horse.

Many objects have served in this role over history: stones, shells, beads, gems; feathers, pelts, tobacco; even human skulls. But most common, at least over the past four thousand years, has been metal: bronze, brass, and iron; copper, silver, and gold. These were first exchanged in the form of pieces and chunks, sometimes even as powder. Later they were worked into crude bars, squares, and discs.

The earliest money in our contemporary sense of it, minted to *serve* as money, to represent something else, be accepted in exchange for goods or services, and function as an agency through which to store wealth, was created in China in the twelfth century B.C.E.: tiny metal replicas of agricultural tools. The first money *qua* money minted in the West was made by the Greeks in the eighth century B.C.E., in the form of coins made from electrum, an alloy of gold and silver.

From the beginning, money possessed powerful spiritual and religious significance: The faces, signs, and names of gods and goddesses appeared on almost all early coins; so did the symbols of creation, fecundity, and vitality. The word *money* itself derives from the divine, from the Roman goddess Moneta (an aspect of Juno, the mother goddess), in whose temples the coins were minted that came to be used throughout the Roman empire and many other parts of the world as well.

In a little time, the faces of rulers and the symbols of state began to appear along with the religious and spiritual imagery on coins, thus linking secular power to supernatural power, legitimizing and strengthening it by virtue of its relationship, its kinship, with the sacred.

Because money was so elementally commingled with spirit and religion, it has been closely associated from the beginning and through its long history with blood, sacrifice, energy, and life, which are the deepest nature of spirit and religion. Early societies prayed and sacrificed for successful hunts and good harvests, burned choice meats, offered up first fruits, spilled human blood. At first, this was probably done in awe, with humility and reverence in the face of what was clearly the overwhelming, incontestable power of nature. Gradually, it came to be done in supplication, entreaty. And then, finally, in the form of corrupted rites and observances, under the auspices of institutionalized, hierarchical religion, as what psychologist William James in his book *The Varieties of Religious Experience* calls "procedures for influencing the disposition of the deity."

This is where money comes from, then—from deep within our psyches or souls, carrying with it all the enormous unrecognized power of its origin. It was money that worshipers paid to purchase animals for sacrifice in the temples, and it was money, even though they or priests slit the animals' throats, that they were actually sacrificing, money that clearly represented the blood, energy, and life being offered up. In tithing, money was given in place of blood and life. So, too, with almsgiving. Money was further sacrificed as taxes, which represented energy, life, and power given over to the representatives, the secular analogs (and in many cases, it was believed, the actual kinfolk) of divinity. Money was passed from hand to hand in place of land surrendered, daughters married off, armies raised. Money was given by one person to another as recompense for the effort and sweat of that second person, sacrificed throughout the day in behalf of the first, who handed over the money (the symbol and storehouse of life and energy) in exchange for the *actual* life and energy: like for like.

Even the ultimate sacrifice in Western mythos, the sacrifice of Christ, was of blood and life in exchange for more blood and life. "I came," said Jesus, "that they might have life, and that they might have it more abundantly." And the coming brought with it the shedding of his blood, without which, the mythos makes clear, there could *be* no life more abundant.

In Greece, the earliest treasuries were temples. And for the next 2,500 years, until only recently, most treasuries and banks were designed and built, consciously or unconsciously, to resemble temples or at least to trigger mental association with them. The same is true of most major buildings of state, too, such as the U.S. Capitol building, Buckingham Palace, and the Kremlin.

The coins and paper money of most nations still carry the likenesses of gods and their symbols, and of the gods' chosen human favorites, our rulers and governors, and of temples, both literal and in the form of buildings of state. They still display the signs and representations of life, energy, and bounty: coiling vegetation, sheaves of wheat, clusters of fruit, fish from the water, game from the plains.

The problem today, says philosopher Jacob Needleman in his book *Money and the Meaning of Life,* is not that we take money too seriously, but that we don't take it seriously *enough.* "The outward expenditure of mankind's energy," he writes, "now takes place in and through money." Not, he says, in the creation of art, as it did in the Renaissance and medieval Europe, nor in the growth of the state, as it did in ancient Rome, nor in construction of monuments, as it did in Egypt. "For anyone who seeks to understand the meaning of our human life on earth," Needleman writes, "for anyone who wishes to understand the meaning of his own individual life on earth, it is imperative that one understand this movement of energy. Therefore, if one wishes to understand life, one *must* understand money—in this present phase of history and civilization."

But *can* one understand money, in its vastness, power, depth, and variegation?

Probably not, at least not in full, not intellectually. What one can do, though, is to recognize the profoundness of money, achieve *an* understanding of it, and learn how to live more in harmony and peace with it than not.

Money and its power cannot be escaped. Like a waterfall, like fire, it itself is neither good nor evil: It is neutral, its character at any instant determined by the eye of the perceiver, the hand of the user.

Practice:
The Best, The Worst, and Change

What have you done with money in your life—fundamentally, from your being? Most of us can't answer that. We might not even understand the question. We are used to thinking of money as something independent of us, which acts upon us and that to a lesser degree we act upon. We are not accustomed to considering our use of it as a reflection of who we are. We don't *want* to consider it that way. For many, our first response is that it would be too intense, unbearable. Yet without knowing who we are with money, what it has meant to us as revealed by what we have done with it, we are handicapped in trying to make peace with it. Here is a way to overcome that handicap.

Pick a day in the coming week in which you're able to set aside an hour or two you can use for quiet reflection. When the time arrives, sit down with a pad and a pen. Relax your mind, your spirit. Become peaceful. Relinquish any thought of either self-congratulation or self-condemnation. Simply accept yourself. Let go of ego. Let go of fear, anger, hopes. For this period, turn your life and your will over to the care of what is best in you. Allow yourself to feel free, tranquil, safe.

Now—with neither justification nor condemnation, and free of denial, of fear—look backward through your life. Look for the worst things you have ever done with money. Look for the things you have done that make you feel ashamed, make you think less of yourself, the things you would least like another human being to know about you. On your pad, list the ten worst of these. Take your time. Be as neutral as you can be while doing this. Be like a camera, simply making a record of what you see.

When you have finished the list, set your pad aside. Stand up. Breathe. Stretch. Relax. Stand quietly a minute or two, breathing easily. Think of yourself as bringing clean, fresh air, new energy, deep into your lungs with each inhale; with each exhale as expelling old, stale air, toxic matter. Think of yourself as exchanging the old for the new, freshening, renewing, revitalizing yourself.

When you're ready, sit and take up your pad again. Relax your mind and spirit. Let go of any thought of congratulation or condemnation of yourself. Be peaceful, accepting of yourself. Let go of your ego. Let go of your fears, angers, hopes. Turn your life and your will over to the care of what is best in you. Let yourself feel free, tranquil, safe.

Once again, look backward through your life—but this time search for the *best* things you have ever done with money, those things about which you are happiest, that make you feel good about yourself, that you are glad you did, even if your act was unknown to any other person. On your pad, list the ten best of them. Again, take your time.

When you have completed the list, set your pad aside. Stand, breathe, stretch. Relax, as you did before. Picture yourself as being freshened, renewed, and revitalized with each inhalation. Then smile and give yourself the pleasure of a deep, extended stretch. Put your pad away in a private place.

There is one more simple action to perform, after which whatever positive changes are to come about as a result of this practice—and there *will be* such changes—will do so of their own accord and at their own pace with no further effort on your part. That action is this: Select a friend, someone trustworthy and understanding, who cares for you and has your best interests at heart. (Don't select your spouse or a relative; the intimate nature of this material could provoke negative family dynamics.) If you can't think of an appropriate person, consider a member of the clergy, some other spiritual counselor, or someone in the helping professions whose empathy and integrity you respect. If you can find someone who has done this kind of process herself or himself, so much the better. Explain to her what you wish to do. Arrange to sit down with her. Then do so, and share with her the two lists you created. Tell her the ten worst things you have ever done with money, then the ten best things you have ever done with it.

The role of the listener is only to serve as witness, to be attentive and compassionate. She is not there to judge or disqualify. She is not there to comment. She is there only to hear and understand you. When you are finished sharing these things with her, she is only to acknowledge that she has heard you. It is best if she simply smiles and says, "Thank you." Nothing more. Nothing less. (She may also wish to express her appreciation of your trust in her and her regard or affection for you. Something like that is all right. Just no commentary.)

If, at a future date, your friend feels a desire or need to share something similar about herself with you, be willing to help her as she did you, serving as a witness for her, attentive and compassionate, empty of judgment or comment, and in the end simply smiling and saying, "Thank you." (And perhaps expressing your appreciation of her trust in you and your regard or affection for her.)

Whatever the case, *you* are finished with this process.

Why do we share these things with another human being? Because it is a profound and liberating thing to do. To sit with another human being and admit to him these things about money that are of such importance to us releases and heals us in the deepest, most significant levels of our being. Without such release, these acts we are ashamed of, that make us think less of ourselves, that we are fearful of other people coming to know about us, can and often do poison us from within. We expend psychic energy trying to repress or justify them; we feel shame, anger, guilt; our sense of isolation increases. Sharing the *best* things we have done with money provides balance and prevents this process from becoming a bill of indictment. These positive acts are just as real as the negative ones. Therefore, it is equally as important that we recognize and be willing to certify them to another person, too.

Nearly everyone who undertakes this practice experiences release and healing. For some, it is immediate and can be almost overpowering. Tim, the owner of a small business, had worked as a hospital orderly when he was young, and in that job had once stolen money from the wallet of an unconscious accident victim. When he finished sharing his lists, he broke into tears. "For the first time in twenty years," he says, "I felt forgiven. I felt like I had a right to walk on the earth again."

For Fred, a mechanic, the most poignant moment came while he was describing an incident at a country flea market. A small boy had been hugging a big stuffed dog at a vendor's table for some time. The boy's father was telling him, with quiet embarrassment, that they couldn't afford the dog and trying to loosen the boy's arms from around it. The boy was stricken. Fred felt sudden pain, felt the sheer *grief* of the boy. The father separated the boy from the dog and led him away.

"How much is that?" Fred asked the vendor. "Ten dollars," she said. Fred had little money of his own at the time, but he took ten dollars from his wallet, put it into the woman's hand, and said, "Give it to him." The woman hurried after the family with the dog and did. The boy flung his arms around the dog. The woman pointed to Fred. "Thank you," the father said awkwardly. "You didn't have to do that." Fred began to move away, feeling awkward himself. "I know," he said. "You're welcome." The boy was staring at Fred, clutching the dog. "I had a dog once myself," Fred said to him. "I really loved him. I know how you feel. I hope he's your good friend."

Several years later, Fred wrote this incident down on his list as one of the best things he had ever done with money. He says, "When I shared the story, it was almost like a mystical experience—I finally knew that I was all right, that I was a good man, I really was."

For others, the release, the healing, is neither immediate nor overwhelming. "I myself felt only a bit of relief as I walked back out into the street afterward," says Joanie, an editor. "In fact, it was a little disappointing. But what happened was that the effect continued to reverberate within me for nearly a year. Its impact was cumulative. Month by month I experienced a lightening of my being. I became progressively freer from images and memories that had oppressed me for years. It was only in retrospect that I became aware that many of these had left me, and that my experience of the ones that remained was less frequent, and their effect less powerful."

I have benefited deeply from this practice myself. I have never seen anyone who did not in some way or another, and most often deeply.

Practice:

The Weekly Review

The goal in this practice is to make you aware on a daily basis of how you handle, think, and feel about money. This awareness will help you make more effective and pleasing decisions about your money, become more capable and comfortable with it, and also make it easier for you to work with the other practices in this book.

At the end of each week, for the next four weeks, conduct a review of the preceding seven days: Was there anything in them concerning money that you regret having done? Or not having done? Was there anything you did that you may want to correct or do differently in the future? Or that you're particularly pleased with or glad of?

If you do find things you're not happy with, negative acts, omissions, don't blame or criticize yourself. There is no judgment in this review. All we want is an increasing *awareness*. That's why we include the positive as well as the negative.

Here is a way such increased awareness played out in my own life. Shortly after publication of my last book, an organization that offers workshops in New York City asked me to present one for them based on material in that book. The money they guaranteed (as opposed to the *potential* earnings if the event was well attended) was much below my normal rates; below, even, what I *needed* to be paid for this kind of work in order not to underearn.

On the other hand, this organization places its promotional catalog into the hands of roughly one million people. What I was really being offered, I needed to see, was not a small payment for an evening-long workshop, but the publicity value of having my name, photograph, and the book's cover appear in a catalog that would be seen by a million people. (Part of being a professional writer involves supporting your books by being willing to do publicity tours, book signings, interviews, and other such activities.) Recognizing this made it easier to evaluate the true offer: one sixth of a page in a twenty-three-page catalog.

That was not enough.

Since my payment was to be primarily in publicity, I had to receive enough of it to justify the time and energy that would go into the workshop. I asked for a half a page. (I was willing to settle for a quarter, though I didn't say that.) The organization said they would try to give me something more than a sixth, but couldn't guarantee that. I offered to accept a sixth of a page if they would raise the guaranteed fee. They tried to persuade me to do it on their terms, and in the end wouldn't meet either of my requests. So, reluctantly, I declined—reluctantly because I *do* need to support my books, and because I know that as someone with an inclination to underearn, I have strong tendency to say no to money.

By mid-afternoon, I had nagging doubt: Had I done the right thing? I reexamined the offer, but remained confused. Clearly nothing momentous hinged on this decision, but because my relationship with money has historically not been easy, and because I *practice* what I preach, I called a friend I respect who could be more objective than I. She not only confirmed my judgment but pointed out that I might actually have devalued myself as a speaker had I accepted, since this organization was known in professional circles for paying low rates to all but their lead people.

It was because of my awareness of how I tended to deal with money, developed through this practice and others, and long before this offer was ever made to me, that I was able to make a sound, self-benefiting decision about it. When lingering discomfort then made me question that decision, calling someone who had worked to make peace with money in her own life—in addition to being a professional peer—removed that doubt and discomfort.

Through this practice, Yvonne, a graphic illustrator, became aware of how she strained to survive on work that didn't really pay her enough to do that, so that she wouldn't be forced into making changes or decisions, which she feared. She had always thought she had a mild tendency in this direction, but was shocked to discover just how powerful these drives were in her.

Noah, an architect, recognized himself as a petty thief, often pilfering some minor item because he felt that somehow he was "owed" it. He saw that this dovetailed with his chronic last-minute rushing to arrive at the office on time, his clock-watching, extended lunch periods, and habit of trying to talk merchants out of charging him sales tax on anything costing more than a few dollars. Through *that* awareness, he discovered the submerged anger he felt toward people who had money and even toward money itself, and the unconscious antagonism he had lived in most of his life toward the rest of the world, over money.

This practice can be so valuable, and pleasurable, that many people end up practicing it on a regular basis—some weekly or even daily, others at less fixed intervals. Whatever you eventually decide to do with this practice, do undertake it formally for at least one month.

Money is always there but the pockets change; it is not in the same pockets after a change, and that is all there is to say about money.

—GERTRUDE STEIN

Money swore an oath that nobody who did not love it should ever have it.

—IRISH

A man was sitting on a rock overlooking the ocean. Beside him was a chest filled with gold coins. He picked a coin out, with tears in his eyes, then flung it into the ocean. With a sob, he picked out another, and flung it too into the sea. A wise man was passing by and stopped to watch this strange sight. After seeing many coins disappear into the sea, he approached the man and said, "What is this?"

"A chest of gold," the man answered.

"But what are you doing?" he asked.

"I'm throwing it into the ocean."

"What do you want to do that for?"

"To learn non-attachment," the man replied, weeping.

"Then why don't you just dump it all in at once?" asked the wise man.

"Oh, no," the man gasped. "That would be too painful!"

—KURDISH

Money is human happiness in the abstract.

—ARTHUR SCHOPENHAUER

What is not in doubt is that the pursuit of money, or any enduring association with it, is capable of inducing not alone bizarre but ripely perverse behavior.

—JOHN KENNETH GALBRAITH

Liking money like I like it, it is nothing less than mysticism. Money is a glory.

—SALVADOR DALÍ

To me it seems clearer every day that the moral problem of our age is concerned with the love of money, with the habitual appeal to the money motive in nine-tenths of the activities of life, with the universal striving after individual economic security as the prime object of endeavour, with the social approbation of money as the measure of constructive success, and with the social appeal to the hoarding instinct as the foundation of the necessary provision for the family and for the future.

—JOHN MAYNARD KEYNES

There are few ways in which a man can be more innocently employed than in getting money.

—SAMUEL JOHNSON

The cost of a thing is the amount of what I call life which is required to be exchanged for it, immediately or in the long run.

—HENRY DAVID THOREAU

Money, what do you signify?
—I am the seal of hearts; a heart once sealed
by me will love no one but me.
When you leave, what becomes of your lover?
—I leave behind a mark on my lover's heart
which remains always as a wound.
Money, what do you like most?
—Changing hands.
Where is your dwelling place?
—In the heart of my worshipper.
Where do you accumulate?
—Where I am warmly welcomed.
Where do you stay?
—Where I am adored.
Money, whom do you seek?
—Him who seeks me.
Money, whom do you obey?
—Him who has risen above me; I become his
slave and lie as dust at his feet.

—HAZRAT INAYAT KAHN

Make money your God, and it will plague you like the devil.

—HENRY FIELDING

It's a kind of spiritual snobbery that makes people think they can be happy without money.

—ALBERT CAMUS

However in every nation there are, and must always be, a certain number of these Fiend's servants, who have it principally for the object of their lives to make money. They are always, as I said, more or less stupid, and cannot conceive of anything else so nice as money. Stupidity is always the basis of the Judas bargain. We do great injustice to Iscariot, in thinking him wicked above all common wickedness. He was only a common money-lover, and, like all money-lovers, did not understand Christ—could not make out the worth of Him, or meaning of Him. He never thought He would be killed. He was horror-struck when he found that Christ would be killed; threw his money away instantly, and hanged himself. How many of our present money-seekers, think you, would have the grace to hang themselves, whoever was killed?

—JOHN RUSKIN

Money is the best bait to fish for man with.

—THOMAS FULLER

Those who set out to serve both God and Mammon soon discover that there is no God.

—LOGAN PEARSALL SMITH

When I was young, I thought that money was the most important thing in life; now that I am old I know that it is.

—OSCAR WILDE

Nothing in the world is worse than money. Money lays waste cities; it sets men to roaming from home; it seduces and corrupts honest men and turns virtue to baseness; it teaches villainy and impiety.

—SOPHOCLES

Money enters in two different characters into the scheme of life. A certain amount, varying with the number and empire of our desires, is a true necessary to each one of us in the present order of society; but beyond that amount, money is a commodity to be bought or not to be bought, a luxury in which we may either indulge or stint ourselves, like any other. And there are many luxuries that we may legitimately prefer to it, such as a grateful conscience, a country life, or the woman of our inclination. Trite, flat, and obvious as this conclusion may appear, we have only to look round us in society to see how scantily it has been recognized; and perhaps even ourselves, after a little reflection, may decide to spend a trifle less for money, and indulge ourselves a trifle more in the article of freedom.

—ROBERT LOUIS STEVENSON

When a man is a beggar, he thinks that small change is a fortune. It is not. In order to rise above beggarhood, he must rise above small

change, even though he uses it as a means. Used as an end it will
become an end.

—IBN IKBAL

A penny saved is a penny to squander.

—AMBROSE BIERCE

It is no accident that banks resemble temples, preferably Greek, and that
the supplicants who come to perform the rites of deposit and with-
drawal instinctively lower their voices into the registers of awe. Even the
most junior tellers acquire within weeks of their employment the offi-
ciousness of hierophants tending an eternal flame. I don't know how
they become so quickly inducted into the presiding mysteries, or who
instructs them in the finely articulated inflections of contempt for the
laity, but somehow they learn to think of themselves as suppliers of the
monetarized DNA that is the breath of life.

—LEWIS H. LAPHAM

We could never imagine what a strange disproportion a few or a great
many pieces of money make between men, if we did not see it every day
with our own eyes.

—JEAN DE LA BRUYÈRE

Money is a new form of slavery, and distinguishable from the old simply
by the fact that it is impersonal—that there is no human relation
between the master and the slave.

—LEO TOLSTOY

Money is as deep and broad as the ocean, the primordially unconscious, and makes us so. It always takes us into great depths, where sharks and suckers, hard-shell crabs, tight clams and tidal emotions abound. Its facets have huge horizons, as huge as sex, and just as protean and polymorphous.

—JAMES HILLMAN

A feast is made for laughter, and wine maketh merry: but money answereth all things.

—ECCLESIASTES

In the early part of the 20th century, because the island yielded no metal, the medium of exchange used by inhabitants of Uap or Yap, a German colony in Micronesia, was *fei*, large solid stone wheels ranging in diameter from a foot to twelve feet, with a hole in the centre wherein a pole was inserted sufficiently large and strong to facilitate transportation.

After concluding a bargain which involved the price of *fei* too large to be conveniently moved, its new owner was quite content to accept the bare acknowledgement of ownership and without so much as a mark to indicate the exchange, the coin remains undisturbed on the former owner's premises.

—MILTON FRIEDMAN

With money in your pocket, you are wise and you are handsome and you sing well too.

—YIDDISH

There was a Sufi teacher, Kilidi, who was distressed to discover that his disciples were spreading stories of his various moral excellencies and extraordinary ability to know just what they were thinking and to anticipate what kind of teaching would benefit them best.

He asked them not to do this. But they were proud of him and admired him greatly. They could not resist the normal human tendency to boast of him.

He told them: "You must stop. This practice only draws crowds of sightseers about me, and worse, makes it very difficult for me to teach you more deeply. If you do not cease, I will have to do something that will make you ashamed of me, that will make you seem foolish for ever having followed me."

His admonition was to no avail; if anything, his pupils began to praise him even more. So shortly after, surrounded one afternoon by a number of his disciples and an even greater number of the general public, Kilidi spied a beggar, summoned him forward, and gave him a hundred pieces of gold.

The beggar returned with the gold only a little time later. "This has done me no good," he said. "My wife demands half of it, or else that she should have a hundred pieces from you herself, since she is just as poor as I am."

Kilidi took the gold from the beggar and handed it to a rich man who was at hand, saying to all who could hear: "Rich people do not complain of their money."

Then he said to the beggar: "I have returned you to your former state. Go. Resume your normal harmonious relationship with your wife.

"Now," he told his disciples, "you see that Kilidi makes mistakes. And everyone else has seen that as well."

—SUFI

Money is not required to buy one necessity of the soul.

—HENRY DAVID THOREAU

If you would like to know the value of money, go and try to borrow some.

—BENJAMIN FRANKLIN

Money, which represents the prose of life, and which is hardly spoken of in parlors without an apology, is, in its effects and laws, as beautiful as roses.

—RALPH WALDO EMERSON

There was a rich man who never gave alms to the poor or contributed to charitable causes. People in his small village never called him by name, they simply referred to him as The Miser.

One day a beggar came to the door of The Miser. "Where do you come from?" he asked.

"I live in the village," answered the beggar.

"Nonsense," cried The Miser. "Everyone in this village knows that I do not support beggars!"

In the same village there lived a poor shoemaker. He was a most generous man who responded to every person in need and every charitable cause that was brought to his attention. No one was ever turned away empty-handed from his door.

One day The Miser died. The village leaders decided to bury him at the edge of the cemetery. No one mourned his passing; no one followed the funeral procession to the place of burial.

As the days passed the rabbi heard disturbing news regarding the shoemaker. "He no longer gives alms to the beggars," complained one man. "He has refused every charity that has approached him," declared another.

"Has anyone asked about his change?" inquired the rabbi.

"Yes," replied the first man. "He says he no longer has money to give away."

Soon the rabbi called on the shoemaker. "Why have you suddenly ceased giving money to worthy causes?"

Slowly the shoemaker began to speak. "Many years ago the man you called The Miser came to me with a huge sum of money and asked me to distribute it to beggars and charities. He made me promise that I would not reveal the source of the money until after he died. Once every month he would visit me secretly and give me additional money to distribute. I became known as a great benefactor even though I never spent a penny of my own money. I am surprised that no one questioned me earlier. How could anyone who earned the wages of a shoemaker give away as much money as I have all these years?"

The rabbi called all of the villagers together and told them the story. "The Miser has lived by the Scriptures, keeping his charity a secret," the rabbi told them. Then they all walked to the grave of The Miser and prayed. When he died the rabbi asked to be buried near the fence, next to the grave of the man known as The Miser.

—HASIDIC

Money is like fire, an element as little troubled by moralizing as earth, air and water. Men can employ it as a tool or they can dance around it as if it were the incarnation of a god. Money votes socialist or monarchist, finds a profit in pornography or translations from the Bible, commissions Rembrandt and underwrites the technology of Auschwitz. It acquires its meaning from the uses to which it is put.

—LEWIS H. LAPHAM

Money, young man, is good for the nerves.

—J. P. MORGAN

The love of money is the root of all evil.

—1 TIMOTHY

People are often reproached for wishing for money above all things, and for loving it more than anything else; but it is natural and even inevitable for people to love that which, like an unwearied Proteus, is always ready to turn itself into whatever object their wandering wishes or manifold desires may for the moment fix upon. Everything else can satisfy only one wish, one need: food is good only if you are hungry; wine, if you are able to enjoy it; drugs, if you are sick, fur for the winter; love for youth, and so on. These are all only relatively good, *ἀγαθὰ πρός τι.* Money alone is absolutely good, because it is not only a concrete satisfaction of one need in particular; it is an abstract satisfaction of all.

—ARTHUR SCHOPENHAUER

There are few sorrows, however poignant, in which a good income is of no avail.

—ADAM SMITH

Through the Eye of the Needle

The camel catches his breath, wipes the sweat from his brow. It was a tight squeeze, but he made it.

Lying back on the unbelievably lush grass, he remembers all those years (how excruciating they were!) of fasting and one-pointed concentration, until finally he was thin enough: thaumaturgically thin, thread-thin, almost unrecognizable in his camelness: until the moment in front of the unblinking eye, when he put his front hooves together. Took one long last breath. Aimed. Dived.

The exception may prove the rule, but what proves the exception? "It is not that such things are possible," the camel thinks, smiling. "But such things are possible for *me*."

(AFTER MARK 10:25)
—STEPHEN MITCHELL

I cannot afford to waste my time making money.

—LOUIS R. AGASSIZ

FLOW

Six

Flow

··············

Money is not static. It must keep moving, must flow. When it ceases to flow, it ceases to be money. It becomes only paper and inert bits of metal, or mathematics frozen in electronic media. In order to flow, money must be *used*: participate in transaction. It cannot be money otherwise. As reward, it must be bestowed; as love, given; as energy, cause reaction; as power, be applied; as benediction, be granted; as wealth, create testimony; as sacrifice, leave. It must *move*.

When we try to capture money, fix it in place, it stops being money; and we, as a consequence, become impoverished and remain so until we set it in motion again. We cannot make peace with money without recognizing that it must stay in motion for it even to *be* money for us. We need, therefore, to become accustomed to the flow and comfortable with it.

Practice:
Cash

Since money continues to declare its connection to spirit and psyche by carrying their symbols, we have been able to maintain at least some small link with its significance and roots, along with a certain intuitive sense of its need to stay in motion.

Even the more abstract financial instruments of the past few centuries—stock certificates, mortgages, and the like—have generally displayed the symbols of divine association: authority, vitality, vegetative abundance. This is true of early bank drafts, or checks, too. In the beginning, only businesses used checks, to make payments to one another. *Personal* checks came into common use only in the past sixty years. Like other financial devices, checks aren't really money at all, but rather, vehicles for *transferring* money. In effect, they are symbols of a symbol. Yet we use them just as we would actual money, currency. As banks have become more architecturally secularized over the past century—shifting from their templelike appearance of most of history to a modern steel and glass angularity—so have the checks they issue become more secularized, too, becoming even more not-money, separating us even further from the symbology and experienced power of money. And the less we recognize the true nature of that power, the more troublesome and even dangerous money becomes in our lives.

Most recently, we have witnessed the birth and explosive growth of credit cards, which has occurred mostly over the past thirty years. Originally, credit cards unconsciously acknowledged the origins of money, and some still do. The first two to achieve national success were Diner's Club and the American Express card. The name Diner's Club summons images of food, abundance, and sharing; in short, of life. On the American Express card was (and still is) the helmeted head of a protecting centurion, harkening back to the divinely sanctioned power of the state. The original American Express card remains green; in this country, where the card was born, the color of money. Today other cards are offered in guises that link them immediately to precious metals: silver, gold, platinum.

But now wholly absent from some cards, and disappearing from others, as it did with checks, is the iconography of money's origins. Plastic cards, in their multiple forms—credit, charge, debit, ATM, and others—are gradually replacing actual money in our lives, depriving us of what contact we have left with the reality of money, no matter how fleeting or unconscious that contact may be.

These cards—especially credit cards—make money less real to us; in the extreme, even unreal. Most people, for example, will spend roughly 10 percent more when they shop with a credit card than they would otherwise. More significantly, though, they will spend—which is to say, sacrifice—life and energy they *do not have*. They will steal it from their future: from tomorrow, next week, next year. They will steal it in the form of repeated and continuing indebtedness.

Looming ahead and ready to break over us at any moment is massive, widespread use of personal electronic funds transfer. Most of the world's business transactions are now accomplished this way, by signals sent over phone lines and through space. Each day, more and more private transactions are being made thus, too, through computer modems and by pressing buttons on telephones. It is nearly inevitable that most American households will conduct most of their financial affairs in this manner within the next ten to fifteen years.

Of even greater potential impact is another form of electronic transfer, which has the power to replace what we have known as money from the beginning almost entirely: the "smart card." The smart card is a piece of plastic electronically encoded to be "worth" a specified amount, similar in concept to prepaid telephone calling cards or transit cards. As the smart card becomes universally accepted and used—which it almost certainly will within the next two or three decades—every transaction you make, from paying for your morning cab to work or filling your car's gas tank to picking up the check at lunch or getting a sandwich from the deli, from buying an afternoon paper or an ice-cream bar from a street vendor, to renting a video or purchasing concert tickets on the way home, and practically anything else you can imagine, will be done by taking your smart card out of your wallet and swiping it through a simple device. That device will deduct the cost of whatever you are purchasing—75 cents for a pack of gum or $75 for a sweater—from your card and automatically add it to either the card or bank account of the vendor. Within a few decades, most people in the United States and the rest of the industrialized world will carry two basic pieces of plastic: a smart card and a credit card. There will be little need left for paper money or coins, though it is unlikely that those will ever disappear altogether, at least not for a long time.

There is nothing objectionable about this. In fact, smart cards and electronic funds transfer, in their purer abstraction, actually come closer to the conceptual reality of money than paper and coins do. But they are *not* money, and that is the crucial difference. In time, they may well *become* money—that is, have the same dynamism and impact for us that what we have thought of as money till now possesses—but at this point they do *not* have those. At this point, they simply divorce us even further from the vital experience and understanding of what money and its use truly are, which harms our relationship with money, making it more difficult for many of us make peace with it.

This practice, "Cash," sets out to remedy that. It is a simple practice, involving nothing more and nothing less than this: For the next thirty days, pay for *everything* in cash. Do not put anything on a credit or charge card. Do not buy groceries at the supermarket with your ATM or debit card. Do not go to the movies on your smart card. Do not even write a check. In the few instances where it's better to send payment through the mail—a utility bill, mortgage payment—go to the post office or your bank and use cash to "buy" a money order or bank check; send that out in place of your personal check, so that you have actually purchased the instrument you're using to pay that bill with cash.

In handling the actual fives, tens, twenties, fifties, and hundreds, paying real currency, in taking time to look at the bills, touch them, rest your awareness on them for a moment, you will gain a vivid sense of the significance, use, power, and enjoyment of money. Using cash, and nothing but cash, for thirty days in this fashion will make you more vividly aware of the living reality of money than most people will ever be, more sensitive to money, more capable with it. Many people find that this practice also gives them a sense of freedom and of true entitlement to their money, some for the first time in their life.

The intent of this practice is not to fight a rear-guard action in behalf of currency. It is to help you reconnect with money's meaning and power, to help you learn to live with that power in ways that vitalize your life rather than oppress or batter it, as always happens when we remain ignorant of the significance and power of money. Whenever you think you have become disconnected from money again in the future, blunted about it, or only partly conscious in employing it, return to this practice and use nothing but cash for thirty days.

With experience—and by consciously bringing it to mind—you will be able to transfer this awareness to your use of checks, credit cards, electronic bill paying, and eventually, use of a smart card, so that the significance of and power of money, as it flows in and out of your life, will not be lost to you.

Practice:

Benediction

At least some of the time, and often much of the time, many of us feel fear or resentment over our need to spend money or even over spending it for something we *want* to spend it on. The underlying sense is: I don't have enough. There won't be enough left. Yet spending is something we all must do on a daily basis. This negative reaction to spending is a steady contributor to the pain and stress we feel about money, to it's being difficult in our life.*

Here is a way to liberate yourself from that fear and resentment. I began this practice many years ago, to deal with my own fear of having to spend. It is powerful. For the next seven days, whenever you hand money over to someone, say silently:

> **"I bless this money.
> I give it to you.
> I wish you pleasure in using it."**

Do the same when you make out a postal money order or bank check, seal it into the envelope, and drop it into the mail. (Remember that you're still involved with the first practice in this chapter, "Cash," by paying for everything in cash.)

---

*We'll deal with the opposite of this problem—compulsive or thrill spending—in chapter 13.

If you wish to continue "Benediction" after you're finished with "Cash," do so. (It is a daily practice in my own life.) Do so by treating the checks you write—for rent, utilities, car payments, an employee's salary—the same way you do cash. After you put the checks into the envelopes, and address, seal, and stamp them, pick them up, one at a time, hold each for a moment lightly in both your hands, and say silently, "I bless this money. I give it to you. I wish you pleasure in using it."

You may feel a hint of pleasure, and a small smile forming on your lips, as you set the envelope aside and pick up the next one. Later, when you drop the envelopes into a mailbox or slot, bring yourself back to this consciousness for an instant, blessing the money and sending it forth. Then smile, turn around, and walk back into the remainder of your day.

Mentally earmark the taxes that are withheld from your salary, if you're employed, or that you must set aside if you're self-employed, for use for health research, botulism control, air traffic safety, or something similar, rather than for anything on which the government spends money that might bother you. Mentally earmark the payment you are making to the telephone company, a department store, or any other institution to serve as part of the salary of an especially deserving employee there.

This is the first part of "Benediction." The second has to do with *receiving* money, which can be distinguished from spending money but not truly separated from it. I instituted this second part about a year after the first, when I was seriously involved with overcoming underearning.

Here is how you do it. When you *receive* money—in whatever amount, from whatever source—take the check or cash in your hands, if you are alone, hold it before you, and say:

> **"I bless this money.**
> **I accept it from you.**
> **I will take pleasure in using it."**

If you are not alone, do this mentally.

Finally, when repaying debts, which is the last part of "Benediction," take the check you are going to send out in hand, and say:

> **"I bless this money.**
> **I return it to you.**
> **I wish you pleasure in using it."**

I created this part about a year after the second part. I still had debts to pay then. I had found that while I had grown much easier with spending and receiving, I was still experiencing some anger, fear, even despondency, when writing out the checks for debt repayment and sending them off, a reluctance to drop them into the mail, a feeling of being deprived, of being taken away from. By including the phrase "I return it to you," in this third part of "Benediction," I was able to see the truth in what I was doing, simply returning to someone his or her own money, which I had used for a while, rather than being forced for some reason to hand over something that was *mine.*[†]

Most people find "Benediction" an exhilarating practice. Many continue it on an ongoing basis. It can be very powerful. Some people have been shocked to discover that it has turned bill paying from something they hated into something almost joyful for them.

You can use this practice with electronic funds transfer, online banking, and smart cards, as well as with currency and checks. You can do it in this fashion: First, commit a brief period each week—five minutes will do—to reflecting on the origin and power of money, and then to recognizing this new activity as the actual spending of money. Second, each time you instruct your computer to send a signal out over a modem to transfer funds from you to someone else or punch a sequence of buttons on your telephone to do the same thing, and each time you use a smart card (or a check card or debit card), pause for a moment just before you do and say silently to yourself, "I bless this money. I give it to you. I wish you pleasure in using it."

[†]Occasionally someone thinks that because she has paid interest on a debt for a long period, perhaps even in an amount exceeding the amount that was originally borrowed, charged, or owed for services, that she has somehow repaid the debt itself and should not be asked to return the original principal. But interest is simply rent, not repayment. Renting an apartment does not entitle anyone to ownership of the apartment after the rental period ends. The apartment still belongs to the landlord. Renting the use of money (paying interest) does not entitle one to ownership of that money when the rental period ends. The money still belongs to the lender.

Money is round; it must roll.

—FRENCH

Once some of the elders came to Scete, and Abbot John the Dwarf was with them. And when they were dining, one of the priests, a very great old man, got up to give each one a little cup of water to drink, and no one would take it from him except John the Dwarf. The others were surprised, and afterward they asked him: How is it that you, the least of all, have presumed to accept the services of this great old man? He replied: Well, when I get up to give people a drink of water, I am happy if they all take it; and for that reason on this occasion I took the drink, that he might be rewarded and not feel sad because nobody accepted the cup from him. And at this all admired his discretion.

—DESERT FATHERS

Annual income twenty pounds, annual expenditure nineteen six, result happiness. Annual income twenty pounds, annual expenditure twenty pounds ought and six, result misery.

—CHARLES DICKENS

We all know how the size of sums of money appears to vary in a remarkable way according as they are being paid in or paid out.

—JULIAN HUXLEY

Remember that you ought to behave in life as you would at a banquet. As something is being passed around it comes to you; stretch out your hand, take a portion of it politely. It passes on; do not detain it. Or it has not come to you yet; do not project your desire to meet it, but wait until it comes in front of you. So act toward children, so toward a wife, so toward office, so toward wealth.

—EPICTETUS

For the kingdom of heaven is as a man traveling into a far country, who called his own servants, and delivered unto them his goods.

And unto one he gave five talents, to another two, and to another one; to every man according to his several ability; and straightway took his journey.

Then he that had received the five talents went and traded with the same, and made them other five talents.

And likewise he that had received two, he also gained other two.

But he that had received one went and digged in the earth, and hid his lord's money.

After a long time the lord of those servants cometh, and reckoneth with them.

And so he that had received five talents came and brought other five talents, saying, Lord, thou deliveredst unto me five talents: behold, I have gained beside them five talents more.

His lord said unto him, Well done, thou good and faithful servant: thou hast been faithful over a few things, I will make thee ruler over many things: enter thou into the joy of thy lord.

He also that had received two talents came and said, Lord, thou deliveredst unto me two talents: behold, I have gained two other talents beside them.

His lord said unto him, Well done, good and faithful servant; thou hast been faithful over a few things, I will make thee ruler over many things: enter thou into the joy of thy lord.

Then he which had received the one talent came and said, Lord, I knew thee that thou art an hard man, reaping where thou hast not sown, and gathering where thou hast not strewed:

And I was afraid, and went and hid thy talent in the earth: lo, there thou hast that is thine.

His lord answered and said unto him, Thou wicked and slothful servant, thou knewest that I reap where I sowed not, and gather where I have not strewed:

Thou oughtest therefore to have put my money to the exchangers, and then at my coming I should have received mine own with usury.

Take therefore the talent from him, and give it unto him which hath ten talents.

For unto every one that hath shall be given, and he shall have abundance: but from him that hath not shall be taken away even that which he hath.

And cast ye the unprofitable servant into outer darkness: there shall be weeping and gnashing of teeth.

—JESUS

A flow will have an ebb.

—ENGLISH

Every one, even the richest and most munificent of men, pays much by cheque more light-heartedly than he pays little in specie.

—MAX BEERBOHM

Ask your purse what you should buy.

—ENGLISH

To keep a lamp burning we have to keep putting oil in it.

—MOTHER TERESA

It was time for the monsoon rains to begin and a very old man was digging holes in his garden.

"What are you doing?" his neighbor asked.

"Planting mango trees," the old man said.

"Do you expect to eat mangoes from those trees?"

"No, I won't live long enough for that. But others will. It occurred to me the other day that all my life I have enjoyed mangoes planted by other people. This is my way of showing them my gratitude."

—SRI LANKAN

Through not spending enough, we spend too much.

—SPANISH

The miser puts all his gold pieces in a coffer; but as soon as the coffer is closed, it's the same as if it were empty.

—ANDRÉ GIDE

We have already noted—in our account of Herodotus—that a first effect of money was to give freedom of movement and leisure to a number of people who could not otherwise have enjoyed these privileges. And that is the peculiar value of money to mankind. Instead of a worker or helper being paid in kind and in such a way that he is tied as much in his enjoyment as in his labour, money leaves him free to do as he pleases amidst a wide choice of purchasable aids, eases, and indulgences. He may eat his money or drink it or give it to a temple or spend it in learning something or save it against some unforeseen occasion. That is the good of money, the freedom of its universal convertibility. But the freedom money gives the poor man is nothing to the freedom money has given to the rich man. With money rich men ceased to be tied to lands, houses, stores, flocks and herds. They could change the nature and locality of their possessions with an unheard of freedom.

—H. G. WELLS

Even though work stops, expenses run on.

—CATO THE ELDER

A miser sold all that he had and bought a lump of gold, which he buried in a hole in the ground by the side of an old wall and went to look at daily. One of his workmen observed his frequent visits to the spot and decided to watch his movements. He soon discovered the secret of the hidden treasure, and digging down, came to the lump of gold, and stole it. The miser, on his next visit, found the hole empty and began to tear his hair and to make loud lamentations. A neighbor, seeing him overcome with grief and learning the cause, said, "Stop your crying, and go find a stone of equal size. Paint it the color of gold and put it back in the earth. Each day you can come and pretend that it is still here. The stone will serve the same purpose since you never meant to use the gold anyway."

—AESOP

A farmer had a cow who gave one pail of milk each day. The man invited guests for a party. In order to save his milk for the special occasion, he refrained from milking the cow for ten days. He expected that on the last day the cow would give ten pails of milk. When he went to milk the animal he found she had dried up and gave less milk than ever before.

—ANATOLIAN

Money knows no day on which it is not welcome.

—AFRICAN

There was once a region where people, houses, and temples had fallen into decay. So the mice, who were old settlers there, occupied the chinks in the floors of stately dwellings with sons, grandsons (both in the male and female line), and further descendants as they were born, until their holes formed a dense tangle. They found uncommon happiness in a variety of festivals, dramatic performances (with plots of their own invention), wedding-feasts, eating-parties, drinking-bouts, and similar diversions. And so the time passed.

But into this scene burst an elephant-king, whose retinue numbered thousands. He, with his herd, had started for the lake upon information that there was water there. As he marched through the mouse community, he crushed faces, eyes, heads, and necks of such mice as he encountered.

Then the survivors held a convention. "We are being killed," they said, "by these lumbering elephants—curse them! If they come this way again, there will not be mice enough for seed. Therefore let us devise a remedy effective in this crisis."

When they had done so, a certain number went to the lake, bowed before the elephant-king, and said respectfully: "O King, not far from here is our community, inherited from a long line of ancestors. There we have prospered through a long succession of sons and grandsons. Now you gentlemen, while coming here to water, have destroyed us by the thousand. Furthermore, if you travel that way again, there will not be enough of us for seed. If then you feel compassion toward us, pray travel another path. Consider the fact that even creatures of our size will some day prove of some service."

And the elephant-king turned over in his mind what he had heard, decided that the statement of the mice was entirely logical, and granted their request.

Now in the course of time a certain king commanded his elephant-trappers to trap elephants. And they constructed a so-called water-trap, caught the king with his herd, three days later dragged him out with great tackle made of ropes and things, and tied him to stout trees in that very bit of forest.

When the trappers had gone, the elephant-king reflected thus: "In what manner, or through whose assistance, shall I be delivered?" Then it occurred to him: "We have no means of deliverance except those mice."

So the king sent the mice an exact description of his disastrous position in the trap through one of his personal retinue, an elephant-cow who had not ventured into the trap, and who had previous information of the mouse community.

When the mice learned the matter, they gathered by the thousands, eager to return the favor shown them, and visited the elephant herd. And seeing king and herd fettered, they gnawed the guy-ropes where they stood, then swarmed up the branches, and by cutting the ropes aloft, set their friends free.

"And that is why I say:

> Make friends, make friends, however strong
> Or weak they be:
> Recall the captive elephants,
> That mice set free."

—HINDU

Taxes are what we pay for civilized society.

—OLIVER WENDELL HOLMES, JR.

Life is short. The sooner that a man begins to enjoy his wealth the better.

—SAMUEL JOHNSON

He that lendeth to all that will borrowe, sheweth great good will, but lyttle wit.

—JOHN LYLY

You know, when you have no money and you really need a cup of coffee, you pray, "God, please give me a quarter for a cup of coffee. I'm really at the end." But when you have a thousand dollars you don't remember to pray for a quarter. What's so special is when you have the money and you still remember to ask God to give. There was a holy rabbi who even when the food was on the table in front of him, before he'd eat it he'd pray, "Please, God, feed me."

— SCHLOMO CARLBACH

The two most beautiful words in the English language are: Check enclosed.

—DOROTHY PARKER

Save your money, die rich.

—AMERICAN

I was born [says the shilling] on the side of a mountain, near a little village of Peru, and made a voyage to England in an ingot, under the convoy of Sir Francis Drake. I was, soon after my arrival, taken out of my Indian habit, refined, naturalized, and put into the British mode, with the face of Queen Elizabeth on one side, and the arms of the country on the other. Being thus equipped, I found in me a wonderful inclination to ramble, and visit all parts of the new world into which I was brought. The people very much favoured my natural disposition, and shifted me so fast from hand to hand, that before I was five years old, I had travelled into almost every corner of the nation. But in the beginning of my sixth year, to my unspeakable grief, I fell into the hands of a miserable old fellow, who clapped me into an iron chest, where I found five hundred more of my own quality who lay under the same confinement. The only relief we had, was to be taken out and counted over in the fresh air every morning and evening. After an imprisonment of several years, we heard somebody knocking at our chest, and breaking it open with a hammer.

This we found was the old man's heir, who, as his father lay a dying, was so good as to come to our release: he separated us that very day. What was the fate of my companions I know not: as for myself, I was sent to the apothecary's shop for a pint of sack. The apothecary gave me to an herb-woman, the herb-woman to a butcher, the butcher to a brewer, and the brewer to his wife, who made a present of me to a nonconformist preacher. After this manner I made my way merrily through the world; for, as I told you before, we shillings love nothing so much as travelling. I sometimes fetched in a shoulder of mutton, sometimes a play-book, and often had the satisfaction to treat a Templar at a twelvepenny ordinary, or carry him, with three friends, to Westminster Hall.

In the midst of this pleasant progress which I made from place to place, I was arrested by a superstitious old woman, who shut me up in a greasy purse, in pursuance of a foolish saying, "That while she kept a Queen Elizabeth's shilling about her, she should never be without money." I continued here a close prisoner for many months, till at last I was exchanged for eight and forty farthings.

I thus rambled from pocket to pocket till the beginning of the civil wars, when, to my shame be it spoken, I was employed in raising soldiers against the king: for being of a very tempting breadth, a sergeant made use of me to inveigle country fellows, and list them in the service of parliament.

As soon as he had made one man sure, his way was to oblige him to take a shilling of a more homely figure, and then practice the same trick upon another. Thus I continued doing great mischief to the crown, till my officer, chancing one morning to walk abroad earlier than ordinary, sacrificed me to his pleasures, and made use of me to seduce a milk-maid. This wench bent me, and gave me to her sweetheart, applying more properly than she intended the usual form of, "To my love and from my love." This ungenerous gallant marrying her within a few days after, pawned for a dram of brandy, and drinking me out next day, I was beaten flat with a hammer, and again set a running.

After many adventures, which it would be tedious to relate, I was sent to a young spendthrift, in company with the will of his deceased father. The young fellow, who I found was very extravagant, gave great demonstrations of joy at the receiving of the will: but opening it, he found himself disinherited and cut off from the possession of a fair estate, by virtue of my being made a present to him. This put him into such a passion, that after having taken me in his hand, and cursed me, he squirred me away from him as far as he could fling me. I chanced to light in an unfrequented place under a dead wall, where I lay undiscovered and useless during the usurpation of Oliver Cromwell.

About a year after the king's return, a poor cavalier, that was walking there about dinner-time, fortunately cast his eye upon me, and to the great joy of us both, carried me to a cook's shop, where he dined upon me, and drank the king's health. When I came again into the world, I found that I had been happier in my retirement than I thought, having probably, by that means, escaped wearing a monstrous pair of breeches.†

Being now of great credit and antiquity, I was rather looked upon as a medal than an ordinary coin; for which reason a gamester laid hold of me, and converted me to a counter, having got together some dozens of us for that use. We led a melancholy life in his possession, being busy at those hours wherein current coin is at rest, and partaking the fate of our master, being in a few moments valued at a crown, a pound, or a sixpence, according to the situation which the fortune of the cards placed us. I had at length the good luck to see my master break, by which means I was again sent abroad under my primitive denomination of a shilling.

I shall pass over many other accidents of less moment, and hasten to the final catastrophe, when I fell into the hands of an artist, who conveyed me under ground, and with an unmerciful pair of shears, cut off my titles, clipped my brims, retrenched my shape, rubbed me to my inmost ring, and, in short, so spoiled and pillaged, that he did not leave me worth a groat. You may think what a confusion, I was in, to see myself thus curtailed and disfigured. I should have been ashamed to have shown my head, had not all my old acquaintance been reduced to the same shameful figure, excepting some few that were punched through

†A new coin of the realm had been issued, bearing a pair of joined shields. These looked to the popular eye like a pair of breeches, which became a standing joke.

the belly. In the midst of this general calamity, when everybody thought our misfortune irretrievable, and our case desperate, we were thrown into the furnace together, and (as it often happens with cities rising out of a fire) appeared with greater beauty and lustre than we could ever boast of before. What has happened to me since this change of sex which you now see, I shall take some other opportunity to relate. In the mean time, I shall only repeat two adventures, as being very extraordinary, and neither of them having ever happened to me above once in my life. The first was, being in a poet's pocket, who was so taken with the novelty of my appearance, that it gave occasion to the finest burlesque poem in the British language, entitled from me, "The Splendid Shilling." The second adventure, which I must not omit, happened to me in the year 1703, when I was given away in charity to a blind man; but indeed this was by a mistake, the person who gave me having heedlessly thrown me into the hat among a pennyworth of farthings.

—JOSEPH ADDISON

Men do not realize how great an income thrift is.

—CICERO

The liberal soul shall be made fat: and he that watereth shall be watered also himself.

—PROVERBS

A wealthy, charitable merchant had many pensioners whom he supported with regular stipends. One poor man received from him ten rubles monthly. Rain, snow, or shine he always came for the money and always got it. In time, he began to take his allowance for granted as though it were an annuity for life.

Once, when he called for his ten rubles, the rich man's secretary gave him only five.

"You've made a mistake!" said the poor man. "I get ten, not five rubles a month."

"Of course you always got ten!" answered the secretary. "But you see, from now on, my employer can give you no more than five."

"What's the reason?"

"My employer is marrying off his youngest daughter, and the dowry he gives her, the cost of her trousseau, and the wedding expenses are so great, he has to cut down on all his charities."

"Is that so!" cried the poor man, trembling with rage. "Then tell your employer that if he wants to marry off his daughter in such grand style he should do it with his own money, not with mine! Who does he think I am—Baron Rothschild?"

—Yiddish

Money is like muck,§ not good except it be spread.

—Francis Bacon

§ Fertilizer.

There were once two brothers, one rich and the other poor. The rich one, however, gave nothing to the poor brother, who barely supported himself by dealing in grain. Things often went so badly for him that his wife and children would have to go without bread.

One day, as he was going through the forest with his wheelbarrow, he noticed a big bald mountain off to the side. Since he had never seen it before, he stopped in amazement and gazed at it. While he was standing there, he saw twelve big, rough men coming toward him. Since he thought that they might be robbers, he pushed his wheelbarrow into the bushes, climbed a tree, and waited to see what would happen. The twelve men went up to the mountain and cried, "Semsi Mountain, Semsi Mountain, open up."

Immediately the bald mountain opened in the middle, and the twelve men entered. Once they were inside, the mountain closed. After a short while, however, it opened up again, and the men came out carrying heavy sacks on their backs. After they were all out in the open, they said, "Semsi Mountain, Semsi Mountain, close together." Then the mountain closed, and there was no more sign of an entrance. The twelve men departed, and when they were completely out of sight, the poor man climbed down from the tree, curious to know what secret things might be hidden in the mountain. So he went up to the mountain and said, "Semsi Mountain, Semsi Mountain, open up," and the mountain opened before him. Then he entered, and the entire mountain was a cavern filled with silver and gold, and in the rear were large piles of pearls and glistening jewels heaped on top of each other like grain. The poor man did not know what to do, nor whether he should take any of the treasure. Finally, he filled his pockets with gold, but he left the pearls and jewels alone. When he came out again, he repeated the words "Semsi Mountain, Semsi Mountain, close together." Then the mountain closed, and he went home with his wheelbarrow. Now his worries disappeared, and he could buy bread and even wine for his wife and children. He lived happily and honestly, gave to the poor, and was kind to everyone. However, when he ran out of money, he went to his brother, borrowed a bushel measure, and fetched more gold. Yet, he refrained from touching any of the precious jewels. When he needed some more gold a third time, he borrowed the bushel measure from his brother once again. But the rich man had long been jealous of his brother's fortune and the beautiful way he had built up his house. He had also been puzzled by his brother's sudden wealth and his need for the bushel measure. So he thought of a trick, and he covered the bottom of the measure with sticky wax. When the measure was returned to him, there was a gold coin stuck to it. Immediately he went to his brother and asked him, "What have you been doing with the measure?"

"I've been measuring wheat and barley," said the other.

Then the rich one showed him the gold coin and threatened to take him to court about this unless he told him the truth. So the poor brother told him how everything had happened. The rich brother had a wagon hitched up at once and drove to the mountain with the idea of taking more advantage of this wonderful opportunity than had his brother and bringing back quite different treasures. When he arrived at the mountain, he cried out, "Semsi Mountain, Semsi Mountain, open up." The mountain opened, and he went inside, where he found all the treasures in front of him. For a long time he could not make up his mind what to grab first. Finally, he took as many jewels as he could carry. He was about to leave with his load of jewels, but his heart and mind had become so occupied by the treasures that he had forgotten the name of the mountain and called out, "Simelei Mountain, Simelei Mountain, open up." But that was not the right name, and the mountain did not budge and remained closed. Then he became frightened, but the more he tried to recall the name, the more confused his thoughts became, and the treasures were of no use to him at all. That evening the mountain opened up, and the twelve robbers entered. When they saw him, they laughed and cried out, "Well, we've finally caught our little bird! Did you think we hadn't noticed that you had slipped in here three times. Maybe we weren't able to catch you then, but you won't escape us now."

The rich man screamed, "It wasn't me, it was my brother!"

But no matter what he said, no matter how he pleaded for his life, they would not listen, and they cut off his head.

—THE BROTHERS GRIMM

Money is congealed energy and releasing it releases life's possibilities.

—JOSEPH CAMPBELL

If small sums do not go out, large sums will not come in.

—Chinese

Shrouds have no pockets.

—Yiddish

> Why is it no one ever sent me yet
> One perfect limousine, do you suppose?
> Ah no, it's always just my luck to get
> One perfect rose.

—Dorothy Parker

If we imagine an ancient road at dusk, a road passing through no-man's land and connecting two towns but itself neither here nor there, we will begin to imagine the ancient Hermes, for he is the God of the Roads, identified not with any home or hearth or mountain but with the traveler on the highway. His name means "he of the stone heap": a traveler seeking the protection of Hermes would pile rocks into a cairn by the road or erect a herma, a stone pillar with a head on top.

At these roadside altars Hermes assumed his other ancient forms, the God of Commerce and the Protector of Thieves. He wants everything to be on the road: travelers, money, and merchandise. And as his patronage of *both* merchants and thieves shows, the moral tone of an exchange does not concern him. Hermes is an amoral connecting deity. When he's the messenger of the gods he's like the post office: he'll carry love letters, hate letters, stupid letters, or smart letters. His concern is the delivery, not what's in the envelope. He wants money to change hands, but he does not distinguish between the just price and a picked pocket. Hermes still appears at a country auction whenever the auctioneer awakens our daydreams of "making a steal," that Hermetic mixture of commerce and larceny that cannot fail to loosen the cash. When we come to our senses later, wondering why we bought a cardboard carton full of pan lids, we know that Hermes was the auctioneer.

Hermes is not greedy, however. He likes the clink of coin but he has no hidden pile. Pictures of Hermes usually show him with a little bag of change, just enough to get the trading started. He's no miser asleep on heaps of gold. He loves the fluidity of money, not the weight.

—LEWIS HYDE

GENEROSITY

Seven

Generosity

Generosity is a quality of unselfishness, *not* self-sacrifice. Self-sacrifice is voluntarily accepting—or even inflicting upon oneself—pain so that someone else may benefit: a mother going without in order to feed her children, a lover stepping in to absorb a blow meant for a beloved, a soldier throwing himself on a hand grenade to save his fellows. Unselfishness, on the other hand, is simply being openhanded, the opposite of fearful, covetous, grasping.

Practicing generosity helps overcome a siege mentality, a belief that there isn't enough for you and that you must defend what little you have. It relaxes the spirit, provides a sense of well-being, and facilitates the flow of money into and through a life. Ultimately, it makes your world a better place to live.

We're going to deal with generosity in this chapter as it relates specifically to money and as it relates to spirit. Both aspects are important in making peace with money.

Practice:

Quietly

Giving away money is a powerful means to counteract the fear—even a long-standing one—that there isn't enough of it for you or that there won't be enough. Giving it away anonymously (especially without an agenda, or even the chance of one) is an especially powerful way to do that. It puts you in contact with the pure act of giving. Here are some effective ways to go about giving money away. Use any or any combination of them that appeals to you.

One: For thirty days, tithe: Give away 10 percent of all the money you net during the month (receive after taxes) from whatever source, paycheck to interest on a savings account to a cash gift from a relative. Give it to any organizations, institutions, or individuals you desire. But do so in a way that makes sure the recipient will never know it was you who gave the money. Use cash, bank checks, or postal money orders.

Two: For ten days, send cash, a bank check, or a money order to every organization or cause that solicits you through the mail during that period.

Three: If you live in a city and are afoot in it during the day, then for one day give money without hesitation to every homeless person or panhandler who asks for something. If you live in a suburb or rural area, get a list from the telephone directory or from a local civic body of all the social welfare organizations in your community that actively feed, shelter, clothe, or in other ways help the disadvantaged, then send cash, a bank check, or a money order to each of them.

Four: Leave a sum of money in a public place—bookstore, movie house, park bench, wherever—and walk away without looking back.

Five: (I created this one for myself many years ago, when I was working to overcome underearning and wanted to engage with giving in as pure a way as I could.)

Get out the residential pages of your telephone directory. Place the book on your desk or a table. Close your eyes. Open the directory at random, and put your finger somewhere on the page. Open your eyes. Write down the name and address your finger has fallen on (most directories include a map with zip code information; if yours doesn't, call the post office for the code).

Place an amount in cash, along with an anonymous note like the one below, inside an envelope. Seal the envelope. Address it to the person you randomly selected from the phone book, put a stamp on it, and mail it.

Give the money away.

To a stranger.

For the sheer sake of giving, of sharing.

You include the note in order to explain what you are doing, so you don't unsettle or alarm the person who receives the money. He or she may be a little uneasy at first, but that will pass quickly, especially if your note is clear. You might want to write something like this:

Dear [Name]:

I don't know you. You don't know me. I picked your name at random out of the telephone book, and will have no record of it, will not keep it in memory after I mail this.

Money comes into my life, and I am grateful for that. I'm expressing my appreciation for it to the universe by passing some of it along, by sharing what I have received.

Bless you. May you know peace, joy.

Type the note if you can, which helps keep it impersonal, but sign it in longhand, which adds a measure of the personal. *Do not sign it with your name.* That would destroy the anonymity and deprive you of the value of this act. You are not seeking acknowledgment or thanks here—you are giving for the sheer sake of giving. You might want to sign the note A Fellow Human Being, Just Someone Else in Life, or something similar. For the return address, repeat the name and address of the recipient.

When you drop the envelope into a mailbox, smile, bless the person who will receive this money, bless the universe from which you received it, and then forget about it. Do not save the recipient's name anywhere. Let the name slip from your mind and be gone. Do not fantasize about how he or she might react, or on what the money might be spent. Be done with it. Your only involvement is with the act of giving, and with blessing this person when you mail the letter.

Some people find the prospect of this practice exhilarating; others are appalled by it. One woman, in a helping profession, refused even to consider the possibility when it was suggested at a workshop. She found the idea of giving money to someone she didn't know, and who would never know it was she who had given it, incomprehensible and infuriating. A young man at the same workshop, a tradesman, was so delighted by the practice that he broke into grins through much of the rest of the day, planning to execute it as soon as he got home that night.

Giving money—especially for someone who doesn't think he or she has enough of it—has much more impact than giving time, services, or personally made gifts. It makes money more real to you, heightens your awareness of it, and increases your confidence in your ability to generate it. But why give it away anonymously? And perhaps even to a stranger? Giving to your church, an environmental fund, a medical cause, or any other program you might support is perfectly fine and a good thing to do. But an *anonymous* act of generosity, particularly toward another human being about whom you know nothing at all except that he or she shares life with you, and with whom you will have contact only for this instant, without an agenda of any kind, puts you most completely into the unadulterated act of giving, something that will resound deeply within you and quite likely in remarkable and unforeseen ways.

When you select an amount of money to give, make it one somewhere between an amount you could toss off easily, like a dollar or two, and one whose loss would really hurt. For many people that may be $20, $30, or $50; for others it might be $5, or $100.

Undertaking any of these exercises at any time is helpful, but they are most effective when undertaken with some regularity. Giving is most beneficial when it becomes a way of being; among other positive effects, it will help you understand on a visceral level that your supply of money is not limited.

Practice:

Friends and Strangers

If any single quality can create a lasting sense of well-being, which is a powerful support in making peace with money, it is generosity of spirit. Generosity of spirit is a liberalness in dealing with others, an affection for them, a compassion, an understanding. It is a willingness to see other people *truly* as human beings—as real as you are, with hopes and fears just like you—and to recognize that all anyone has ever truly wanted is to be happy. That is true of every one, no matter how dark or twisted the person might have become, how terrible his or her actions. Here are three exercises that can foster generosity of spirit.

One: Pick one day out of every two months, say the fifteenth of each odd-numbered month or something equally easy to remember. Mark those days on your calendar for the coming twelve months. When that day arrives, for the entire day, see every friend you encounter or deal with as a stranger. He looks familiar, but his physical being is inhabited by someone else, someone unknown. See how many new things you can notice about him: how he smiles, how he frowns, how he gestures; what makes him do those things; the way his eyes move; the flow of his emotions, the play of his intelligence. Notice as many things about him as you can. Discover this human being.

Conversely, see every stranger upon whom your attention rests for more than a few moments as a lifelong friend: You remember her birth, her childhood, the pains and disappointments she's had, her joys and triumphs. You remember her times of need, of tenderness, of strength. Deal with her, feel about her, from this knowledge and relationship.

This practice helps reclaim a sense of kinship, of community, of tribal belonging, which encourage emotional and spiritual generosity.

Two: Metta is the Pali word for lovingkindess, or unlimited friendliness. (Pali was a language contemporary with Sanskrit; much spiritual literature was written in both.) Here are the words of a basic lovingkindness meditation, to be said mentally. The mediation begins with lovingkindess toward oneself:

> May I be safe and free from danger.
> May I be physically happy.

May I be mentally happy.
May I live joyfully, and with ease of well-being.

If you are inexperienced with meditation, a basic technique is described in chapter 2, page 32. You might wish to reread the appropriate paragraphs there, starting with the one that says, "Begin by relaxing, clearing your body of tension . . ." and continuing through two more, through the one that begins, "Then, very gently, begin to focus . . ."

Once you've focused on your breathing in the manner described for a minute or two, bring the words above to mind. Say them silently to yourself. Say them slowly, listening to each word, contemplating each phrase. When you have, say them again, in the same focused manner; and then again; and then again. Continue this way for ten minutes if you can, or longer if you wish. Undertake this meditation each day for a week (it's easier to maintain if you do it at the same time each day).

On the eighth day, after you've spent about half the meditation period practicing lovingkindess on yourself, bring up the image of a benefactor in your mind, someone who has helped you greatly or done something wonderful for you, and spend the remainder of the period practicing lovingkindess on him.

May [Name] be safe and free from danger.
May he be physically happy.

May he be mentally happy.
May he live joyfully, and with ease of well-being.

Continue this way through the second week.

On the fifteenth day, spend a third of your meditation period practicing lovingkindness on yourself, a third on a benefactor, and the remaining third on your children, if you have children. (If you don't, then spend the time on your parents, assuming you have a good relationship with them, or a kind relative like a grandmother or uncle. If you do have children, bring your parents or a kind relative into your meditation the following week and extend the progression below accordingly.) Finish the third week this way.

Each week add a new person or kind of person to the meditation—the fourth week, a friend; the fifth, someone neutral like the mail carrier; the sixth, all people who are strangers to you; the seventh, someone who has been difficult or troublesome in your life; the eighth, an enemy; and last, all beings.

When you have progressed to including all beings in your meditation, you can begin by practicing lovingkindess for yourself—saying the four lines silently to yourself once or twice—then moving on to each person or class of people in turn, saying the lines once or twice for all your benefactors, for all your children or relatives, for all your friends, and so on, through all beings. Many people practice this meditation on an ongoing basis. It is powerful.

Three: I have written about this particular practice before, in *Earn What You Deserve.* But it is so fundamentally important to making peace with money—no matter from what point one begins, debt-ridden to managing a family fortune—that it would be irresponsible not to repeat it here. So I do:

Resentment has been called the root of all spiritual disease, and it may be. Certainly it is toxic: physically, emotionally, psychologically, and spiritually. Resentment can generate, for example: gastritis (physical), rage (emotional), obsession (psychological), and disconnection (spiritual).

Resentments militate against making peace with money, and violently: They dominate your consciousness, consume your energy, blind you to possibilities, and even cause you to maintain yourself in a state of deprivation out of a desire to punish someone ("Look how badly you hurt me—you crippled me, made me incapable and miserable!") or, less frequently, out of guilt over having the resentment.

Resentment is not the same thing as anger. Anger is a temporary flare of hostility or wrath. Resentment is an *abiding* anger. A *bitter* anger. It is hatred. Blame. A burning sense of grievance. A hunger for retribution. The word comes from the Latin prefix *re*—("again") and the verb *sentir* ("to feel"). Literally, resentment means to feel again. And again, and again. Over and over, endlessly.

Marge, a severe underearner through most of her adult life, now in her sixties, was speaking bitterly about a painful injustice she had suffered at the hands of her older sister when she was fourteen. Her listener had heard this tale several times. Marge," he said, "that was *half a century* ago—and your sister's been *dead* for twenty years."

"Yes!" Marge said, mouth twisted in fury. "And I'll *never* forget!"

Sadly, she probably never will.

Resentment, for anyone, is a costly luxury—it steals away delight, peace, joy; it makes comfort unavailable, love impossible. For people trying to make peace with money, it is deadly: If any single factor in itself can stop you from making peace with money, it is resentment. The bile, acid, spite, virulence, shrieking fury, and agony of resentment wreak most of their damage not upon the person who is resented but upon the one who holds the resentment. Resentment is a form of self-destruction. With people who do not have a peaceful relationship with money, this destruction nearly always manifests at least in part in debting, overspending, or underearning, sometimes all three.

Resentment needs to be gotten free of—for your own sake.

The most effective way to free yourself of resentment is through forgiveness, by forgiving whomever you feel resentful toward. Actually, forgiveness will never fail to free you.

"But how can I possibly forgive *him*!"

"After what she *did* to me?"

Forgiveness is an alien concept to some people, particularly those whose resentments are deep and intense or who have been clinging to them for years. It is important to know this: The point of forgiving is not to earn heaven-points or to become virtuous, but *to free yourself from pain*—to help *you* in your process of making peace with money. It's also important to know that to forgive does not mean to condone or excuse behavior. You may indeed have been treated shamefully, even hideously. But that is not the point. The point is for *you* to become free of the resentment, so that *you* can live a better, happier, and more prosperous life.

Here is an effective way to achieve forgiveness. In bed, just before sleep, relax. Quiet your mind. Become still. Then, using the first name of whomever you feel resentful toward, say silently to yourself, and with as much sincerity and genuineness as you can muster:

"[Name], I fully and freely forgive you. I completely loose you and let you go. I do not wish to hurt you. I wish you no harm. So far as I am concerned, this incident [trouble] between us is over forever. You are free, and I am free, and all is well again between us."

Even the *thought* of saying such a thing makes some people gag—which only indicates how powerful and deeply entrenched the resentment is. The final phrase—"and all is well again between us"—does not mean that you need to embrace this person or welcome him back into your life. It might mean that, it might not. It may mean that you never see or deal with him again. But what it definitely *does* mean is that you will be at peace over the issue, and that a blocked channel will have been opened, through which more life can now flow.

For many people this technique can be very difficult at first. If that is your experience, don't fret about it: just summon up however much sincerity you can as you say the words, even if that isn't much at all. You'll find that more will come as you proceed, until finally you will be able to forgive the person completely. Sometimes the experience of that—of total forgiveness—lasts only an instant, is experienced as a kind of epiphany. Other times, it is a slower, more abiding thing.

Work with a single resentment at a time. Stay with it until you feel the forgiveness is complete. Many people find they can realize forgiveness—and through it, release—by practicing this exercise with a given resentment each night for a week or so. Occasionally someone discovers she accomplishes forgiveness almost instantly. Other resentments require more time.

Use this procedure to forgive all the offenses you have ever suffered—real or perceived. Some never *did* take place, but were only a matter of our interpretation. Often there is what *I* think happened, what *you* think happened, and what *really* happened. Begin with resentments that revolve around money or work, such as alimony you have to pay, having been passed over for a promotion, or cheated by a business partner. Later you can go on to others. (*All* resentments are obstacles to making peace with money.)

Of course human nature is fundamentally good! Why am I so sure of this? That is what I want to tell you. The proposition "Human nature is fundamentally good" is a logical consequence of two other propositions, both of which are as self evident to me as any axioms, but either or both of which the reader is, of course, free to reject.

The first of my two axioms is that *I* am fundamentally good. This to me is so utterly obvious! By "fundamentally" good, I mean, of course, that I was born good. I say this because I distinctly remember coming into the world in complete good faith, loving and trusting everybody, with good will to all and malice towards none. I only developed hostilities, hatreds, pettinesses, envies, jealousies, etc. as a result of having been mistreated and distrusted. Now, I haven't been all that badly treated and that's why I'm not half bad as I now stand. But whatever badness I have, 'tis nothing more nor less than a reaction to the badness I have experienced. I did not bring this badness into the world when I arrived! Of this I am certain. Thus my first axiom is unequivoacably, "I am fundamentally good."

My second axiom is that it is obvious that I am no better than anyone else! Fundamentally better, I mean. Of course, I sometimes act better than other people and sometimes worse. But it is inconceivable to me that human natures can be so radically different that some are good and others bad at birth! No, that is ridiculous! So, if I am fundamentally good, then everyone is fundamentally good. And since I *am* fundamentally good, then *everyone* is fundamentally good.

—RAYMOND M. SMULLYAN

The old miser was overheard at his prayers: "If the Almighty, may His holy name be blessed forever, would give me a hundred thousand dinars, I would give ten thousand to the poor. I promise I would. And if the Almighty, may He be glorified forever, were not to trust me, let Him deduct the ten thousand in advance and just send me the balance."

—MIDDLE EASTERN

Hatred does not cease with hatred.

—BUDDHA

Did you give, forget it; did you accept, mention it.

—HUNGARIAN

A poor shoemaker had only enough leather for a single pair of shoes. He cut the leather but was too weary to work more and went to bed.

In the morning, he was astonished to find a perfect pair of finished shoes on his workbench. Not a stitch was out of place! So beautiful were the shoes that the cobbler's first customer fell in love with them on sight and paid him a handsome price for them. The shoemaker had enough money to buy leather for two pair of shoes. He cut the leather that night and went to bed. The next morning, to his amazement, he found *two* pairs of perfect finished shoes on his bench—which he sold that day for such a price that he could afford to buy leather for four pairs of shoes.

And so it went for many months, and the shoemaker prospered.

One winter evening, he could no longer abide his ignorance over the

source of his good fortune so he prevailed upon his wife to sit up with
him in hiding through the night and spy upon his workbench. What
they saw by the light of the candle they had left burning amazed them!

Two naked elves appeared. Humming and singing, the little men tapped
and sewed through the night, finishing one beautiful pair of shoes after
another. Just before dawn, they cleaned up, set the shoes out smartly,
returned the cobbler's tools to their proper places, then opened the door
a little and scampered away into the night.

"The little men have made us rich," said the shoemaker's wife, "and we
should show our gratitude. They're running about in this cold winter
with nothing on. They might freeze, and surely they must be uncomfortable! I am going to make them each a shirt, a coat, a jacket, trousers,
and stockings. Why don't you make them each a pair of little shoes?"

The cobbler was happy to agree, and he and his wife cut and sewed and
fashioned the tiniest and finest clothes and shoes they had ever made,
and when they were done they put them out at night on the workbench
in place of the leather the shoemaker usually left, then hid themselves to
spy again.

The elves clapped their hands and jumped up and down when they discovered the clothes. They put them on, pulled the shoes onto their feet.
They held each other's hands and whirled in a circle, singing:

> "We're sleek, we're fine, we're out the door,
> We won't be cobblers any more!"

And danced and tumbled and sang and then were out the door and into the night.

They never did return, but all was well with the shoemaker and his wife, who prospered with all they turned their hand to.

—THE BROTHERS GRIMM

The longer we dwell on our misfortunes, the greater is their power to harm us.

—VOLTAIRE

Anticipate charity by preventing poverty; assist the reduced fellowman, either by a considerable gift, or a sum of money, or by teaching him a trade, or by putting him in the way of business, so that he may earn an honest livelihood, and not be forced to the dreadful alternative of holding out his hand for charity. This is the highest step and the summit of charity's golden ladder.

—MAIMONIDES

You may give in the spirit of light
Or as you please,
But if you care how another man gives,
Or how he withholds,
You trouble your quietness endlessly.

—THE *DHAMMAPADA*

Giving is the highest expression of potency.

—ERICH FROMM

Though I speak with the tongues of men and angels,
And have not love,
I am no better than a clanging gong
   or a brass bell.
And though I have the gift of prophesy,
   and know every hidden mystery;
   and though I have faith strong enough to move
   mountains,
And have not love,
   I am nothing.
And though I give away all I own to the poor,
   and offer my body to be burned,
And have not Love,
   I do not gain a thing.
Love is patient, Love is kind;
Love knows not jealousy,
Love is never boastful,
   nor proud, nor unseemly.
Love is not selfish nor easily provoked.
Love knows nothing of wrong,
   does not rejoice at the misfortune of others,
   and only delights in the Truth.
There is nothing Love cannot bear;
   no limit to its faith, its hope, or its endurance.

The reign of Love will never end.
But where there are prophesies, they will end;
Where there are tongues of ecstasy, they will end;
Where there is knowledge, it will end.
For our knowledge is only of a part,
   and our prophesies tell of but a part.
And that which is a part vanishes
   with the arrival of the whole.
When I was a child,
   I spoke as a child, I saw as a child,
   and I thought as a child.
When I grew up, I put away childish things.
Now we see everything through a murky glass,
   one day we will see God clearly,
   face to face.
Now my knowledge is incomplete,
   one day it will be perfect,
   like God's knowledge of me.
In a word,
   there are three things you are never to let go of:
Faith, hope, and love;
   but the greatest of these
   will always be love.

—St. Paul

Once a man and his wife were sitting by the entrance to their house. They had a roasted chicken in front of them and were about to eat it when the man saw his father coming toward them. So the man quickly grabbed the chicken and hid it because he did not want to give him any. The old man came, had a drink, and went away. As the son reached to put the roasted chicken back on the table, he found that it had turned into a toad, which then sprang onto his face, sat there, and would not leave him. If anyone tried to take it off, the toad would look at the person viciously as if it wanted to spring right into his face too. So nobody dared touch it. And the ungrateful son had to feed the toad every day; otherwise, it would have eaten away part of his face. Thus the son wandered about the world without a moment of rest.

—THE BROTHERS GRIMM

Give, and it shall be given unto you; good measure, pressed down, and shaken together, and running over . . .

—JESUS

Behold! I do not give lectures on a little charity.
When I give, I give myself.

—WALT WHITMAN

Should not the giver be thankful that the receiver received? Is not giving a need? Is not receiving, mercy?

—FRIEDRICH WILHELM NIETZSCHE

There were once two brothers who farmed together. They shared equally in all of the work and split the profits exactly. Each had his own granary. One of the brothers was married and had a large family; the other brother was single.

One day the single brother thought to himself, "It is not fair that we divide the grain evenly. My brother has many mouths to feed, while I have but one. I know what I'll do, I will take a sack of grain from my granary each evening and put it in my brother's granary." So, each night when it was dark, he carefully carried a sack of grain, placing it in his brother's barn.

Now the married brother thought to himself, "It is not fair that we divide the grain evenly. I have many children who will care for me in my old age, and my brother has none. I know what I'll do, I will take a sack of grain from my granary each evening and put it in my brother's granary." And he did.

Each morning the two brothers were amazed to discover that though they had removed a sack of grain the night before, they had just as many.

One night the two brothers met each other halfway between their barns, each carrying a sack of grain. Then they understood the mystery. And they embraced, and loved each other deeply. That place has ever since been hallowed ground.

—Hasidic

That best portion of a good man's life,
His little, nameless, unremembered acts
of kindness and of love.

—WILLIAM WORDSWORTH

At the deepest level, there is no giver, no gift, and no recipient . . . only the universe rearranging itself.

—HENRY DAVID THOREAU

When thou doest alms, do not let thy left hand know what they right hand doeth.

—JESUS

The devotee knelt to be initiated into discipleship. The guru whispered the sacred mantra into his ear, warning him not to reveal it to anyone.

"What will happen if I do?" asked the devotee.

Said the guru, "Anyone to whom you reveal the mantra will be liberated from the bondage of ignorance and suffering, but you yourself will be excluded from discipleship and suffer damnation."

No sooner had he heard those words than the devotee rushed to the marketplace, collected a large crowd around him, and repeated the sacred mantra for all to hear.

The disciples later reported this to the guru and demanded that the man be expelled from the monastery for his disobedience.

The guru smiled and said, "He has no need of anything I can teach. His action has shown him to be a guru in his own right."

—ANTHONY DE MELLO

Once upon a time there was an old woman. Of course, you've seen old women go begging before. Well, this woman begged too, and whenever she got something, she said, "May God reward you." Now, this beggar woman came to a door where a friendly young rascal was warming himself inside by a fire. As she stood shivering at the door the youngster spoke kindly to the old woman, "Come in, grandma, and warm yourself."

She entered but went too close to the fire so that her old rags began to burn without her noticing it. The youngster stood there and watched. He should have put out the fire, don't you think? And even if there was no water at hand, he should have wept out all the water in his body through his eyes. That would have made for two nice streams of water, and with that he could have extinguished the fire.

—THE BROTHERS GRIMM

Rabbi Shelomo said: "If you want to raise a man from mud and filth, do not think it is enough to keep standing on top and reaching down to him a helping hand. You must go all the way down yourself, down into mud and filth. Then take hold of him with strong hands and pull him and yourself out into the light."

—HASIDIC

Then came Peter to him, and said, Lord, how oft shall
my brother sin against me, and I forgive him? till seven times?

Jesus saith unto him, I say not unto thee, Until seven
times: but, Until seventy times seven.

Therefore is the kingdom of heaven likened unto a
certain king, which would take account of his servants.

And when he had begun to reckon, one was brought unto
him, which owed him ten thousand talents.

But forasmuch as he had not to pay, his lord commanded
him to be sold, and his wife, and children, and all that he
had, and payment to be made.

The servant therefore fell down, and worshipped him,
saying, Lord, have patience with me, and I will pay thee all.

Then the lord of that servant was moved with
compassion, and loosed him, and forgave him the debt.

But the same servant went out, and found one of his
fellowservants, which owed him an hundred pence: and he laid
hands on him, and took him by the throat, saying, Pay me
that thou owest.

And his fellowservant fell down at his feet, and
besought him, saying, Have patience with me, and I will pay
thee all.

And he would not: but went and cast him into prison,
till he should pay the debt.

So when his fellowservants saw what was done, they were
very sorry, and came and told unto their lord all that was done.

Then his lord, after that he had called him, said unto
him, O thou wicked servant, I forgave thee all that debt,
because thou desiredst me:

Shouldest not thou also have had compassion on thy
fellowservant, even as I had pity on thee?

And his lord was wroth, and delivered him to the
tormentors, till he should pay all that was due unto him.

—MATTHEW 18:21–34

A teacher's work is like a gardener's, who takes care of various plants.
One plant loves the sunshine, the other the cool shade; one loves the
bank of a stream, the other a barren mountain peak. One thrives in
sandy soil, the other in rich loam. Each requires the care best suited for
it; otherwise the result is unsatisfactory.

—ABDU'L-BAHÁ

We should give as we would receive, cheerfully, quickly, and without
hesitation; for there is no grace in a benefit that sticks to the fingers.

—SENECA

One must be poor to know the luxury of giving!

—GEORGE ELIOT

I don't know what your destiny will be, but one thing I know: the only ones among you who will be really happy are those who have sought and found how to serve.

—ALBERT SCHWEITZER

There is one type of person who, whenever he does a kind deed, will not hesitate to ask for some reward. Another type of person, though not so bold, will keep track of everything he has done for you, feeling deep down that you are in his debt. Then there are those who give without any remembrance of what they have done. They are like the vine that has brought forth a cluster of grapes, and having once borne its delicious fruit, seeks nothing more. As the horse that runs its race, the hound that tracks its game, and the bee that hives its honey, so should a man be when he has done an act of kindness: not seeking reward, not proclaiming his virtues, but passing on to the next act, as the vine passes on to bear another cluster of summer grapes.

—MARCUS AURELIUS

An invalid girl asked,
"How do I dance?"
We told her:
let your heart dance.

Then the crippled girl asked,
"How do I sing?"
We told her:
let your heart sing.

A poor dead thistle asked,
"How do I dance?"
We told it,
let your heart fly in the wind.

God asked from on high,
"How do I come down from this blueness?"
We told Him:
come dance with us in the light.

The entire valley is dancing
in a chorus under the sun.
The hearts of those absent
return to ashes.

—GABRIELA MISTRAL

The only gift is a portion of thyself.

—RALPH WALDO EMERSON

When people grow gradually rich their requirements and standard of
living expand in proportion, while their present-giving instincts often

remain in the undeveloped condition of their earlier days. Something showy and not-too-expensive in a shop is their only conception of the ideal gift.

—SAKI

He who learns and does not teach is like a myrtle which grows in the desert: no one receives enjoyment from it.

—ROSH HA-SHANAH, 23A

In nothing do men approach so nearly to the gods as in doing good to men.

—CICERO

If you straighten out some trouble between two individuals, that is an alms. If you help a lame man with his beast, mounting him thereon, or hoisting up on to it his baggage, that is an alms. A good word is an alms. In every step you take while walking to prayers there is an alms.

Your smiling in your brother's face, is charity; and your exhorting mankind to virtuous deeds, is charity; and your prohibiting the forbidden, is charity; and your showing men the road, in the land in which they lose it, is charity; and your assisting the blind, is charity.

—MUHAMMAD

Love, and do as you please.

—THOMAS AQUINAS

GRACE

Eight

Grace

....

Grace is an inner beauty; effortlessness, good will. It is the activity some have looked upon as a divine love or protection, bestowed freely. It is what others have called the dharma, the law, the way things work. It is what still others have seen as being in a state of at-one-ment with whatever vitalizes the universe. Grace is what flows between you and another human being. It is a state of harmony with what is. It is awareness. Perception. Realization.

The Latin root word for grace is *gratia*: pleasing and welcome. *Gratia* itself derives from the Greek for the Three Graces, three divine sisters who personified charm and loveliness, physically and in moral behavior. The elemental qualities the Three Graces represented were brightness, joyfulness, and fruitfulness.

To suggest the magnitude and sweep, and perhaps even the essence of grace, here are some of the many words and notions with which it has been linked over the centuries:

fitness   benevolence
goodwill   helpfulness

mercy	harmlessness
compassion	innocence
forgiveness	benignity
indulgence	kindliness
immunity	charity
sanctification	empathy
to honor, favor	responsiveness
divine function	love
inspiration	leniency
regeneration	tenderness
comfort	humaneness
strengthening	philanthropy
consolation	hospitality
atonement	generosity
redemption	gentleness
creation	tolerance
salvation	forgiveness
intercession	blessing

A disposition toward generosity
Rendering a favor when not obligated to
Excellence or power granted by God
Granting beauty, elegance, charm

A life in which grace is present—or probably more correctly, in which one consciously engages with grace—is a life in which money becomes progressively less difficult and painful. Whatever the ultimate nature of grace, its presence can't be forced or created: It is already there. You *can* cultivate it, though, make yourself receptive to its activity, uncover it within yourself, remove impediments to its flow.

Practice:
If Only This Were Mine

"If only I had this. If only things were that way. Then I would be happy." These are common sentiments. Everyone gets caught up in them at one time or another. But when we are overwhelmed by them, we feel impoverished, bereft, and alone. And when we experience ourselves thus, we become blind to grace.

In his private journal of musings on life and death, never intended for publication but which we now know as the brilliant *Meditations*, the Roman emperor and philosopher Marcus Aurelius, a strong, sensitive, and humble mind, wrote: "Reckon up the chief of the blessings you possess, and then thankfully remember how you would crave for them if they were not yours."

And that is what this practice is about, doing what Marcus Aurelius suggests—consciously, deliberately.

For the next three months, sit down once each month with a pad. On it, list fifteen things in your life that you deeply enjoy, deeply appreciate, that are important to you. These may be as profound as your child, as simple as the luster of your hair, or as mundane as your answering machine. All that matters is that they be among the things that you most enjoy, appreciate, and that are the most important to you.

Look at the first entry on your list. Think about it. Picture it. Then consciously, very deliberately, feel how much you would long for it, how much you would crave it, if you did not have it. *Feel* that longing, that craving, that hollowness. Truly *feel* it. Then realize that you have this thing. And as you do, feel the *release* from that craving, the joy of having that lack filled, that want satisfied. Truly *feel* it. Now do the same, one at a time, with the remaining items on the list. Understand that you are not impoverished, not bereft, not alone. Understand that there *is* grace in your life.

After three months, convert this practice into a simple, occasional listing of all the things in your life that you enjoy, appreciate, and are grateful for. After you write out the list, just look it over and let the realization that there is much in your life that is good and valuable settle into your consciousness. Do this particularly whenever you find yourself beginning to feel that your life is small, dark, and constrained.

Practice:

To You, and You, Freely and with Good Will

Pick a day in the coming week. From start to end of it, mentally give to each person on whom your attention settles for more than a few moments—a salesclerk, a pedestrian, a passenger across from you on the bus—something you think he or she wants. It can be anything: love, a CD player, a new car, children, freedom from fear, a business of her own, fame, tickets to a movie, dancing lessons; anything at all. Just make it something you think this person wants or would like to have.

Give it to her or to him.

Freely.

As is given to you in your life.

It is this kind of effort, this kind of opening of yourself, that permits grace to flow into and through your life. The universe is not an aggressor. It won't force its love—or grace—upon you. You have to open the door and invite that in.

The Vedic rites, as everyone knows, were so precise and so powerful that when the sages prayed for rain there was never a drought. It was in this knowledge that a worthy man set himself to pray to the goddess of wealth, Lakshmi, begging her to make him rich.

He prayed to no effect for ten long years, after which period he suddenly saw the illusory nature of wealth and adopted the life of a renunciate in the mountains.

He was sitting in meditation one day when he opened his eyes and saw before him a wondrously beautiful woman, all bright and shining as if she were made of gold.

"Who are you?" he asked. "Why are you here?"

"I am the goddess Lakshmi to whom you recited hymns for ten years," said the woman. "I have appeared to grant you your desire."

"Ah, my dear goddess," said the man, "I have since attained the bliss of meditation and lost my desire for wealth. You come too late. Tell me, why did you delay so long in coming?"

"To speak the truth," said the goddess, "given the nature of those rites you so faithfully performed, you had fully earned the wealth. But, in my love for you and my desire for your welfare, I held it back."

—HINDU

An elephant broke loose from the herd and charged across a little wooden structure that stretched across a ravine.

The worn-out bridge shivered and groaned, barely able to support the elephant's weight.

Once it had gone safely to the other side, a flea that had lodged itself in the elephant's ear exclaimed in mighty satisfaction, "Boy, did we shake that bridge!"

—HINDU

God did not deprive thee of the operation of his love, but thou didst deprive him of thy cooperation.

—ST. FRANCIS DE SALES

Great crises show us how much greater our vital resources are than we had supposed.

—WILLIAM JAMES

The elves had stolen a mother's child from the cradle and had replaced the baby with a changeling who had a fat head and glaring eyes and would do nothing but eat and drink. In her distress the mother went to her neighbor and asked for advice. The neighbor told her to carry the changeling into the kitchen, put him down on the hearth, start a fire, and boil water in two eggshells. That would make the changeling laugh, and when he laughed, he would lose his power. The woman did everything the neighbor said, and when she put the eggshells filled with water on the fire, the blockhead said:

> "Now I'm as old
> as the Westerwald,

and in all my life I've never seen
eggshells cooked as these have been."

And the changeling began to laugh. As soon as he laughed, a bunch of
elves appeared. They had brought the right child with them and put him
down on the hearth and took the changeling away.

—THE BROTHERS GRIMM

In the midst of winter I finally learned that there was in me an invinci-
ble summer.

—ALBERT CAMUS

I have heard it said that if in your heart you keep a green bough, will
come one day to stay a singing bird.

—CHINESE

The Props assist the House
Until the House is built
And then the Props withdraw
And adequate, erect,
The House support itself
And cease to recollect
The Auger and the Carpenter—
just such a retrospect
Hath the perfected Life—

A past of Plank and Nail
And slowness—then the Scaffolds drop
Affirming it a Soul.

—EMILY DICKINSON

In a large town there were two merchants who were fierce competitors. Their shops were across the street from each other. The sole method each man had of determining the success of his business was not daily profit, but how much more business he had than his competitor.

If a customer made a purchase at the store of one merchant, he would taunt his competitor when the sale was complete. The rivalry grew with each succeeding year.

One day God sent an angel to one of the merchants with an offer. "The Lord God has chosen to give you a great gift," the angel said. "Whatever you desire, you will receive. Ask for riches, long life, or healthy children, and the wish is yours. There is one stipulation," the angel cautioned. "Whatever you receive, your competitor will get twice as much. If you ask for 1,000 gold coins, he will receive 2,000. If you become famous, he will become twice as famous." The angel smiled. "This is God's way of teaching you a lesson."

The merchant thought for a moment. "You will give me anything I request?" The angel nodded. The man's face darkened. "I ask that you strike me blind in one eye."

—RUSSIAN

**How God comes
to the soul**

I descend on my love
As dew on a flower.

—MECHTILD OF MAGDEBURG

Once upon a time Zeus, in human shape, visited the land of Phrygia, and with him Hermes, without his wings. They presented themselves as weary travelers at many a door, seeking rest and shelter, but found all closed; for it was late, and the inhospitable inhabitants would not rouse themselves to open for their reception. At last a small thatched cottage received them, where Baucis, a pious old dame, and her husband, Philemon, had grown old together. Not ashamed of their poverty, they made it endurable by moderate desires and kind dispositions. When the two guests crossed the humble threshold and bowed their heads to pass under the low door, the old man placed a seat, on which Baucis, bustling and attentive, spread a cloth, and begged them to sit down. Then she raked out the coals from the ashes, kindled a fire, and prepared some potherbs and bacon for them. A beechen bowl was filled with warm water, that their guests might wash. While all was doing, they beguiled the time with conversation.

The old woman with trembling hand set the table. One leg was shorter than the rest, but a piece of slate put under restored the level. When it was steady she rubbed the table down with sweet-smelling herbs. Upon it she set some of chaste Athena's olives, some cornel berries preserved in vinegar, and added radishes and cheese, with eggs lightly cooked in the ashes. The meal was served in earthen dishes; and an earthenware pitcher, with wooden cups, stood beside them. When all was ready the stew, smoking hot, was set on the table. Some wine, not of the oldest, was added, and for dessert, apples and wild honey.

Now while the repast proceeded, the old folks were astonished to see that the wine, as fast as it was poured out, renewed itself in the pitcher of its own accord. Struck with terror, Baucis and Philemon recognized their heavenly guests, fell on their knees, and with clasped hands implored forgiveness for their poor entertainment. There was an old goose, which they kept as the guardian of their humble cottage, and they bethought them to make this a sacrifice in honor of their guests. But the goose, too nimble for the old folk, with the aid of feet and wings eluded their pursuit and at last took shelter between the gods themselves. They forbade it to be slain, and spoke in these words: "We are gods. This inhospitable village shall pay the penalty of its impiety; you alone shall go free from the chastisement. Quit your house and come with us to the top of yonder hill."

Baucis and Philemon hastened to obey. The country behind them was speedily sunk in a lake, only their own house left standing. While they gazed with wonder at the sight, that old house of theirs was changed. Columns took the place of the comer posts, the thatch grew yellow and appeared a gilded roof, the floors became marble, the doors were enriched with carving and ornaments of gold. Then spoke Zeus in benign accents: "Excellent old man, and woman worthy of such a husband, speak, tell us your wishes. What favor have you to ask of us?" Philemon took counsel with Baucis a few moments, then declared to the gods their common wish. "We ask to be priests and guardians of this thy temple, and that one and the same hour may take us both from life." Their prayer was granted. When they had attained a great age, as they stood one day before the steps of the sacred edifice and were telling the story of the place, Baucis saw Philemon begin to put forth leaves, and Philemon saw Baucis changing in like manner. While still they exchanged parting words, a leafy crown grew over their heads. "Farewell, dear spouse," they said together, and at the same moment the bark closed over their mouths. The Tyanean shepherd still shows the two trees—an oak and a linden, standing side by side.

—GREEK

Many times a day I realize how much my own outer and inner life is built upon the labors of my fellow men, both living and dead, and how earnestly I must exert myself in order to give in return as much as I have received.

—ALBERT EINSTEIN

Some old men came to see Abba Poemen, and said to him: Tell us, when we see brothers dozing during the sacred office, should we pinch them so they will stay awake? The old man said to them: Actually, if I saw a brother sleeping, I would put his head on my knees and let him rest.

—DESERT FATHERS

Religion is a defense against having a religious experience.

—CARL GUSTAV JUNG

i thank You God for most this amazing
day:for the leaping greenly spirits of trees
and a blue true dream of sky;and for everything
which is natural which is infinite which is yes

(i who have died am alive again today,
and this is the sun's birthday;this is the birth
day of life and of love and wings:and of the gay
great happening illimitably earth)

how should tasting touching hearing seeing
breathing any—lifted from the no
of all nothing—human merely being
doubt unimaginable You?

(now the ears of my ears awake and
now the eyes of my eyes are opened)

—E.E. CUMMINGS

A small rock holds back a great wave.

—HOMER

A Zen Master was invited to a great Catholic monastery to give instructions in Zen practice. He exhorted the monks there to meditate and try to solve their koan or Zen question with great energy and zeal. He told them that if they could practice with full-hearted effort, true understanding would come to them. One old monk raised his hand. "Master," he said, "our way of prayer is different than this. We have been meditating and praying in the simplest fashion without effort, waiting instead to be illuminated by the Grace of God. In Zen is there anything like this illuminating grace that comes to one uninvited?" he asked. The Zen Master looked back and laughed. "In Zen," he said, "we believe that God has already done his share."

—CHRISTINA FELDMAN AND JACK KORNFIELD

In the autumn,
on retreat at a mountain temple

Although the wind
blows terribly here,
the moonlight also leaks
between the roof planks
of this ruined house.

—IZUMI SHIKIBU

A seed offers itself for the tree which grows from it. Seen from without, the seed is lost, but the same seed that is sacrificed is embodied in the tree, its branches, blossoms, and fruits. If the continued existence of that seed had not been sacrificed for the tree, no branches, blossoms, or fruits could have developed.

—ABDU'L-BAHÁ

One moon shows in every pool; in every pool, the one moon.

—ZEN

> I was alone on a sunny shore
> by the forest's pale blue lake,
> in the sky floated a single cloud
> and on the water a single isle.
> The ripe sweetness of summer dripped
> in beads from every tree
> and straight into my opened heart
> a tiny drop ran down.

—EDITH SÖDERGRAN

It was a time of turmoil and slaughter. An especially fierce general led his troops through valley after valley, overrunning everything before him. Knowing of his cruelty, and told that he was coming, all the people of one town fled into the hills. The general led his troops into the empty town. His scouts returned to report that the only person left was a Zen priest. The general strode with his bodyguard to the temple, threw open the doors, and advanced upon the priest, drawing his sword. "Don't you know who I am?" he demanded. "I am one who can run you through without batting an eye."

The Zen master looked back and calmly responded, "And I, sir, am one who can be run through without batting an eye."

The general, hearing this, bowed and left.

—ZEN

The superior man blames himself; the inferior man blames others.

—CONFUCIUS

There was something formless and perfect
before the universe was born.
It is serene. Empty.
Solitary. Unchanging.
Infinite. Eternally present.
It is the mother of the universe.
For lack of a better name,
I call it the Tao.
It flows through all things,

inside and outside, and returns
to the origin of all things.

The Tao is great.
The universe is great.
Earth is great.
Man is great.
These are the four great powers.

Man follows the earth.
Earth follows the universe.
The universe follows the Tao.
The Tao follows only itself.

—Lao Tzu

God *must* act and pour himself into you the moment he finds you ready.
Don't imagine that God can be compared to an earthly carpenter, who
acts or doesn't act, as he wishes; who can will to do something or leave it
undone, according to his pleasure. It is not that way with God: where
and when God finds you ready, he must act and overflow into you, just
as when the air is clear and pure, the sun must overflow into it and cannot refrain from doing that.

—Meister Eckhart

Your first aim in life here on earth should be to be at peace with all men,
Jew and Gentile alike. Contend with no one. Your home should be a
place of quietude and happiness, where no harsh word is ever heard, but
love, amity, modesty, and a spirit of gentleness and reverence reigns all
the time. This spirit must not end with the home, however. In your deal-
ings with the world you must allow neither money nor ambition to dis-
turb you. Forgo your rights, if need be, and envy no man. For the main
thing is peace, peace with the whole world. Show all men every possible
respect, deal with them in the finest integrity and faithfulness. . . .

It was oft my way at assemblies to raise my eyes and regard those present from end to end, to see whether in truth I loved everyone among them, whether my acceptance of the duty to love was genuine. With God's help I found that indeed I loved all present. Even if I noticed one who had treated me improperly, then, without a thought of hesitation, without a moment's delay, I pardoned him. Immediately I resolved to love him. If my heart forced me to refuse my love, I addressed him with spoken words of friendship, until my heart became attuned to my word. So, whenever I met one to whom my heart did not incline, I forced myself to speak to him kindly, so as to make my heart feel affection for him. What if he were a sinner? Even then I would not quarrel with him, for I wonder whether there exists in this age one who is able to reprove another! On the other hand, if I conceived that he would listen to advice, I drew near to him, turning towards him a cheerful countenance. If, however, I fancied that he would resent my advances, I did not intrude on him. As there is a duty to speak, so is there a duty to be silent.

—JOEL BEN ABRAHAM SHEMARIAH
(IN HIS LAST WILL AND TESTAMENT)

Our deepest fear is not that we are inadequate. Our deepest fear is that we are powerful beyond measure. It is our light, not our darkness, that most frightens us. We ask ourselves, who am I to be brilliant, gorgeous, talented and fabulous? Actually, who are you not to be? You are a child of God. Your playing small doesn't serve the world. There's nothing enlightened about shrinking so that other people won't feel insecure around you. We are born to manifest the glory of God that is within us. It's not just in some of us; it's in everyone. And as we let our own light shine, we consciously give other people permission to do the same. As we are liberated from our own fear, our presence automatically liberates others.

—MARIANNE WILLIAMSON

I must study politics & war that my sons may have liberty to study mathematics and philosophy. My sons ought to study mathematics & philosophy, geography, natural history, naval architecture, navigation, commerce, and agriculture, in order to give their children a right to study painting, poetry, music, architecture, statuary, tapestry, and porcelain.

—JOHN ADAMS

The sage* was asked, "Why do we never perceive in thee a trace of anxiety?" He replied, "Because I never possessed a thing over which I would grieve had I lost it."

—IBN GABRIOL

A father complained to the Besht (the Baal Shem Tov) that his son had forsaken God. "What, Rabbi, shall I do?"

"Love him more than ever," was the Besht's reply.

—HASIDIC

*Diogenes; also attributed to Socrates.

Concerning all acts of initiative (and creation) there is one elementary truth, the ignorance of which kills countless ideas and splendid plans: that the moment one definitely commits oneself, then Providence moves too. All sorts of things occur to help one that would never otherwise have occurred. A whole stream of events issues from the decision, raising in one's favor all manner of unforeseen incidents and meetings and material assistance, which no man could have dreamed would have come his way.

—JOHANN WOLFGANG VON GOETHE

Always fall in with what you're asked to accept. Take what is given, and make it over your way. My aim in life has always been to hold my own with whatever's going on. Not against: with.

—ROBERT FROST

Keep cool: it will all be over 100 years hence.

—RALPH WALDO EMERSON

Awakening is not possible so long as the mind is constantly distracted from Truth by remaining habitually egocentric, by instinctively seeking personal gratification. Divine Grace, the healing and illuminating energy that rains down ceaselessly upon the human mind, heart, and soul, cannot be absorbed or assimilated by the high, rocky hill of personal interest and personal importance. This precious, life-giving water runs off the high ground of ego, without ever penetrating its hard, barren soil.

—RAMAKRISHNA

PERCEPTION

Nine

Perception

Our perception of life comprises our attitudes, beliefs, and convictions—what we *think* life is, what we *think* is real. We encounter a snake in the grass at dusk and leap back. An instant later we discover it is not a snake but a piece of rope. Our *perception* created the reality we experienced—but that reality in no way corresponded to the actual world.

When our perceptions of ourselves, money, or ourselves in relationship to money are distorted, money becomes difficult for us. We grow uncomfortable with it, struggle with it. Several years ago, I went to Florida to help create the template for a new magazine. While Floridians didn't wear their hearts on their sleeves, they did seem to wear them then on their bumpers, in the form of stickers. Among the bumper stickers that struck me in particular were: *I'll Shop and I'll Buy, in Debt till I Die; A Woman's Place Is in the Mall; I'm So Broke I Can't Even Pay Attention; I Owe, I Owe, It's Off to Work I Go,* and the erudite *Veni. Vidi. Visa. I came. I saw. I shopped.* All of these made me smile, as they probably did most people, but what they were, actually, were affirmations, instructions to the subconscious, beliefs, truthful declarations by the people who mounted them on their bumpers. I doubt that any of these people had a peaceful relationship with money.

Prior to 1954, it was believed that it was not physically possible for a human being to run a mile in less than four minutes. But then a British runner named Roger Bannister did just that; once he showed it could be done, several other runners duplicated the feat within months. Today, breaking the four-minute mile barrier is commonplace. Had human anatomy changed? No. What happened was that the *perception* of what was possible changed. And with it, reality itself.

Some of the common distorted perceptions many of us have about ourselves or money are: *There isn't enough of it. You can't make money in this kind of economy. I'm no good (or I'm incapable, undereducated, too old, and the like). You have to be corrupt to get ahead.* With these or any of the many others like them you will hear in the words of other people, or even from your own mouth, operating within you with any kind strength, your relationship with money will not be peaceful.

But some of them are true, aren't they?

Man can't fly. The Gods live on Mount Olympus. "Everything that can be invented has been invented"—Charles H. Duell, Commissioner, United States Office of Patents, in 1899, recommending that the office be closed. I'm not disciplined enough. Life sucks. I'll never have money.

Perceptions, all: beliefs, attitudes, convictions.

Just as is your thinking that the table on which you eat your dinner is solid. It isn't. It is composed of rapidly moving molecules with great spaces between them; the molecules themselves are composed of whirling atoms with even more empty spaces between them; and the atoms are made up of streaking neutrons, protons, and electrons, with empty spaces between them: Ultimately, your table is reducible to a mathematical configuration of pure energy. Without argument, it is useful and practical for us to perceive a table as solid even if we know there is "another reality" to it, too. But it is *not* useful or practical for us to perceive ourselves or money in limited or distorted ways.

Practice:
Opening Your Eyes

Pick a problem or question you have about money. Perceive it from several points of view: What would H. Ross Perot think of it, do about it? Your grandfather? The last street person to ask you for a handout, the president, Mother Teresa, Karl Marx, a ten-year-old child, your sister-in-law, Betty Friedan, your financially most successful friend?

Examine the problem or question from the perspective of ten different people with differing backgrounds and values. Write out a paragraph for each one, describing how he or she would be likely to approach the matter. Do this practice periodically, whether you have a particular situation you wish to resolve or not. Accustom yourself to opening your eyes and learning to look beyond your own limited perception—which is just that, only a perception.

Practice:
I Understand

Mentally select two people you don't know well or don't know not at all. Pick them from among people with whom you normally conduct or will conduct a financial transaction. They could be a bank teller, a ticket seller at a movie house, the person who will handle your online purchase of shares of stock, the collector of donations at a church, a cabdriver, whoever signs your payroll check, a newspaper vendor, and the like. One at a time, contemplate each in this way: Imagine his or her childhood, fears, hopes, pains; imagine what he treasures, what he has suffered; imagine what he loves, what he longs for. Know him, or her. Do this once a month, with a different set of people, for at least three months, longer if you'd like. This will begin to alter your perceptions of other people involved in and around your money, which is valuable in itself, but just as valuably, of yourself, as you see yourself mirrored in them.

A poor peasant returned to his tiny hut where there was not even fire-wood. His wife and son were huddled under a blanket eating the last crumbs of bread. He told them that men from the city wished to buy their bull to fight in the bullring.

"Oh no!" cried the boy. "Not the bool. Not my favorite thing in the whole world, not my friend. Not the bool I raised from a little calf!"

"But, my son," said the peasant, "we have no money left and nothing to eat. They will pay us twenty thousand dollars for him. We can move to a house. You will have shoes, a bicycle. You will be able to go to movies, to go to school, to have all the things you never had before."

"Twenty thousand dollars?" the boy asked.

"Yes, my son."

"Shoes? A bicycle? School?"

"Everything, my son."

The boy reflected a moment, then said brightly, "Keel the bool."

—SPANISH

Experience is not what happens to a man, it is what a man does with what happens to him.

—ALDOUS HUXLEY

Just above a mountain valley stood a great dam. The dam began to crack, soon to give way completely, and water began to roar down into the valley. A National Guard unit was rushed in to evacuate the valley's residents.

The water was already several feet high and rising. The first guardsmen were working from rubber rafts. One raft-full came upon a house where a man was sitting on the sill of a second-floor window, the water swirling just below his feet.

"Hurry up!" yelled a guardsman. "Get in. The whole valley's going under in four minutes!"

With a serene smile the man waved them off. "No. Go away," he said. "I put all my trust in the Lord."

The guardsmen left to help others.

Two minutes later another group came by in a powerboat. The man was now standing on his roof, the water lapping at his shoes. "Come on, get in!" a guardsman shouted. "The valley's going under in two minutes!"

The man shook his head. "No. Go away," he said. "I put all my trust in the Lord."

The guardsmen left.

Two minutes later another group returned in a helicopter. By now the man was standing on his chimney, the water rising up over his ankles. A guardsman tossed out a rope ladder from the helicopter. "Hurry up!" he shouted. "Grab the ladder! The valley's going under in seconds!"

"No. Go away," the man shouted back. "I put all my trust in the Lord."

The helicopter left. . . .

A few minutes later the man woke up in heaven, just outside the Pearly Gates. "What happened!" he demanded angrily of God. "I put all my trust in you!"

God shrugged. "I sent you a raft, I sent you a boat, I sent you a helicopter: What do you want?"

—AMERICAN

The man who never alters his opinion is like standing water, and breeds reptiles of the mind.

—WILLIAM BLAKE

I have lost my favorite teacup. I can have lost my favorite teacup and be miserable, or I can have lost my favorite teacup and be all right. Either way, my teacup is gone.

—ZEN

It's never too late to have had a good childhood.

—JIM ROI

The day is cold, and dark, and dreary;
It rains, and the wind is never weary;
The vine still clings to the moldering wall,
But at every gust the dead leaves fall,
    And the day is dark and dreary.

My life is cold, and dark, and dreary;
It rains, and the wind is never weary;
My thoughts still cling to the moldering Past,
But the hopes of youth fall thick in the blast,
   And the days are dark and dreary.

Be still, sad heart! and cease repining;
Behind the clouds is the sun still shining;
Thy fate is the common fate of all,
Into each life some rain must fall,
   Some days must be dark and dreary.

—HENRY WADSWORTH LONGFELLOW

The world is as we are.

—HINDU

Poor Byron, who had only three happy hours in his life! He was either
of a morbid and enormously unbalanced spirit, or else he was affecting
merely the fashionable *Weltschmerz* of his decade. Were the feeling of
Weltschmerz not so fashionable, I feel bound to suspect that he must
have confessed to at least thirty happy hours instead of three.

—LIN YUTANG

What men commonly call their fate is mostly their own foolishness.

—ARTHUR SCHOPENHAUER

An intelligent young man, thirsty for knowledge and wisdom, had
studied physiognomy, the science of deducing temperament from out-

ward appearance. His studies, which lasted six years, took place in Egypt and cost him many sacrifices far from his homeland. But finally he completed his exams with excellent results. Filled with pride and joy, he rode back to his home. Everyone he met on the way he looked at through the eyes of his science, and, in order to extend his knowledge, he read the facial expressions of all the people he encountered.

One day he met a man whose face was stamped by six qualities: envy, jealousy, greed, covetousness, stinginess, and inconsideration. "My God, what a monstrous expression! I've never seen or heard of anything like that before. I could test my theory here."

While he was thinking this, the stranger approached with a friendly, kind, and modest demeanor, saying, "Oh, sheik. It is already very late and the next village is far away. My cottage is small and dark, but I will carry you in my arms. What an honor it would be for me if I could consider you my guest for the night. And how happy I would be in your presence!"

Amazed by this, the traveler thought to himself, "How astonishing! What a difference between this stranger's speech and his horrible facial expression." This realization frightened him very much. He began to doubt the things he had learned in the past six years. In order to gain some certainty, he accepted the stranger's invitation. The man pampered the scholar with tea, coffee, fruit juices, pastries, and a waterpipe. He overwhelmed his guest with kindness, with attention, goodness, and politeness. For three days and three nights, the host succeeded in keeping our traveler there. Eventually the scholar was able to resist his host's politeness. He firmly decided to continue his journey. When the time had come for him to leave, his host handed him an envelope and said, "O lord. Here is your bill."

"What bill?" the scholar asked, surprised.

As fast as a person can draw a sword form its sheath, the host suddenly showed his true face. He wrinkled his brow sternly and screamed with an angry voice, "What impudence! What were you thinking when you ate everything here? Did you think it was all free?" Upon hearing these words, the scholar suddenly came to his senses. Without saying a word, he opened the letter. There he saw that everything he had eaten and not eaten had been billed to him a hundred times over. He did not even have half the money that was demanded of him. Forced by necessity, he climbed down from his horse and gave it to his host. Then he took off his traveling clothes and set off on foot. As if in ecstasy, he bowed his torso with every step of the way. From far off, one could hear him saying, "Thank God, thank God my six years of study were not in vain!"

—AFTER ABDU'L-BAHÁ

They are able because they think they are able.

—VIRGIL

It is easier to put on sandals than it is to carpet the world.

—HINDU

Mullah Nasrudin wished to have a flower garden. He turned the soil and planted the seeds of many beautiful flowers. But when they emerged from the ground, they were not alone: with them came an army of dandelions. Mullah struggled mightily against the dandelions, but without effect. They sprang up again and again. Mullah sought advice from gardeners in all quarters and tried every method known to them, to no avail. Finally he journeyed to the capital to speak with the royal gardener at the sheik's palace. This wise old man who had counseled generations of gardeners suggested a number of potent remedies to evict the dandelions. But Mullah had tried them all. They sat together in silence a long time and finally the gardener looked at Nasrudin and said, "Well, then I suggest you learn to love them."

—SUFI

Once a man was about to cross the sea. Bibhishana wrote Rama's name on a leaf, tied it in a corner of the man's wearing-cloth and said to him: "Don't be afraid. Have faith and walk on the water. But look here, the moment you lose faith you will be drowned." The man was walking easily on the water. Suddenly he had an intense desire to see what was tied in his cloth. He opened it and found only a leaf with the name of Rama written on it. "What is this?" he thought. "Just the name of Rama!" As soon as doubt entered his mind he sank under the water.

—RAMAKRISHNA

Our destination is never a place, but rather a new way of looking at things.

—HENRY MILLER

I've known a lot of troubles in my life, and most of them never happened.

—MARK TWAIN

Chicken Little was in the woods one day when an acorn fell on her head. It scared her so much she trembled all over. She shook so hard, half her feathers fell out.

"Help! Help!" she cried. "The sky is falling! I must go tell the king!" So she ran in great fright to tell the king.

Along the way she met Henny Penny. "Where are you going, Chicken Little?" Henny Penny asked.

"Oh, help!" Chicken Little cried. "The sky is falling!"

"How do you know?" asked Henny Penny.

"Oh! I saw it with my own eyes, and heard it with my own ears, and part of it fell on my head!"

"This is terrible, just terrible!" Henny Penny clucked. "We'd better run." So they both ran away as fast as they could.

Soon they met Ducky Lucky. "Where are you going, Chicken Little and Henny Penny?" he asked.

"The sky is falling! The sky is falling! We're going to tell the king!" they cried.

"How do you know?" asked Ducky Lucky.

"I saw it with my own eyes, and heard it with my own ears, and part of it fell on my head," Chicken Little said.

"Oh dear, oh dear!" Ducky Lucky quacked. "We'd better run!" So they all ran down the road as fast as they could.

Soon they met Goosey Loosey waddling along the roadside.

"Hello there, Chicken Little, Henny Penny, and Ducky Lucky," called Goosey Loosey. "Where are you all going in such a hurry?"

"We're running for our lives!" cried Chicken Little.

"The sky is falling!" clucked Henny Penny.

"And we're running to tell the king!" quacked Ducky Lucky.

"How do you know the sky is falling?" asked Goosey Loosey.

"I saw it with my own eyes, and heard it with my own ears, and part of it fell on my head," Chicken Little said.

"Goodness!" squawked Goosey Loosey. "Then I'd better run with you." And they all ran in great fright across a meadow.

Before long they met Turkey Lurkey strutting back and forth.

"Hello there, Chicken Little, Henny Penny, Ducky Lucky, and Goosey Loosey," he called. "Where are you all going in such a hurry?"

"Help! Help!" cried Chicken Little.

"We're running for our lives!" clucked Henny Penny.

"The sky is falling!" quacked Ducky Lucky.

"And we're running to tell the king!" squawked Goosey Loosey.

"How do you know the sky is falling?" asked Turkey Lurkey.

"I saw it with my own eyes, and heard it with my own ears, and part of it fell on my head," Chicken Little said.

"Oh dear! I always suspected the sky would fall someday," Turkey Lurkey gobbled. "I'd better run with you."

So they all ran with all their might, until they met Foxy Loxy.

"Well, well," said Foxy Loxy. "Where are you rushing on such a fine day?"

"Help! Help!" cried Chicken Little, Henny Penny, Ducky Lucky, Goosey Loosey, and Turkey Lurkey. "It's not a fine day at all. The sky is falling, and we're running to tell the king!"

"How do you know the sky is falling?" said Foxy Loxy.

"I saw it with my own eyes, and heard it with my own ears, and part of it fell on my head," Chicken Little said.

"I see," said Foxy Loxy. "Well then, follow me, and I'll show you the way to the king."

So Foxy Loxy led Chicken Little, Henny Penny, Ducky Lucky, Goosey Loosey, and Turkey Lurkey across a field and through the woods. He led them straight to his den, and they never saw the king to tell him the sky was falling.

—ENGLISH

This time, like all times, is a very good one, if we but know what to do with it.

—RALPH WALDO EMERSON

So long as a man imagines that he cannot do this or that, so long is he determined not to do it: and consequently, so long it is impossible to him that he should do it.

—BARUCH SPINOZA

The setting sun will always set me to rights—or if a sparrow come before my window, I take part in its existence and pick about the gravel.

—JOHN KEATS

The solution of the problem that you see in life is to live in a way that will make what is problematic disappear.

The fact that life is problematic means that your life doesn't fit into life's shape. So you must change your life, and when it fits into the shape, what is problematic disappears.

But don't we have the feeling that someone who doesn't see a problem in life is blind to something important, to the most important thing of all? Don't I want to say that someone like this is just going along with his life—blindly, like a mole, and if only he could see, he would see the problem?

Or shouldn't I say rather: that whoever lives rightly, experiences the problem not as sorrow, and therefore not problematic, but rather much more as a joy; therefore, so to speak, as a bright halo around his life, not as a questionable background.

—LUDWIG WITTGENSTEIN

The mighty ruler was bedridden with illness, and all the doctors feared his rage. At wits' end, a servant pleaded, cajoled, and then finally threatened a frightened hakim into coming to the sickbed. There, the king roared at him with a mighty voice, saying, "You are famed everywhere for your skill. Show it to us now. But remember whom you have in front of you." The hakim carefully examined the fearsome king.

"Here, only one thing will help," he said. "Get everything ready for an enema."

"What? An enema?" shouted the king. "Who is supposed to have an enema?"

The frightful glance of the ruler made the hakim tremble. "The enema is for me, O lord."

The king allowed it to take place, and lo, from that hour on, the ruler's condition began to improve. And every time an illness plagued him, he summoned the hakim so that the doctor could have an enema.

—PERSIAN

Every man takes the limits of his own field of vision for the limits of the world.

——ARTHUR SCHOPENHAUER

In the day of prosperity there is a forgetfulness of affliction: and in the day of affliction there is no more remembrance of prosperity.

—APOCRYPHA

No two people see the external world in exactly the same way. To every separate person a thing is what he thinks it is—in other words, not a thing, but a think.

—PENELOPE FITZGERALD

Look to this day,
For it is life,
The very life of life.
In its brief course lie all
The realities and verities of existence,
The bliss of growth,
The splendor of action,
The glory of power —

For yesterday is but a dream
And tomorrow is only a vision.
But today, well lived,
Makes every yesterday a dream of happiness
And every tomorrow a vision of hope.

Look well, therefore, to this day

—SANSKRIT

A man whose axe was missing suspected his neighbor's son. The boy walked like a thief, looked like a thief, and spoke like a thief. But the man found his axe while he was digging in the valley, and the next time he saw his neighbor's son, the boy walked, looked, and spoke like any other child.

—GERMAN

So much is a man worth as he esteems himself.

—FRANÇOIS RABELAIS

A merry heart doeth good like medicine; but a broken spirit drieth the bones.

—PROVERBS

One comes to be of just such stuff as that on which the mind is set.

—UPANISHADS

ENLIGHTENMENT

Ten

Enlightenment

Enlightenment is a state of being, a deeper knowing. Its nature, ultimately, is ineffable. Experience of it, and the means through which that experience is achieved, vary. Commonly, people who live it or who have tasted it know to one degree or another a serenity, a bliss, a peace, a freedom, a confidence, a calmness, a happiness. That is not to say that they do not know dark nights of the soul also; or doubts, fear, or other forms of suffering. Buddha nearly died of asceticism, Christ sweated blood at Gethsemane.

Enlightenment is vast. All we are going to say about it in relation to money is this: Money becomes easier for the person who is at least conscious that such a state exists—even better, makes some effort to move toward it.

Practice:
Body, Mind

That body and mind are deeply interrelated and have a powerful effect on one another is not a recent discovery: Twenty-four hundred years ago, Hippocrates prescribed exercise and outdoor activity for melancholy. The Romans said, *mens sana in corpore sano;* a sound mind in a sound body. Eighteenth-century French philosopher Jean-Jacques Rousseau wrote, *un corps debile affaiblit l'âme;* a feeble body makes a mind weak. And over the past two decades, a torrent of scientific evidence has confirmed the relationship—from physical cures by placebo effect to the strengthening of the immune system though visualization to the altering of mood through exposure to light.

Clearly a powerful mind is not always joined with a powerful body. Most people tend toward one or the other; biology is not to be denied. And in the case of disease, such as with Stephen Hawking, the brilliant, intellectually active physicist whose body is ravaged to near uselessness by Lou Gehrig's disease, the equation collapses. Nevertheless, improvement in either mind or body generally results in improvement in the other; as damage to one—through abuse or neglect—generally results in damage to the other.

Body and mind do not act independent of spirit. It is not possible to cull one from the other two in any living person and still have what we know as a human being. All three of these elements are interrelated, and affect each other. This practice addresses mind and body; the following addresses spirit. Effort applied to any of the three will have its most immediate and observable impact upon that element in particular, but will also reverberate beneficially in the other two.

Body: The simplest way to work with the body is through exercise. Nearly any form will do, from formal workouts in a gym or on a piece of home equipment to participation in sports, long walks, or even dancing. The key is to do the activity consistently, for at least twenty minutes three or four times a week. Many people find yoga particularly helpful. "Yoga," as a word, means yoke, or union, joining together. Yoga is just that, a system of exercises specifically designed to strengthen both the body and the mind. Another way to work through the body is to learn a new physical skill that requires strength or ability in areas in which you're weak, such as coordination or reflexes; this causes new neural pathways to form in the brain. Addressing your physical nature is especially beneficial when the emphasis in your life, your primary activity, is mental.

Mind: For mental strengthening, learning a new intellectual skill is helpful, from a branch of mathematics to computer programming or a language, or even working crossword or jigsaw puzzles. What is important is to keep the mind supple and dynamic through use and new learning.

Some people will find psychotherapy useful, maybe even critical. There are many forms available, from intrapersonal through behavioral to classical analysis. The individual will have to determine which would be best for him or her. Central in the decision should be simple pragmatism: Have others you know gotten lasting relief and changed for the better in this form of therapy, or working with this practitioner? After you have been in the therapy awhile, ask yourself if *you* are experiencing relief and getting demonstrably better. If you aren't, then this form of therapy or this practitioner is not for you. Many people in therapy get caught up in what could be called the Vietnam Syndrome—after all that investment, it's hard to admit a mistake has been made and pull out.

Finally, meditation is a way of strengthening the mind, especially the forms that employ the kind of concentration known as one-pointedness, such as counting your breaths, working with a mantra, or focusing on an object. (Meditation is much more than a simple tool through which to strengthen the mind, of course—vastly more—and is more properly placed in the following practice, but some forms can be used for this purpose, and if that is how an individual chooses to use them, there is nothing wrong with that, and he or she will benefit.)

Practice:

Spirit

This practice is simple to describe, but challenging and powerful to do:

Select a spiritual path that is appropriate for you—Christian, Judaic, Buddhist, humanist, whatever. Then for the next three months *actively* practice or participate in it: read, chant, pray; meditate; give, help, love; volunteer; comfort, bless. You needn't be intense or urgent about it. Just maintain awareness of the path you are on, place yourself on it anew each morning, and do what it would have you do, as you can. This modest three-month practice can have great transformative impact on your life.

Historically, the two most common ways people have used to achieve some kind of conscious contact or alignment with a power greater than themselves, whatever they imagine that to be, are prayer and meditation. You don't need a creed or even a belief in anything in particular to undertake either. Prayer has been called talking to God (or the universe); meditation, listening (to Him or it). Both are helpful, to *anyone* who undertakes them. The section at the end of this book, "For Further Reading" cites some works that will be of assistance on these subjects.

One major effect of leading a spiritual life, or one in which spirituality plays at least a part, is that you become more fully present, more aware. This has positive ramifications across the entire spectrum of your engagements, including—though it might seem a narrow concern in the face of such an immense theme—your relationship with money, the degree of peace that is in it.

Where logic and evidence clash, it seems prudent to stick with evidence, for this holds the prospect of leading to a wider logic, whereas the opposite approach closes the door to discovery.

—HUSTON SMITH

Man was once divine. But because of a grievous offense, Bhraman decided to punish him by taking his divinity from him.

"Where shall I hide it?" Brahman wondered.

"In the ocean," the other, lesser gods answered.

"No—for man will surely someday plumb the deepest parts of all the oceans."

"On the highest mountain top," the others suggested.

"No—for man will inevitably conquer all the peaks of the world."

"Out among the farthest stars!" cried the gods.

"No—for man will someday travel even there, and beyond, in his search for it."

The other gods went mute, utterly confounded.

Brahman thought and thought.

"I have it!" he said at last. "I will hide man's divinity deep within himself. That is the one place he will never think to look for it."

—HINDU

You cannot step twice into the same river.

—HERACLITUS

Nothing burns in hell except the self.

—*THEOLOGIA GERMANICA*

The most beautiful and profound emotion we can experience is the sensation of the mystical. It is the sower of all true science. He to whom this emotion is a stranger, who can no longer wonder and stand rapt in awe, is as good as dead. To know that what is impenetrable to us really exists, manifesting itself as the highest wisdom and the most radiant beauty, which our dull faculties can comprehend only in their primitive forms—this knowledge, this feeling, is at the center of true religion.

—ALBERT EINSTEIN

The good-natured sensualist is better than the bad-tempered saint.

—AL-JUNAID OF BAGHDAD

A person works in a stable. That person has a breakthrough. What does she do? She returns to the stable.

—MEISTER ECKHART

When the guru sat down to worship each evening, the ashram cat would get in the way and distract the worshipers. So he ordered that the cat be tied during evening worship. After the guru died the cat continued to be tied during evening worship. And when the cat expired, another cat was brought to the ashram so that it could be duly tied during evening worship. Centuries later, learned treatises were written by the guru's scholarly disciples on the liturgical significance of tying up a cat while worship is performed.

—HINDU

To say there is an afterlife is to miss the mark. To say there isn't an afterlife is to miss the mark. To say either there is or there isn't is to miss the mark. To say that there both is and isn't is to miss the mark. All these have no bearing on the real problem, which is salvation.

—BUDDHA

Trials and revelations is what it's all about.

—JOSEPH CAMPBELL

> Play all the symphonies you like
> On the marshlands of Thung-Ting.
> The birds will fly away
> In all directions;
> The animals will hide;
> The fish will dive to the bottom;
> But men
> Will gather around to listen.

Water is for fish
And air for men.
Natures differ, and needs with them.

Hence the wise men of old
Did not lay down
One measure for all.

—CHUANG TZU

All we are is the result of what we have thought.

—THE *DHAMMAPADA*

He deserves paradise who can make his companions laugh.

—THE KORAN

It is a test of a good religion whether you can make a joke about it.

—G. K. CHESTERTON

Contemplation for an hour is better than formal worship for sixty years.

—MUHAMMAD

Those who seek the truth by means of intellect and learning only get further and further away from it.

—HUANG PO

We should tackle reality in a slightly joking way . . . otherwise we miss its point.

—LAWRENCE DURRELL

The Universe is not only queerer than we suppose, but queerer than we
can suppose.

—J. B. S. HALDANE

Mother, Mother, Mother!* Everyone foolishly assumes that his clock
alone tells correct time. Christians claim to possess exclusive truth. . . .
Countless varieties of Hindus insist that their sect, no matter how small
and insignificant, expresses the ultimate position. Devout Muslims maintain that Koranic revelation supersedes all others. The entire world is
being driven insane by this single phrase: "My religion alone is true."
O Mother, you have shown me that no clock is entirely accurate. Only the
transcendent sun of knowledge remains on time. Who can make a system
from Divine Mystery? But if any sincere practitioner, within whatever culture or religion, prays and meditates with great devotion and commitment
to Truth alone, Your Grace will flood his mind and heart,
O Mother. His particular sacred tradition will be opened and illuminated.
He will reach the one goal of spiritual evolution. Mother, Mother,
Mother! How I long to pray with sincere Christians in their churches and
to bow and prostrate with devoted Muslims in their mosques! All religions are glorious!

—RAMAKRISHNA

*Ramakrishna often invoked Divine Reality as Mother.

All things hang like a drop of dew
Upon a blade of grass.

—WILLIAM BUTLER YEATS

The true value of a human being can be found in the degree to which
he has attained liberation from the self.

—ALBERT EINSTEIN

That is perfect. This is perfect. Perfect comes from perfect. Take perfect from perfect, the remainder is perfect.

—UPANISHADS

The tao that can be told
is not the eternal Tao.
The name that can be named
is not the eternal Name.

The unnamable is the eternally real.
Naming is the origin
of all particular things.

Free from desire, you realize the mystery.
Caught in desire, you see only the manifestations.

Yet mystery and manifestations
arise from the same source.
This source is called darkness.

Darkness within darkness.
The gateway to all understanding.

—LAO TZU

Absolutely unmixed attention is prayer.

—SIMONE WEIL

True religion is surrender.

—MUHAMMAD

You possess only whatever will not be lost in a shipwreck.

—EL-GHAZALI

I met a traveler from an antique land
Who said: Two vast and trunkless legs of stone
Stand in the desert. . . . Near them, on the sand,
Half sunk, a shattered visage lies, whose frown,
And wrinkled lip, and sneer of cold command,
Tell that its sculptor well those passions read
Which yet survive, stamped on these lifeless things,
The hand that mocked them, and the heart that fed:
And on the pedestal these words appear:
"My name is Ozymandias, king of kings:

Look on my works, ye Mighty, and despair!"
Nothing beside remains. Round the decay
Of that colossal wreck, boundless and bare
The lone and level sands stretch far away.

—PERCY BYSSHE SHELLEY

If on earth there be
    a Paradise of Bliss,
It is this,
It is this,
It is this.

—FIRADUSI

Are you looking for me? I am in the next seat.
My shoulder is against yours.
You will not find me in stupas, not in Indian shrine rooms, nor in
        synagogues, nor in cathedrals:
not in masses, nor kirtans, not in legs winding around your own
        neck, nor in eating nothing but vegetables.
When you really look for me, you will see me instantly —
you will find me in the tiniest house of time.
Kabir says: Student, tell me, what is God?
He is the breath inside the breath.

—KABIR

When I dance, I dance; when I sleep, I sleep; yes, and when I walk alone in a beautiful orchard, if my thoughts have been concerned with extraneous incidents for some part of the time, for some other part I lead them back again to the walk, to the orchard, to the sweetness of this solitude, and to myself. Nature has in motherly fashion observed this principle, that the actions she has enjoined on us for our need should also give us pleasure; and she invites us to them not only through reason, but also through appetite. It is wrong to infringe her laws.

. . . We are great fools. "He has passed his life in idleness," we say. "I have done nothing today." What! haven't you lived? That is not only the fundamental but the most illustrious of your occupations. "Had I been put in a position to manage great affairs, I would have shown what I could do." Have you been able to think out and manage your life? You have performed the greatest work of all. In order to show and release her powers, Nature has no need of fortune; she shows herself equally on all levels, and behind a curtain as well as without one. To compose our character is our duty, not to compose books, and to win, not battles and provinces, but order and tranquility in our conduct. Our great and glorious masterpiece is to live appropriately. All other things, to rule, to lay up treasure, to build, are at most but little appendices and props.

—MICHEL EYQUEM DE MONTAIGNE

The kingdom of God is within you.

—JESUS

A wanderer was trudging along an endless road. He was weighted down with many burdens: a heavy knapsack of sand hung from his shoulders on his back; a long waterskin was wound around his torso. In his right hand, he carried a rock, in his left, a larger one. An old millstone was suspended from a rope that went round his neck. Rusty chains were fastened to clamps around his ankles, and at the end of them were iron weights, which he dragged through the dusty sand. On his head, the man was balancing a rotting pumpkin. With every step he took, the chains clanked. Moaning, groaning, he moved forward one step at a time, complaining of his hard fate, the weariness that plagued him. In the shimmering heat of midday, a farmer came upon him on the road. The farmer asked, "Oh, tired wanderer, why do you burden yourself with those rocks you carry?"

"Quite thickheaded of me," replied the wanderer, "but I hadn't noticed them before." With that, he threw the rocks away and felt much lighter.

After he had gone a long way farther down the road, another farmer met him and asked, "Tell me, tired wanderer, why do you vex yourself with that rotting pumpkin on your head, and why do you drag those iron weights behind you on chains?"

The wanderer answered, "I'm very glad you pointed that out to me. I didn't realize what I was doing to myself." He threw the pumpkin into a ditch beside the road, then opened the clamps around his ankles and took off the chains with their attached weights. Again, he felt lighter.

But the farther he went, the less was his relief and the more he began to suffer again.

A farmer came from a field to the edge of the road to watch him in amazement. The farmer said, "Oh, good man, you are carrying sand in the sack, but what you see ahead of you in the distance is more sand than you could ever carry. And your big waterskin—it's as if you planned to cross a great desert, while all the while there's a clear stream flowing alongside you on this road, which will accompany you on your way for as long as you can imagine." Hearing this, the wanderer removed his waterskin, opened its spout, and emptied its brackish water onto the path. Then he took off his knapsack and poured out the sand from it, filling up a hole in the road. He stood there pensively, looking toward the sinking sun, whose last rays sent their light washing over him. He glanced down at his chest, and saw the heavy millstone that hung there from around his neck, and suddenly realized the stone was causing him still to walk bent over. He unfastened it and threw it as far as he could, into the river. Freed from his burdens, he set off into the cool of the evening to find lodging.

—Persian

The fact that there is nothing but a spiritual world deprives us of hope and gives us certainty.

—Franz Kafka

The Father maketh his sun to rise on the evil and on the good, and sendeth rain on the just and on the unjust.

—JESUS

The first step in the acquisition of wisdom is silence, the second listening, the third memory, the fourth practice, the fifth teaching others.

—IBN GABRIOL

I will teach you the best way to say Torah. You must be nothing but an ear that hears what the universe of the word is constantly saying within you. The moment you begin to hear what you yourself are saying, you must stop.

—DOV BAER OF MEZRITCH

A mullah wanted to protect his daughter from the dangers of life. When the time had come and she had grown into a true flower of beauty, he took her aside and told her about the baseness and malice of the world. "My dear daughter," he said, "remember what I tell you. All men want only one thing. Men are cunning. They set traps wherever they can. You don't realize how you sink deeper and deeper into the swamp of their desires. I want to show you the way of unhappiness. First the man swoons about your best features, and he admires you. Then he invites you to go out with him. Then the two of you pass his house, and he mentions that he just wants to fetch his coat. He asks you if you wouldn't like to come in the house with him. Upstairs he invites you to have a seat, and he offers you some tea. The two of you listen to music, and, when the time is right, he suddenly throws himself on you. In this way you are violated, and we are violated, your mother and I. Our family is violated, and our good reputation is gone."

The daughter took these words of her father to heart. Some time later she came up to her father and smiled proudly. "Dear Father," she asked, "are you a prophet? How did you know how everything happens? It was just as you described it. First he admired my beauty. Then he asked me out. As if by coincidence we passed his house. There the poor man noticed he had forgotten his coat. And so I wouldn't be alone, he invited me to come on into his apartment. As good manners require, he offered me tea and brightened the day with beautiful music. At that point, I thought of your words and I knew exactly what would happen. But you see, I am worthy to be your daughter. When I felt the moment coming, I threw myself on him and violated him, his parents, his family, his good reputation, and his esteem!"

—PERSIAN

In the autumn,
on retreat at a mountain temple

Although I try
to hold the single thought
of Buddha's teaching in my heart,

I cannot help but hear
the many crickets' voices calling as well.

—IZUMI SHIKIBU

Long ago, a mouse was in constant distress because of its fear of the cat.
A magician took pity on it and turned it into a cat. But then it became
afraid of the dog. So the magician turned it into a dog. Then it began to
fear the panther. So the magician turned it into a panther. Whereupon it
was full of fear of the hunter. At this point the magician gave up. He
turned it into a mouse again saying, "Nothing I do for you is going to be
of any help. The problem is not in your circumstances but in your heart."

—HINDU

Thou wilt keep him in perfect peace whose mind is stayed on thee.

—ISAIAH

Throw away sacredness and wisdom, and people will be a hundred times
happier.

—LAO TZU

Beyond a certain point there is no return. This point has to be reached.

—FRANZ KAFKA

Certainly Adam in Paradise had not more sweet and curious apprehen-
sions of the world than I when I was a child. All appeared new, and
strange at the first, inexpressibly rare, and delightful, and beautiful. I was

a little stranger, which at my entrance into the world was saluted and surrounded with innumerable joys. My knowledge was divine. I knew by intuition those things which since my apostasy I collected again, by the highest reason. My very ignorance was advantageous. I seemed as one brought into the estate of innocence. All things were spotless and pure and glorious: yea, and infinitely mine, and joyful and precious. I knew not that there were any sins, or complaints, or laws. I dreamed not of poverties, contentions or vices. All tears and quarrels were hidden from my eyes. Everything was at rest, free, and immortal. I knew nothing of sickness or death, or exaction, in the absence of these I was entertained like an angel with the works of God in their splendor and glory; I saw all in the peace of Eden; heaven and earth did sing my Creator's praises, and could not make more melody to Adam than to me. All time was eternity, and a perpetual sabbath. Is it not strange that an infant should be heir of the world, and see those mysteries which the books of the learned never unfold?

The corn was orient and immortal wheat, which never should be reaped, nor was ever sown. I thought it had stood from everlasting to everlasting. The dust and stones of the street were as precious as gold. The gates were at first the end of the world, the green trees when I saw them first through one of the gates transported and ravished me; their sweetness and unusual beauty made my heart to leap, and almost mad with ecstasy, they were such strange and wonderful things. The men! O what venerable and reverend creatures did the aged seem! Immortal cherubims! And young men glittering and sparkling angels, and maids strange seraphic pieces of life and beauty! Boys and girls tumbling in the street, and playing, were moving jewels. I knew not that they were born or should die. But all things abided eternally as they were in their proper places. Eternity was manifest in the light of the day, and something infinite behind everything appeared: which talked with my expectation and moved my desire. The city seemed to stand in Eden, or to be built in heaven. The streets were mine, the temple was mine, the people were mine, their clothes and gold and silver were mine, as much as their sparkling eyes, fair skins and ruddy faces. The skies were mine, and so were the sun and moon and stars, and all the world was mine, and I the only spectator and enjoyer of it. I knew no churlish properties, nor bounds nor divisions: but all properties and divisions were mine: all treasures and the possessors of them. So that with much ado I was corrupted; and made to learn the dirty devices of this world. Which now I unlearn, and become as it were a little child again, that I may enter into the kingdom of God.

—Thomas Traherne

Be still, and know that I am God.

—Psalms

Do not seek after truth. Merely cease to hold opinions.

—Zen

The amount of hostility I have encountered [to the idea of enlighten-
ment] is fantastic! Why are people so unbelievably uneasy and disturbed
about this? . . . I believe I can easily (though not quickly) convey the . . .
notion of enlightenment to anybody who is sympathetic to it. But in a
hundred million kalpas,[†] no words of mine can convey it to one who is
not. For any such words I can find, he can find more clever words to
show that what I am saying is as empty as the babbling of a stream. The
curious thing, though, is that the babble of a stream is itself something
so remarkably close to enlightenment!

—RAYMOND M. SMULLYAN

The only important thing is liberation—people should not be attached
to the means.

— ZEN MASTER YUANWU

Out of mist, God's
Blind hand gropes to find
Your face. The fingers
Want to memorize your face. The fingers
Will be wet with the tears of your eyes. God

Wants only to love you, perhaps.

—ROBERT PENN WARREN

[†]Kalpa—the period of time it would take an angel who descended from heav-
en once a year and brushed its wings once across the top of a mile-high mountain to wear the mountain down.

You who assume that you have at last found the best religion, or rather the best teachers, and fixed your credulity on them, how do you know that they are the best among those who have taught other religions, or now teach or shall hereafter teach them? Have you examined all those religions both ancient and modern which are taught here and in India and all the world over? And supposing you have duly examined them, how do you know you have chosen the best?

—BARUCH SPINOZA

Those who are regarded as believers or religious people, and who are incapable because of habit from behaving in any other manner, may be called religious but cannot be regarded as having faith. If, on the other hand, this is faith, then some other word should be used to convey the kind of faith which is not produced by the parents or surroundings of a person.

—PAHLAWAN-I-ZAIF

Master Shaku Soen liked to take an evening stroll through a nearby village. One day he heard loud lamentations from a house and, on entering quietly, realized that the householder had died and the family and neighbors were crying. He sat down and cried with them. An old man noticed him and remarked, rather shaken on seeing the famous master crying with them: "I would have thought that you at least were beyond such things." "But it is this which puts me beyond it," replied the master with a sob.

—ZEN

What a wonderful life I've had! I only wish I'd realized it sooner.

—COLETTE

Before enlightenment, I chopped wood and carried water; after enlightenment, I chopped wood and carried water.

—ZEN

The birds have vanished into the sky,
and now the last cloud drains away.

We sit together, the mountain and me,
until only the mountain remains.

—LI PO

Nasrudin was now an old man. Sitting with his friends in a tea shop, he was looking back on his life.

"When I was young," he said, "I was fiery—I wanted to awaken everyone. I prayed to Allah to give me the strength to change the world.

"In my middle age, I realized one morning that my life was half over and that I had changed no one. So I prayed to Allah to give me strength to change those around me, who were in so much need of it."

"Now, alas, I am old and my prayer is simpler. 'Allah,' I ask, 'please give me the strength to at least change myself.'"

—SUFI

I will to know you, unknown one,
You who seize me deep in my soul,
You who roam through my life like a storm,
You, inconceivable, are kin to me!
I will to know you, even serve you.

—FRIEDRICH WILHELM NIETZSCHE

All human evil comes from a single cause, man's inability to sit still in a room.

—BLAISE PASCAL

Why do you hasten to remove anything which hurts your eye, while if something affects your soul you postpone the cure until next year?

—HORACE

A man walking along a high road sees a great river, its near bank dangerous and frightening, its far bank safe. He collects sticks and foliage, makes a raft, paddles across the river, and reaches the other shore. Now suppose that, after he reaches the other shore, he takes the raft and puts it on his head and walks with it on his head wherever he goes. Would he be using the raft in an appropriate way? No; a reasonable man will realize that the raft has been very useful to him in crossing the river and arriving safely on the other shore, but that once he has arrived, it is proper to leave the raft behind and walk on without it. This is using the raft appropriately.

In the same way, all truths should be used to cross over; they should not be held on to once you have arrived. You should let go of even the most profound insight or the most wholesome teaching; all the more so, unwholesome teachings.

—BUDDHA

Be patient toward all that is unresolved in your heart and try to love the *questions themselves.* . . .

—RAINER MARIA RILKE

As you watch it, your life turns to dust.

—KABIR

Do not cherish the unworthy desire that the changeable might become the unchanging.

—BUDDHA

Nevertheless the flowers fall with our attachment
And the weeds spring up with our aversion.

—DŌGEN

To every thing there is a season,
    and a time to every purpose under the heaven.
A time to be born, and a time to die;
    a time to plant, and a time to pluck up that which is
    planted;

A time to kill, and a time to heal; a time to break down,
    and a time to build up;
A time to weep, and a time to laugh; a time to mourn,
    and a time to dance;
A time to cast away stones, and a time to gather stones
    together; a time to embrace, and a time to refrain from
    embracing;
A time to get, and a time to lose; a time to keep, and a
    time to cast away;
A time to rend, and a time to sew; a time to keep silence,
    and a time to speak:
A time to love, and a time to hate; a time of war, and a
    time of peace.

—ECCLESIASTES

We are not troubled by things, but by the opinions which we have of things.

—EPICTETUS

The last and most important branch of non-verbal education is training in the art of spiritual insight. . . .To know the ultimate Not-Self, which transcends the other not-selves and the ego, but which is yet closer than breathing, nearer than hands and feet—this is the consummation of human life, the end and ultimate purpose of individual existence.

—ALDOUS HUXLEY

There are two ways of spreading light: to be
The candle or the mirror that reflects it.

—EDITH WHARTON

When a man takes one step toward God, God takes more steps toward that man than there are sands in the worlds of time—this is called the Welcoming of God, or the Kaballah.

—*THE WORK OF THE CHARIOT*

Gratitude is heaven itself.

—WILLIAM BLAKE

May God multiply for me all that I desire for you.

—CHRISTIAN

We shall not cease from exploration
And the end of all our exploring
Will be to arrive where we started
And know the place for the first time.

—T. S. ELIOT

The mind is its own place, and in itself can make a heaven of hell, a hell of heaven.

—JOHN MILTON

There lives more faith in honest doubt,
Believe me, than in half the creeds.

—ALFRED, LORD TENNYSON

Our life is frittered away by detail . . . Simplify, simplify.

—HENRY DAVID THOREAU

If enlightenment is not where you are standing, then where will you look?

—ZEN

A man whose mind feels that it is captive would prefer to blind himself to the fact. But if he hates falsehood, he will not do so; and in that case he will have to suffer a lot. He will beat his head against the wall until he faints. He will come to again and look with terror at the wall, until one day he begins afresh to beat his head against it; and once again he will faint. And so on endlessly and without hope. One day he will wake up on the other side of the wall.

—SIMONE WEIL

We found the Great Reality deep down within us. In the last analysis it is only there that it may be found.

—*ALCOHOLICS ANONYMOUS*[†]

[†] Known commonly as the "Big Book."

God fulfills himself in many ways,
Lest one good custom should corrupt the world.

—ALFRED, LORD TENNYSON

No one who has lived even for a fleeting moment for something other than life in its conventional sense and has experienced the exaltation that this feeling produces can then renounce his new freedom so easily.

—ANDRÉ BRETON

It is only when we realize that life is taking us nowhere that it begins to have meaning.

—P. D. OSPENSKY

It all comes back to this—just let it all be. Step over here where it is cool, out of the battle. Why not give it a try? Do you dare?

—ACHAAN CHAH

Well I am certainly wiser than this man. It is only too likely that neither of us has any knowledge to boast of; but he thinks that he knows something which he does not know, whereas I am quite conscious of my ignorance. At any rate it seems that I am wiser than he is to this small extent, that I do not think that I know what I do not know.

—SOCRATES

I don't know Who-or-What put the question, I don't know when it was put. I don't even remember answering. But at some moment I did answer Yes to Someone-or-Something—and from that hour I was certain that existence is meaningful and that, therefore, my life, in self-surrender, had a goal.

—DAG HAMMARSKJÖLD

Truth has no special time of its own. Its hour is now-always.

—ALBERT SCHWEITZER

What could begin to deny self, if there were not something in man different from self?

—WILLIAM LAW

The function of prayer is not to influence God, but rather to change the nature of the one who prays.

—SØREN KIERKEGAARD

> Since everything is but an apparition
>   Perfect in being what it is,
> Having nothing to do with good or bad,
> Acceptance or rejection,
> One may well burst out in laughter.

—LONGCHENPA

WEALTH

Eleven

Wealth

Wealth is money in great amount—not just enough with which to be financially comfortable or even affluent, but in truly great amount: tens of millions of dollars; these days, even billions. Wealth is the wherewithal to cause things to be done: businesses to be bought and sold, politicians to be elected, public opinion to be swayed, social policy to be set.

Wealth is a two-edged sword. It offers much, threatens more. You can build a cathedral with wealth, you can build a death camp with it. You can give a hundred million dollars to Save the Children, or corrupt a judiciary. Some wealthy families have looked upon their wealth as a kind of a sacred trust, administering large parts of it for the public good, like the Rockefellers and Carnegies; others have brutalized themselves with it and torn themselves apart over it, like many of the Johnson & Johnson heirs or John E. du Pont, who shot Olympic wrestler David Schultz to death.

Wealth is powerful. It is also rarely what people who don't have it imagine it to be.

F. Scott Fitzgerald wrote: "Let me tell you about the very rich. They are different from you and me. They possess and enjoy early, and it does something to them, makes them soft where we are hard, and cynical where we are trustful, in a way that, unless you were born rich, it is very difficult to understand. They think, deep in their hearts, that they are better than we are because we had to discover the compensations and refuges of life for ourselves. Even when they enter deep into our world or sink below us, they still think that they are better than we are. They are different."

In response, Ernest Hemingway, Fitzgerald's contemporary and friend, wrote in one of his own stories, "He remembered poor Julian [Fitzgerald] and his romantic awe of them and how he had started a story once that began, 'The very rich are different from you and me.' And how someone had said to Julian, 'Yes, they have more money.'"

Of the two, nearly anyone who has ever studied wealth and the wealthy would more agree with Fitzgerald.

Even on a much reduced scale, simple affluence, the possession of money remains two-edged: It can contribute to a peacefulness and sense of well-being, facilitate the enjoyment of life, and be used for self-improvement or to help others, or it can promote arrogance, bullying, callousness, selfishness, and a hunger for more.

It's unlikely that anyone reading this book—unless born to wealth—is going to become wealthy: not in the magnitude of the *truly* wealthy like Bill Gates, at $40 billion; investment genius Warren Buffett, at $21 billion; or even Oprah Winfrey, at $550 million. It is possible, but improbable. There just aren't that many Ted Turners or

Estée Lauders around, or even Kim Basingers or Michael Jordans, for that matter.

It *is* entirely possible, though, that anyone reading this book might become affluent or at least what he or she and most others would call financially comfortable. It's difficult to put a dollar figure to that, but what most people these days would consider a good or even large amount of money would be an income, say, of $125,000 a year and up and a net worth of more than $2 million. Possessing money is powerful, but rarely what people who do not have it imagine it to be. While having it in a good amount may be a part of making peace with money, it also may not—that's as much a matter of election as anything else.

Practice:
The Key

Whether creating wealth, affluence, or even simple financial comfort, the key is the same: You have to start with savings. That's a depressing thought for many people, probably most of us. The majority of people in the United States don't save any money at all, or else very little. Yet it is easier to create savings than you might think. Actually it isn't difficult at all, once you know how.

The first need is to reconceive saving: Saving is not money you're putting away, being prevented from spending, or that's being removed from you.

Saving is *spending*.

It is spending on investments. It is *buying* an investment. Even if all you do with the money is put it into a passbook savings account, you are still *spending* it. You are spending it on *yourself*. But if that's true, what are you buying with it? Profit—the interest the bank will pay you.

Buying profit is one of the best kept secrets about savings there is. The more profit you buy, the more profit you *can* buy. And of all the things money can be spent on, profit is one of the most helpful in gaining a happier and more prosperous relationship with money. Money you save is not money you're being deprived of—it is *spending*. Spending on *yourself*.

Saving doesn't have anything to do with working hard, squirreling away what you can, and using the rest to pay bills. That's drudgery and none of us will stay with it very long. Yet that is how most people *attempt* to save. No wonder they throw up their hands in frustration and give up.

When you save, when you spend on yourself this way, what you do is put money to work for you (which is only fair, since you've spent a lot of time working for it). Each of your saved dollars is like an employee—only you don't pay your employees, *they* pay *you*. They go out into the marketplace to find work. And when they do, each sends his salary back to you. Happily! You can have hundreds, thousands of employees out there working for you, even hundreds of thousands and more in this new life with money you're beginning to lead.

Consider: Spend $1,000 on savings this year, and you'll be sending 1,000 employees out to work for you. If each makes a salary of 10 percent (not unreasonable to expect in the long run), those 1,000 employees will turn $100 over to you every year. And if you allow those dollars (which you didn't have to do anything to get) to remain with your existing employees, to become *new* employees, you'll now have 1,100 employees working for you. Next year, those 1,100 employees will send back to you $110. Even if you do nothing but let your employees be, never spend another dime on them, simply allow the salary they earn to become new employees, at the end of five years you'll have *1,611* of them; at the end of ten years, *2,594*; at the end of twenty years, *6,727*;

at the end of thirty years, *17,449*! And all you did to get that was to spend a thousand dollars on yourself—on savings, on buying an investment.

Here's an even more interesting possibility: Let's say you spend $1,000 a year on savings for five years, buying yourself 1,000 employees each year to go out and work for you at the same 10 percent salary. At the end of five years, having spent $5,000, you'll have 6,507 employees; if you spend $1,000 a year for ten years, you'll have *17,213* employees; for twenty years, *63,808*; for thirty years, 189,943!

If, at the end of say twenty years you never wanted to spend another dollar on another employee, the 63,808 you *already* have would continue to send their salary of nearly *$6,500* a year to you every year for the rest of your life.

These are best kinds of employees in the world, each and every one of them devoted to working entirely on your behalf.

Echoing chapter 1, "Debt," here is something important to know about savings: You will never be able to create any if you keep incurring unsecured debt—if you keep putting dinners on a credit card, charging clothes to your department store account, falling behind on your rent, or in any other way. You cannot create savings by borrowing money; and that's what carrying unsecured debt or falling behind in your obligations is—borrowing money. Unfortunately, most people who have never saved anything, or who have saved very little, have gotten into the habit of spending money they don't have, other people's money. Then, not only must they pay that money back eventually (which gives them even less than they had before) but they must pay interest on it too—taking a double hit. It is nearly impossible to create savings when you're paying that kind of surcharge on your life.

If you have never created any savings, the best possible time to begin is somewhere between the time you finished reading the preceding sentence and the moment you begin the paragraph that follows this one. I'm serious. Take a dollar out of your wallet, or fifty cents out of your pocket, and set it aside: That's your first employee, if you don't already have any. (If you already do, but their number keeps rising and falling, and you never seem able to get it above a certain amount, then this is the time, right now, to begin increasing their number on a regular basis.)

The most important thing in creating, or increasing, savings—always—is to begin right now, no matter how plainly or on how small a scale. Here are six simple ways to do that:

The Best Deal in Town. The first step in creating savings, and by far the best deal in town, is to pay off your unsecured debt. Unsecured debt is nearly always more costly than secured debt—often carrying an interest rate of 20 percent or more. That is killer interest. Unstopped, it can wipe you out. But if you wipe out that *debt* instead, the impact on your life—the cash benefit you will reap—will be the same as if you had *invested* that money at a guaranteed 20 percent. This means that for every hundred dollars of high-interest unsecured debt you pay off, you will have about twenty dollars more each year to spend on anything you like—forever! For simply paying off your unsecured debt.

A Tip of the Hat. There are many ways to acknowledge people: jump up and down and scream when you see them, run forward through a wheat field to embrace them, pump their hand, or as in polite days gone by give them a tip of the hat as you pass. The latter is a good way to create savings. You don't have to make a great big deal of it—you can do it without much more effort than would be required by tipping your hat to them. Let's say you have $100 to spend this weekend. If we were to reduce that amount to $95, would you be seriously restricted? Not really. Most people would scarcely notice the $5 reduction at all; they'd have just as much fun and do just as well on $95 as they would have on $100. The missing $5 would be hardly more than a tip of the hat. This is an easy way to create savings, and one you'll barely notice: From every $100 you receive, remove $5—and put them into your savings account. "Top o' the morning to you." (He tips his hat and moves on.)

Out of Sight, Out of Mind. Many employers will deduct whatever amount you request from your paycheck and deposit it directly into a company-sponsored pension or savings plan, or into your own savings account or investment fund. In this arrangement, your saving is done automatically. You never get the money in hand, never have to set it aside and put it into a savings account. You deposit all of your paycheck into your checking account and spend it as you normally would, without giving a single thought to saving. Out of sight, out of mind. Since you have never even seen that money, you have little or no sense of doing without it—yet your savings keep growing. All by themselves, as if by magic. If your company offers such an arrangement, opt for it.

Thanks for a Job Well Done. Pay yourself. Pay yourself $1 (or more) each day for a task such as making your bed. Pay yourself five days a week, and take the weekend off. (You can still make your bed on the weekend if you wish, but you're on holiday and not getting paid for it.) At the end of each week, for the first three weeks of each month, put your week's pay into your savings account. The fourth week, put it into your wallet, and spend it over the weekend. On something frivolous. Be sure to spend the money *that* weekend, and on something strictly for fun, not on anything "sensible" or utilitarian. Follow this system every month: three weeks' pay into savings, one week's pay out on the town.

A Bit Extra. Decide to work one overtime hour a week, or four each month. (Assuming you get paid for overtime, preferably at a premium.) Place 80 percent of the extra money those hours bring you into savings. With the remaining 20 percent, buy yourself a gift. If you work at a profession where overtime isn't paid, then decide that once a month you'll work for half a day on a Saturday or Sunday at something that *will* bring in extra money, whatever that may be. Put 80 percent of that income into savings, and spend 20 percent on a gift for yourself.

Good, Sound Stuff. Saving money for a rainy day is a bad idea.

Surprised? Many of us were taught early that we'd better sock money away toward catastrophe or old age. But people who do that live in increasing fear of catastrophe (or subconsciously trigger one in order to release the money back into their lives) or come to resent the obligation this kind of saving represents and swing to the opposite pole, begin to spend up to limit of their income or even beyond it. I'm not suggesting that you say to hell with tomorrow and live strictly for today. But I am suggesting that you begin to look upon your savings in a new way: not as savings—but as investment money. Investing has nothing to do with get-rich-quick schemes or making a killing in the market. Investing is nothing more than putting money to work for you, rather than you working for it: safely, in ways that bring you a return that exceeds the rate of inflation. This means putting it to work in good, sound stuff. Conservative stuff. Stuff that earns you more than a savings account ever can or will. You don't need to know much about the financial markets in order to do this effectively and without risk, or with very little risk. All you do need to know is fairly simple, and most of it you'll pick up naturally as you go. The next practice, "Multiplying," will get you started.

Practice:

Multiplying

First, if you don't already have a savings account, open one. Keep your extra money there, where it will earn interest, rather than in your personal checking account, where in most cases it will not.

Then, moving up the ladder, here are the basic tools for you to use:

Free Checking Account. At the least, your checking account should be free. You should pay neither a monthly fee nor a per-check fee. Different banks have different minimum-balance requirements for this, but it shouldn't be very high. Even in New York City, one of the most expensive places in the country to live, one bank, Amalgamated, offers a completely free checking account for no minimum balance at all.

Interest-Bearing NOW Account. This is the next step up, a checking account that is not only cost-free, but which earns interest for you on your balance. Some banks require a high balance to be maintained for that privilege, in the thousands, while others a balance of only $100 to $500. Shop around.

CD. A CD is a certificate of deposit, a document from a bank certifying that you have loaned the bank a specified amount of money for a specified period of time, usually a few months to a few years. In exchange, the bank guarantees that it will pay you a higher rate of interest on the money than you could currently obtain from a simple savings account.

Treasury Securities. Treasury securities—bills, notes, and bonds—are financial instruments issued and backed by the United States Government. They offer a higher rate of return at time of purchase than could be received from a savings account. The lowest denomination is usually a note or bond, for $1,000. Maturity dates (when the instrument can be redeemed or cashed in) range from three months to thirty years. Treasury bills, notes, and bonds can all be purchased from Federal Reserve banks, from some local banks, and some brokerage houses.

Money-Market Fund. A money-market fund is a mutual fund that invests in financial instruments such as treasury bills, giant certificates of deposit, and similar, safe securities. Your money remains completely liquid—meaning you can take it out any time you wish. Money-market funds always pay more interest than savings accounts. The big ones, even though they may not be federally insured, are very safe.

401(k) Plan. The 401(k) plan is a retirement plan. Many companies sponsor them and offer them to their employees. The employee can make *tax-deductible* contributions to the plan (which is like an investment fund) that will grow *tax-deferred* until she withdraws them. Not only that, but most employers will match from 15 to 100 percent of the amount the employee puts in. For most people, 401(k) plans are a very good deal.

IRAs and Keoghs. These are private pension funds individuals can set up for themselves. Both offer certain tax benefits. IRAs are available to anyone, Keoghs only to self-employed people or employees of unincorporated businesses. (They can be a bit complicated; get qualified guidance.)

Mutual Funds. A mutual fund is a fund managed by an investment company. You and other people (shareholders) invest money in the fund, which itself then invests that money—into *what* depends on the nature of the fund. There are many kinds of funds. Some buy stocks, others bonds; some buy treasury securities or property such as mortgages, others precious metals. Some funds are ultra-conservative. Others are highly speculative. Each shareholder in a fund shares in its profits (or losses).

Bonds. A bond is a promise to pay, backed up by collateral. You loan money to a company, it issues you a bond representing the loan, and guarantees to pay you a set rate of interest twice a year over a number of years, usually ten to forty. When the bond matures, the company will redeem it by giving you your money back. You are a creditor of the company, not a stockholder (owner) in it. The company has to pay you your interest before it can pay its shareholders their dividends. If the company files for bankruptcy, its bondholders get their share of the proceeds from the sale first, before stockholders get anything. (Note: Bonds are rated for safety by agencies such as Standard & Poor's. No investment-grade—high-rated—bond has ever defaulted.) Bonds can be bought or sold by anyone at any time in the life of the bond through brokerage houses.

Stocks (Equities). When you buy stock in a company you become a part owner of it. Thus the term "shareholder"—someone who has a share in the company. Thus, also, the word *equities*, which is sometimes used in place of the word *stocks*; equity means ownership. As a shareholder (a genuine owner, no matter how tiny a fraction of the company you own), you are entitled to share in the company's earnings. You receive your part of those earnings in the form of dividend payments, which are usually distributed four times a year. You also profit from the company's growth through the rising market value of its stock. Conversely, of course, you can lose money if the value of a company's stock—and thus of the shares you own—declines.

Probably the most desirable of the basic tools presented here for most people is the 401(k) plan, offering a good return, tax advantages, and safety. Mutual stock funds, like those put forward by Vanguard, Fidelity, T. Rowe Price, and others may offer greater potential profit, but they also carry a greater risk of loss. Some funds, in their conservatism, are nearly as safe as the government, others are a cut above gambling. An axiom in all investing is: The greater the potential return, the greater the potential risk; the smaller the potential risk, the smaller the return. Nothing is ever certain in investing. It is still worth noting, however, that over the past seventy-five years the equities market has increased in value by an average of roughly 12 percent a year. That is *several times* higher than even the best savings accounts returned. It is also the long-term *average;* any given year, or cluster of years, can be catastrophic.

You will probably do well with almost *any* investment if you observe the following three rules: First, keep it simple. Learn everything you can about the kind of investment you're interested in—such as growth funds—but don't try to master the world of investments. You can't and will only drive yourself crazy if you try. Second, be conservative. Your first consideration is always safety. (So is your second, third, fourth, and fifth, for that matter.) Last, never invest in anything you don't fully understand.

Finally, to complete this practice, select three good books on investing that appeal to you, and read them over the coming year. *Inform yourself.*

Wealth is like a viper, which is harmless if a man knows how to take hold of it; but if he does not it will twine round his hand and bite him.

—St. Clement

The wise man understands equity; the small man understands only profits.

—Confucius

'Tis pitiful the things by which we are rich or poor—a matter of coins, coats and carpets, a little more or less stone, wood or paint, the fashion of a cloak or hat.

—Ralph Waldo Emerson

Socrates: There seem to be two causes of the deterioration of the arts.

Adeimantus: What are they?

Wealth, I said, and poverty.

How do they act?

The process is as follows: When a potter becomes rich, will he, think you, any longer take the same pains with his art?

Certainly not.

He will grow more and more indolent and careless?

Very true.

And the result will be that he becomes a worse
    potter?
Yes; he greatly deteriorates.
But, on the other hand, if he has no money, and
    cannot provide himself with tools or instruments, he
    will not work equally well himself, nor will he teach
    his sons or apprentices to work equally well.
Certainly not.
Then, under the influence either of poverty or of
    wealth, workmen and their work are equally liable to
    degenerate?
This is evident.
Here, then, is a discovery of new evils, I said,
    against which the guardians will have to watch, or
    they will creep into the city unobserved.
What evils?
Wealth, I said, and poverty: the one is the parent
    of luxury and indolence, and the other of meanness
    and viciousness, and both of discontent.

—PLATO

A long cry at midnight near the mosque,
        a dying cry.
The young man sitting there hears
and thinks, "That doesn't make me afraid.

Why should it?
          It's the drumbeat announcing a celebration!
It means,
          we should start cooking the joy-soup!"

He hears beyond his death-fear, to the Union.
"It's time for that Merging in me now,
or it's time to leave my body."

He jumps up and shouts to God,
If You can be human, come inside me now!

The signal of a death-yell splits him open.
Gold pours down, many kinds, from all directions,
gold coins, liquid gold, gold cloth, gold bars.
They pile up, almost blocking the doors of the mosque.

The young man works all night carrying the gold away
in sacks and burying it, and coming back for more.
The timid church-members sleep through it all.

If you think I'm talking about actual gold,
you're like those children who pretend that pieces
of broken dishes are money, so that anytime they see
pottery shards, they think of money, as when you hear
the word *gold* and think "Goody."

This is the other gold
that glows in your chest when you love.

The enchanted mosque is in *there*, and the pointed cry
is a candleflame on the altar.
                              The young man is a moth
who gambles himself and wins. A True Human Being
is not human! This candle does not burn.
                                        It illuminates.

Some candles burn themselves, and one another, up,
Others taste like a surprise of roses in a room
and you just a stranger who wandered in.

—JALAL AD-DIN RUMI

It is not the man who has too little who is poor, but the one who han-
kers after more. What difference does it make how much there is laid
away in a man's safe or in his barns, how many head of stock he grazes
or how much capital he puts out at interest, if he is always after what is
another's and only counts what he has yet to get, never what he has
already. You ask what is the proper limit to a person's wealth? First, having what is essential, and second, having what is enough.

—SENECA

It would be well, also, to collect the scattered stories of the ways in which individuals have succeeded in amassing a fortune; for all this is useful to persons who value the art of getting wealth.

—ARISTOTLE

A man is rich in proportion to the number of things which he can afford to let alone.

—HENRY DAVID THOREAU

My father's generation grew up with certain beliefs. One of those beliefs is that the amount of money one earns is a rough guide to one's contribution to the welfare and prosperity of our society. I grew up unusually close to my father. Each evening I would plop into a chair near him, sweaty from a game of baseball in the front yard, and listen to him explain why such and such was true and such and such was not. One thing that was almost always true was that people who made a lot of money were neat. Horatio Alger and all that. It took watching his son being paid 225 grand at the age of twenty-seven, after two years on the job, to shake his faith in money. He has only recently recovered from the shock.

I haven't. When you sit, as I did, at the center of what has been possibly the most absurd money game ever and benefit out of all proportion to your value to society (as much as I'd like to think I got only what I deserved, I don't), when hundreds of equally undeserving people around you are all raking it in faster than they can count it, what happens to the money belief? Well, that depends. For some, good fortune simply reinforces the belief. They take the funny money seriously, as evidence that they are worthy citizens of the Republic. It becomes their guiding assumption—for it couldn't possibly be clearly thought out—that a talent for making money come out of a telephone is a reflection of merit on a grander scale. It is tempting to believe that people who think this way eventually suffer their comeuppance. They don't. They just get richer. I'm sure most of them die fat and happy.

For me, however, the belief in the meaning of making dollars crumbled; the proposition that the more money you earn, the better the life you are leading was refuted by too much hard evidence to the contrary. And without that belief, I lost the need to make huge sums of money. The funny thing is that I was largely unaware how heavily influenced I was by the money belief until it had vanished.

—MICHAEL LEWIS

A penny saved is a penny earned.

—BENJAMIN FRANKLIN

You never find people laboring to convince you that you may live very happily upon a plentiful fortune.

—SAMUEL JOHNSON

Truth will properly blame those who without discrimination shun all concern with the life of the State, and say that they despise the acquisition of good repute and pleasure. They are only making grand pretensions, and they do not really despise these things. They go about in torn raiment and with solemn visage, and live the life of penury and hardship as a bait, to make people believe they are lovers of good conduct, temperance, and self-control. Therefore, be drunk in a sober manner.

—PHILO

It is physically impossible for a well-educated, intellectual, or brave man to make money the chief object of his thoughts; just as it is for him to make his dinner the principal object of them. All healthy people like their dinners but their dinner is not the main object of their lives. So all healthily-minded people like making money—ought to like it, and to enjoy the sensation of winning it: but the main object of their life is not money; it is something better than money.

—JOHN RUSKIN

If you should put even a little on a little, and should do this often, soon this too would become big.

—HESIOD

I cannot call riches better than the baggage of virtue; the Roman word is better, *impedimentia*: for as the baggage is to an army, so is riches to virtue; it cannot be spared nor left behind, but it hindereth the march; yea and the care of it sometimes loseth or disturbeth the victory.

—FRANCIS BACON

Riches are chiefly good because they give us time.

—CHARLES LAMB

No wealth can satisfy the covetous desire of wealth.

—JEREMY TAYLOR

The pulpit and the press have many commonplaces denouncing the thirst for wealth; but if men should take these moralists at their word, and leave off aiming to be rich, the moralists would rush to rekindle, at all hazards, this love of power in the people lest civilization should be undone.

—RALPH WALDO EMERSON

Ask a great money-maker what he wants to do with his money—he never knows. He doesn't make it to do anything with it. He gets it only that he *may* get it. "What will you make of what you have got?" you ask. "Well, I'll get more," he says. Just as, at cricket, you get more runs. There's no use in the runs, but to get more of them than other people is the game. And there's no use in the money, but to have more it than other people is the game.

—JOHN RUSKIN

We have profoundly forgotten everywhere that *Cash-payment* is not the sole relation of human beings; we think, nothing doubting, that it absolves and liquidates all engagements of man. . . .Verily Mammon-worship is a melancholy creed.

—THOMAS CARLYLE

Once upon a time a poor, pious peasant died and arrived at the gate to heaven. At the same time, a very rich man showed up and wanted to enter heaven too. Then St. Peter came with a key, opened the gate and let the rich man in. Apparently he did not see the peasant there and shut the gate again. Soon the peasant could hear from outside how the rich man was welcomed with great joy into heaven and how they played music and sang. Finally, it became quiet again, and St. Peter came, opened up the gate to heaven, and let the peasant in. The peasant thought that there would now be music and singing for him, but everything remained silent. Of course, he was welcomed with a great deal of love, and the angels came to meet him, but nobody sang. Then the peasant asked St. Peter, why nobody had sung for him the way they had for the rich man. It seemed to him that things were exactly the same in heaven as they had been on earth, where certain people were favored.

"Not at all," said St. Peter. "You're just as dear to us as anybody else, and you are entitled to all the heavenly joys just as much as the rich man. But, look, poor fellows like you come to heaven every day, while a rich man like this one comes to us only once in a hundred years."

—THE BROTHERS GRIMM

Inherited wealth is a big handicap to happiness. It is as certain death to ambition as cocaine is to morality.

—WILLIAM K. VANDERBILT

I am opposed to millionaires, but it would be dangerous to offer me the position.

—MARK TWAIN

I have no complex about wealth. I have worked hard for my money, producing things people need.

—J. PAUL GETTY

A dervish, whose joy was self-denial and whose hope was paradise, once met a prince, whose wealth exceeded everything the dervish had ever seen. The nobleman's tent, pitched outside the city for recreation, was made of precious fabrics, and even the spikes that held it up were solid gold. The dervish, who was used to preaching asceticism, attacked the prince with a flood of words about the futility of earthly wealth, the vanity of the golden tent spikes, and the fruitlessness of human endeavor. How eternal and majestic, on the other hand, were the holy places. Renunciation, he said, was the greatest happiness. The prince listened seriously and with great thought. He took the dervish's hand and said, "For me your words are like the fire of the midday sun and the clarity of the evening breeze. Friend, come with me, accompany me on the way to the holy places." Without looking back, without taking money or a servant, the prince set out on the way.

Astonished, the dervish hurried along behind him. "Lord," he cried, "tell me, are you really serious about making a pilgrimage to the holy places? If you are, then wait for me so I can go get my pilgrim's cloak."

Smiling kindly, the prince answered, "I left behind my wealth, my horses, my gold, my tent, my servants, and everything I owned. Do you have to go back just because of your cloak?"

"Lord," replied the dervish with surprise. "Please explain to me—how you could leave all your treasures behind and even go without your princely cloak?"

The prince spoke slowly but with a steady voice, "We sank the golden tent spikes into the earth, but not into our heart."

—PERSIAN

The larger the income, the harder it is to live within it.

—RICHARD WHATELY

Some of God's noblest sons, I think, will be selected from those that know how to take wealth, with all its temptations, and maintain godliness therewith. It is hard to be a saint standing in a golden niche.

—HENRY WARD BEECHER

And a certain ruler asked him, saying, Good Master,
   what shall I do to inherit eternal life?
And Jesus said unto him, Why callest thou me good? none
   is good, save one, that is, God.
Thou knowest the commandments, Do not commit adultery,
   Do not kill, Do not steal, Do not bear false witness, Honour
   thy father and thy mother.

And he said, All these have I kept from my youth up.
Now when Jesus heard these things, he said unto him,
  Yet lackest thou one thing: sell all that thou hast, and
  distribute unto the poor, and thou shalt have treasure in
  heaven: and come, follow me.
And when he heard this, he was very sorrowful: for he
  was very rich.
And when Jesus saw that he was very sorrowful, he said,
  How hardly shall they that have riches enter into the
  kingdom of God!
For it is easier for a camel to go through a needle's
  eye, than for a rich man to enter into the kingdom of God.

—LUKE 18:18–25

Adversity is something hard upon a man; but for one man who can stand prosperity, there are a hundred that will stand adversity.

—THOMAS CARLYLE

For just as poets love their own works, and fathers their own children, in the same way those who have created a fortune value their money, not merely for its uses, like other persons, but because it is their own production. This makes them moreover disagreeable companions, because they will praise nothing but riches.

—PLATO

To be clever enough to get all that money, one must be stupid enough to want it.

—G. K. Chesterton

The moral flabbiness born of the exclusive worship of the bitch-goddess SUCCESS. That—with the squalid cash interpretation put on the word success—is our national disease.

—William James

Believe not much them that seem to despise riches, for they despise them who despair of them; and none are worse than they when riches come to them.

—Francis Bacon

The love of money as a possession—as distinguished from the love of money as a means to the enjoyments and realities of life—will be recognized for what it is, a somewhat disgusting morbidity, one of those semi-criminal, semi-pathological propensities which one hands over with a shudder to the specialists in mental disease.

—John Maynard Keynes

He [the businessman] is the only man above the hangman and the scavenger who is forever apologizing for his occupation. He is the only one who always seeks to make it appear, when he attains the object of his labors, *i.e.*, the making of a great deal of money, that it was not the object of his labors.

—H. L. Mencken

He that trusteth in his riches shall fall.

—PROVERBS

To own is to fear.

—SPANISH

Among all the emotions, the rich have the least talent for love. It is possible to love one's dog, dress or duck-shooting hat, but a human being presents a more difficult problem. The rich might wish to experience feelings of affection, but it is almost impossible to chip away the enamel of their narcissism. They take up all the space in all the mirrors in the house. Their children, who represent the most present and therefore the most annoying claim on their attention, usually receive the brunt of their irritation.

—LEWIS H. LAPHAM

Consider the little mouse, how wise an animal it is which never entrusts its life to one hole only.

—PLAUTUS

Do not despise the world, for the world too is God.

—MUHAMMAD

Probably the greatest harm done by vast wealth is the harm that we of moderate means do ourselves when we let the vices of envy and hatred enter deep into our own natures.

—THEODORE ROOSEVELT

Wealth is not without its advantages and the case to the contrary, although it has often been made, has never proved widely persuasive.

—JOHN KENNETH GALBRAITH

Money is of a prolific generating nature. Money can beget money, and its offspring can beget more.

—BENJAMIN FRANKLIN

This, then, is held to be the duty of the man of wealth: First, to set an example of modest, unostentatious living, shunning display or extravagance; to provide moderately for the legitimate wants of those dependent upon him; and, after doing so, to consider all surplus revenues which come to him simply as trust funds, which he is called upon to administer, and strictly bound as a matter of duty to administer in the manner which, in his judgment, is best calculated to produce the most beneficial results for the community—the man of wealth thus becoming the mere trustee and agent for his poorer brethren, bringing to their service his superior wisdom, experience and ability to administer, doing for them better than they would or could do for themselves. . . .

The day is not far distant when the man who dies leaving behind him millions of available wealth, which was free for him to administer during life, will pass away "unwept, unhonored, and unsung," no matter to what uses he leaves the dross which he cannot take with him. Of such as these the public verdict will then be: "The man who dies thus rich dies disgraced." Such, in my opinion, is the true gospel concerning wealth, obedience to which is destined some day to solve the problem of the rich and the poor.

—ANDREW CARNEGIE

If all the rich men in the world divided up their money amongst themselves, there wouldn't be enough to go around.

—CHRISTINA STEAD

I have been poor and I have been rich. Rich is better.

—SOPHIE TUCKER

Most of the luxuries and many of the so-called comforts of life are not only not indispensable, but positive hindrances to the elevation of mankind.

—HENRY DAVID THOREAU

There must be a reason why some people can afford to live well. They must have worked for it. I only feel angry when I see waste.

—MOTHER TERESA

The saddest thing I can imagine is to get used to luxury.

—CHARLIE CHAPLIN

ABUNDANCE

Twelve

Abundance

For something to be in abundance is for it to be in great or plentiful supply, present to the point of overflowing. You can have that. To a degree, abundance is subjective; one person's vision of it is another's of deprivation. Further, anyone's idea of it will change as time passes, as her life changes. Still, each of us knows for himself or herself what abundance is. We each have a clear sense of what abundant happiness feels like, what an abundance of sunlight would be; spilled out of a boat and underwater, none of us would perceive an abundance of air.

As abundance relates to money, we can use here the same threshold definition we established in chapter 2, "Earning," in defining what we meant by a beneficial amount of money: enough to meet our basic needs on a humane level, with at least some left over to spend on items exceeding those needs or on items of higher quality, some for recreation and relaxation, and some to put into savings. That is a minimal starting point for abundance—as it relates to money. But it is difficult to restrict the concept of abundance to money alone. Nor, in making peace with money, should we.

Practice:
Making Its Acquaintance

There is already a great deal of abundance in your life—in *everyone's* life. But many of us can't see that or experience it. This is especially true when our relationship with money has not been peaceful. The first step in knowing, or having, abundance is to become acquainted with it.

To begin, practice abundance for ten days. Practice it by becoming aware of it and of your use of it. Start by identifying a single area in your life where there is abundance. There *is* one, regardless of your circumstances. If you look for it, you will find it. The easiest way to recognize it is to narrow your field of focus. Look at a specific part of your life, your personal library, for example. Let's say you are someone for whom reading is important and that you have a great many books. You have hardcovers and paperbacks, oversize books, books in good bindings, old and rare books, new books, books both read and unread, books that are your favorites, books that are pleasurable simply to take down from the shelves and touch. You have books in plentiful number, in much more than sufficient supply; you have an abundance of books.

Or it might be the greenery around your house: an expanse of lawn, trees, shrubs, plants—an abundance of greenery. Or perhaps you like to dance, are graceful, instinctively respond to music with movement, inner and outer, *feel* rhythm, are moved to express something, demonstrate something, delight in the feel of your body as you dance—ability in abundance. Or you might have an abundance of youth, physical strength, or height; or an abundance of wisdom and insight, of the kind that can come only through experience and age. There may be an abundance of sunlight in your days, of empty space on your hard drive, of dinnerware in your kitchen cabinets, of love from your dog.

Each day in this ten-day period identify, in the morning, a new area in your life in which there is abundance. Then throughout the day, consciously bring awareness of this abundance to mind at different times; contemplate it for several moments; think about it; picture it; let yourself *feel* it—the fullness and reality of this abundance in your life.

While looking over your life for an area in which there is abundance, don't pause if you come across one that seems not only *not* abundant but in fact downright impoverished. You already know how to feel lack and deprivation. Here we're learning to recognize and experience abundance. And anyway, we'll be addressing lack and deprivation in the next practice. Before we do, though, there are two more parts of *this* practice to complete.

After you have finished your ten-day period of identifying and experiencing separate areas of abundance in your life, begin another set of ten days. This time, pick an area each day that is *outside* yourself or your immediate life. Pick one that offers abundance you *could* partake of, if you wished to: a park, an ocean or river to walk by, public concerts, your library system, sports teams, meditation training, the company of

friends, opportunities to spend time with children or animals,
comedians on television, long baths, places to learn new crafts and
skills or master intellectual material. Each day, consciously bring
awareness of this particular abundance to mind. Contemplate it for
several moments. Think about it. Picture it. Let yourself *feel* it—the
fullness and reality of it as abundance that is available to you, that you
could partake of.

After you have completed this second set of days, undertake a third
and final set. This time, bring to mind each day at different times the
knowledge, the *awareness* of abundance as a sea in which you live, as
something very literally all about you. Contemplate it. Think about it.
Picture it. Let yourself *feel* it. Know the reality and fullness of it; know
it mentally, spiritually, and emotionally.

Practice:

Why Is There Not?

Recognizing and understanding abundance—having the internal
experience of it—which was the point of the previous practice, is valuable and pleasurable in itself. It is also a necessary preparation for *this*
practice, which is a way to bring abundance into places in your life
where there is none: Before we can do that, we need to know that
abundance exists. We need to know it is all about us. We need to know
what it feels like to have it.

This practice is simple. Pick one area, not money at first, where you feel there is not abundance in your life. It can be anything: romance, friendships, time, towels, recreation, artworks, energy, computers, cooking ware. Then ask yourself: Why is there not? Answer the question. Write down all the reasons. Then ask: What could I do to change that? Answer the question. Write down as many things you could do as you can think of, large or small. Then finally: Do those things.

Do not undertake this practice with money until you have completed it in half a dozen other areas of your life. After that, with experience behind you, you'll be more effective at it. And by then, doing it with money might well be superfluous.

I laugh when I hear the fish in the water is thirsty.

—KABIR

I desire it may be understood that I am now speaking, not of that inferior species of amity which occurs in the common intercourse of the world (although this, too, is not without its pleasures and advantages), but of that genuine and perfect friendship, examples of which are so extremely rare as to be rendered memorable by their singularity. It is this sort alone that can truly be said to heighten the joys of prosperity, and mitigate the sorrows of adversity, by a generous participation of both; indeed, one of the chief among the many important offices of this connection is exerted in the day of affliction, by dispelling the gloom that overcasts the mind, encouraging the hope of happier times, and preventing the depressed spirits from sinking into a state of weak and unmanly despondence. Whoever is in possession of a true friend sees the exact counterpart of his own soul. In consequence of this moral resemblance between them, they are so intimately one that no advantage can attend either which does not equally communicate itself to both; they are strong in the strength, rich in the opulence, and powerful in the power of each other. They can scarcely, indeed, be considered in any respect as separate individuals, and wherever the one appears the other is virtually present. I will venture even a bolder assertion, and affirm that in despite of death they must both continue to exist so long as either of them shall remain alive; for the deceased may, in a certain sense, be said still to live whose memory is preserved with the highest veneration and the most tender regret in the bosom of the survivor, a circumstance which renders the former happy in death, and the latter honored in life.

If that benevolent principle which thus intimately unites two persons in the bands of amity were to be struck out of the human heart, it would be impossible that either private families or public communities should subsist—even the land itself would lie waste, and desolation overspread the earth. Should this assertion stand in need of a proof, it will appear evident by considering the ruinous consequences which ensue from discord and dissension; for what family is so securely established, or what government fixed upon so firm a basis, that it would not be overturned and utterly destroyed were a general spirit of enmity and malevolence to break forth amongst its members?—a sufficient argument, surely, of the inestimable benefits which flow from the kind and friendly affections.

—CICERO

I'd like to live like a poor man with lots of money.

—PABLO PICASSO

Hell is the state in which we are barred from receiving what we truly need because of the value we give to what we merely want.

—JACOB NEEDLEMAN

Abundance is from activity.

—TURKISH

The rich, visiting industrialist was horrified to find a local fisherman lying lazily beside his boat, smoking a pipe.

"Why aren't you out fishing?" said the industrialist.

"Because I've caught enough fish for the day," said the fisherman.

"Why don't you catch some more?"

"What would I do with it?"

"Earn more money. And with that, you could get a motor for your boat so you could go out into deeper waters and catch more fish.

"Then you'd make enough to buy nylon nets. These would bring you even more fish and more money. Soon you would have enough to own two boats . . . even a fleet of boats. You would be a rich man like me."

"What would I do then?"

"Why, really enjoy life!"

"What do you think I'm doing right now?"

—AMERICAN

The animals met in assembly and began to complain that humans were always taking things away from them.

"They take my milk," said the cow. "They take my eggs," said the hen. "They take my flesh for bacon," said the hog. "They hunt me for my oil," said the whale.

Finally the snail spoke. "I have something they would certainly take away from me if they could. Something they want more than anything else. I have *time*."

—HINDU

I am indeed rich, since my income is superior to my expense, and my expense is equal to my wishes.

—EDWARD GIBBON

Human felicity is produced not so much by great pieces of good fortune that seldom happen, as by little advantages that occur every day.

—BENJAMIN FRANKLIN

One time, investigating in the backyard of our house in Temuco the tiny objects and minuscule beings of my world, I came upon a hole in one of the boards of the fence. I looked through the hole and saw a landscape like that behind our house, uncared for, and wild. I moved back a few steps, because I sensed vaguely that something was about to happen. All of a sudden a hand appeared—a tiny hand of a boy about my own age. By the time I came close again, the hand was gone and in its place there was a marvelous white sheep.

The sheep's wool was faded. Its wheels had escaped. All of this only made it more authentic. I had never seen such a wonderful sheep. I looked back through the hole but the boy had disappeared. I went into the house and brought out a treasure of my own: a pinecone, opened, full of odor and resin, which I adored. I set it down in the same spot and went off with the sheep.

I never saw either the hand or the boy again. And I have never again seen a sheep like that either. The toy I lost finally in a fire. But even now, in 1954, almost fifty years old, whenever I pass a toy shop, I look furtively into the window, but it's no use. They don't make sheep like that anymore.

I have been a lucky man. To feel the intimacy of brothers is a marvelous thing in life. To feel the love of people whom we love is a fire that feeds our life. But to feel the affection that comes from those whom we do not know, from those unknown to us, who are watching over our sleep and solitude, over our dangers and our weaknesses—that is something still greater and more beautiful because it widens out the boundaries of our being, and unites all living things.

That exchange brought home to me for the first time a precious idea: that all of humanity is somehow together. That experience came to me again much later; this time it stood out strikingly against a background of trouble and persecution.

It won't surprise you then that I attempted to give something resiny, earthlike, and fragrant in exchange for human brotherhood. Just as I once left the pinecone by the fence, I have since left my words on the door of so many people who were unknown to me, people in prison, or hunted, or alone.

That is the great lesson I learned in my childhood, in the backyard of a lonely house. Maybe it was nothing but a game two boys played who didn't know each other and wanted to pass to the other some good things of life. Yet maybe this small and mysterious exchange of gifts remained inside me also, deep and indestructible, giving my poetry light.

—PABLO NERUDA

Lives based on having are less free than lives based either on doing or on being.

—WILLIAM JAMES

The luxury of doing good surpasses every other personal enjoyment.

—JOHN GAY

There were two old men who had lived together for many years, and they never quarreled. Now one of them said: Let us try to quarrel once just like other people do. And the other replied: I don't know how a quarrel happens. Then the first said: Look, I put a brick between us, and I say, This is mine, and you say, No, it's mine, and after that a quarrel begins. So they placed a brick between them, and one of them said: This is mine, and the other said: No, it's mine. And he replied: Indeed, it's all yours, so take it away with you! And they went away unable to fight with each other.

—DESERT FATHERS

A dog was given a fine meaty bone by a friendly neighbor. On his way home, with the bone firmly between his teeth, the animal had to cross a bridge over a narrow stream. When he reached the middle of the bridge the dog paused to look into the water and saw his own reflection magnified. Thinking that the other dog had a larger bone, the animal decided to take it by force. He leaned over and snapped at his own reflection. As he did so, the bone between his teeth fell into the water and was lost.

—AESOP

Phaedrus:	But let us go, now that it has become less oppressively hot.
Socrates:	Shouldn't we first offer a prayer?
Phaedrus:	Of course.
Socrates:	Dear Pan, and all you other gods who live here, grant that I may become beautiful within, and that whatever outward things I have may be in harmony with the spirit inside me. May I understand that it is only the wise who are rich, and may I have only as much money as a temperate person needs. —Is there anything else that we can ask for, Phaedrus? For me, that prayer is enough.
Phaedrus:	Make it a prayer for me too, since friends have all things in common.
Socrates:	Let's be going.

—PLATO

I love laughing.

—William Blake

Blessed are the man and the woman
   who have grown beyond their greed
   and have put an end to their hatred
   and no longer nourish illusions.
But they delight in the way things are
   and keep their hearts open, day and night.
They are trees planted near flowing rivers,
   which bear fruit when they are ready.
Their leaves will not fall or wither.
   Everything they do will succeed.

—Psalm 1

It is over. What is over?
   Nay, how much is over truly:
Harvest days we toiled to sow for;
   Now the sheaves are gathered newly,
   Now the wheat is garnered duly.
It is finished. What is finished?
   Much is finished known or unknown:
Lives are finished; time diminished;
   Was the fallow field left unsown?
   Will these buds be always unblown?

It suffices. What suffices?
   All suffices reckoned rightly:
Spring shall bloom where now the ice is,
   Roses make the bramble sightly,
   And the quickening sun shine brightly,
   And the latter wind blow lightly,
And my garden teem with spices.

—Christina Rossetti

A man who is very busy seldom changes his opinions.

—Friedrich Wilhelm Nietzsche

Laughter, like jesting, is mere pleasure; and therefore is in itself good, so it be not excessive. Surely 'tis but an ill-favored and sour superstition that forbids rejoicing. For why is it a better deed to quench thirst and hunger than to drive out melancholy? This is my way of life, and thus have I attuned my mind. No deity, nor anyone but an envious churl hath delight in my infirmity and inconvenience, nor reckons toward our virtues weeping, sobs, fear, and other such matters which are tokens of a feeble mind; but on the contrary, the more we are moved with pleasure, the more we pass to greater perfection, that is, the more must we needs partake of the divine nature. Therefore it is the wise man's part to use the world and delight himself in it as he best may, not indeed to satiety, which is no delight. A wise man, I say, will recruit and refresh himself with temperate and pleasant meat and drink, yea and with perfumes, the fair prospect of green woods, apparel, music, sports and exercises, stage-plays and the like, which every man may enjoy without harm to his neighbor. For the human body is compounded of very many parts different of kind, which ever stand in need of new and various nourishment, that the whole body alike may be fit for all actions incident to its kind, and that by consequence the mind may be equally fit for apprehending many things at once.

—BARUCH SPINOZA

Scatter Joy.

—RALPH WALDO EMERSON

If I had my life to live over, I would start barefoot earlier in the spring and stay that way later in the fall. I would go to more dances. I would ride more merry-go-rounds. I would pick more daisies.

—NADINE STRAIN

I have laid aside business, and gone a-fishing.

—IZAAK WALTON

Here is God's plenty.

—JOHN DRYDEN

Look, children, hailstones!
Let's rush out!

—BASHO

A MISCELLANY OF PRACTICES

Thirteen

A Miscellany of Practices

This chapter is a miscellany of practices that can help you in special circumstances. To be successful with them, you will need already to have worked with or at least be working with the practices and material in the previous chapters. I can't overstress the importance of that.

These distinct circumstances are:

1. Inheritance Money
2. Trust Fund or Family Money
3. Compulsive Shopping or Thrill Spending
4. Being Out of Work
5. Anorectic Spending
6. Excessive Giving
7. Service and Community
8. Self-Employment
9. Unequal Incomes in a Marriage or Partnership
10. De-Evilizing Money

Practices For:

Inheritance Money

Many people run through money they inherit in as little as three years, two, or even one. The amount doesn't make much difference, whether it's $50,000, $500,000, or $5 million. They wake up and the money is gone. They may have a closetful of good clothes, a couple of costly toys, and maybe a house or co-op that's too expensive for them to maintain left, but not much more. The money is gone.

Any of several reasons, or a combination of them, can be responsible for this in a given person: no history of ever having handled money well, giddiness or disorientation in the face of greatly increased possibilities, fear of the responsibility, a triggering of greed and unrestricted appetite, or a feeling of guilt or wrongness about the inheritance, a sense that it is undeserved, shouldn't be possessed, that it came only through the death of a loved one. The last is especially powerful in people who coveted the money they knew was going to come to them someday or who disliked the person—most often a parent—who left it to them; or worse, both.

Know the Psychological Dynamics. Be aware that these psychological dynamics exist. Recognizing them at work in you goes a good way toward not falling victim to them. If they are particularly strong, you may want to consider a few months of psychotherapy focused directly on your inheritance and your feelings about it to help you deal with them.

A Planner. Consider working with a certified financial planner, too. You will want to establish a long-range strategy for using and managing the money before you make any significant expenditures. In the case of large inheritances—in the several millions or more—work with a planner, adviser, or counselor who specializes in just such estates.

Tithing. A powerful corrective for people who feel guilty or wrong about an inheritance, that they shouldn't have it, that they don't deserve it, is to tithe it—give away 10 percent of it. This can be tremendously liberating. For many people, it purifies or cleanses the remaining money, freeing them to accept it and use it with gratitude and little lingering encumbrance.

Thirds. If the inheritance is small—and what constitutes that is a subjective call—you might want to put a third of it toward paying off unsecured debts (if you still have any of those left) or into investments, a third into upgrading or improving your home or the furnishings in it, and the final third, over the coming twelve months, into spending in those categories that most contribute to your sense of well-being and enjoyment of life: dining out, entertainment, travel, a retreat, a skiing vacation, and the like.

Trio Press. Trio Press* publishes six specialized titles in this area, including *For Love and/or Money: The Impact of Inherited Wealth on*

*Trio Press, The Inheritance Project, P.O. Box 933, Blacksburg, VA 24063-0933.

Relationships, and *Inheritors and Work: The Search for Purpose*. You may find their books helpful.

Practice for:

Trust Fund or Family Money

Having a trust fund or access to family money can be a blessing; it can also be, and often is, a curse. Of the people I have known personally over the past two decades who had monthly incomes from trust funds and/or received regular cash gifts or support from wealthy parents—frequently in amounts more, sometimes much more, than enough on which to live humanely—*all* were in unsecured debt and nearly each felt that he or she was not being given enough. Obviously none of these people was living in peace with money. Some later went on to do so, eventually paying off their debts, surrendering or losing their sense of deprivation or victimization, and, in the main, bringing more money into their lives, earning it, on a regular basis than they ever had before. Those who did, did it using many of the practices and other material in this book.

Now, my experience with such people—even over many years of working and writing in the areas of debt, earning, and making peace with money—is clearly not a large scientific study. And I have no doubt that there are some people in similar circumstances who *do* live peacefully with money, and naturally. But consider: What is your *own* experience of trust funds or access to family money, and the experience of people you know? And consider: The research of Thomas J. Stanley, Ph.D., and William D. Danko, Ph.D.[†] demonstrates conclusively that grown children from affluent or wealthy families who receive regular cash gifts or supplements from their parents are more likely to be in debt than those who don't, are less productive, spend more profligately, save little or nothing at all, often can't distinguish between their wealth and the wealth of their gift-giving parents, and are more significantly dependent on credit than their peers. Here is a way to remedy that.

Through Your Own Contributions. Few things are as satisfying and pleasurable as being wholly self-supporting through your own contributions—especially when you've had a history of not being so, of relying on gifts, debt, and stipends to supplement what you earn. The German proverb is, "Whose bread I eat, his song I sing." The old English proverb is, "He who pays the piper calls the tune." Both are painfully true. If a parent or anyone else supports you, or even contributes to your support, he or she is going to want a say in your life. (Just as you would, sooner or later, if you were supporting or helping to support someone else.) Feeling dependent on this support, you become highly sensitive to anything that person says about how you live or what you do with your money. You grow angry, you become resentful, and probably guilty and ashamed as well.

[†] Summarized in their book *The Millionaire Next Door.*

The only real remedy for this is to become self-supporting through your own contributions. This does not mean renouncing income from a trust fund or refusing cash gifts from your family (though in the latter case, where the relationship is difficult, turning down the gifts might be best). It does mean, though, that eventually you will need to give up basic monthly support from your family, if you're receiving that now.

The first step in becoming wholly self-supporting through your own contributions is to determine what your monthly expenses would be if you were so—if you were bringing in enough money yourself with which to live on a humane level. Not necessarily the one on which you're living now, but one that *most* people would consider humane. (You may find my book *How to Get Out of Debt, Stay Out of Debt & Live Prosperously* useful here.)

The second step is to begin earning that amount. Chapters 2 and 3 in this book will help you in that. (You may also find my book *Earn What You Deserve: How to Stop Underearning & Start Thriving* useful in *this* step.)

The third step, to be taken only after you're earning enough on which to support yourself humanely, is to let go of the monthly or periodic support you have been receiving from your family. Give it up, even if that means you will have to reduce the scale on which you have been living till now. You do *not* need to surrender the income from a trust fund—that trust fund is yours, it belongs to you—or to turn down an occasional cash gift, providing you're not soliciting such gifts, either subtly or not so subtly, and providing that you could live without them.

The last step—now that you are wholly self-supporting, able to meet all your own needs humanely yourself—is to use the income from your trust fund or the occasional family gift to complement or upgrade your style of living, put into investments, contribute to charities and other good causes, or a combination of those. One very satisfying thing you might do with some of it is to establish a little charitable foundation, make an endowment, or set up a grant or prize of some kind.

I have never had a trust fund or family money myself, but I have on occasion, despite a history of debt and underearning, been fortunate enough to make more money than I had anticipated or immediately needed. Once, when I lived in the mountains of upstate New York, I established anonymously at the local high school and junior high a literary prize for fiction. (It was named after the dominant local river, the Esopus, situated across the road from the schools.) The prize carried small cash awards for the top three entries in both schools. The contest stimulated about forty entries from each, some quite good, all showing effort and thought, and nearly all, I was told by my liaison at the school, being a source of pleasure or self-esteem for their writers. I and my then-wife (who was also a writer) read every entry. In addition to picking the winners, we wrote a short paragraph of comment for each author, finding something to praise in each story and offering constructive suggestions.

Now it's true that my wife and I put a fair amount of time into that prize as well as the cash I contributed, but we got a lot back, too, in personal satisfaction, from seeing the fullness, care, and enthusiasm of response of the preteen and teenage students who entered. I sustained the prize over the next few years until my life changed, and I no longer lived in that area. Establishing the prize was one of the things I have done over the course of my life that I like best. You might find that you enjoy doing something like this, too.

Becoming wholly self-supporting through your own contributions, when you have not been so, is tremendously liberating—psychologically, emotionally, and spiritually.

"Whose bread I eat, his song I sing." Your bread, your song.

"He who pays the piper calls the tune." True. What tune would you like?

Practices for:

Compulsive Shopping or Thrill Spending

In the main, compulsive shopping and thrill spending are attempts to fill an internal emptiness (surrogates for love, security, meaning, recognition, or other perceived lacks); are done for excitement; are used as mood changers (to cure boredom, escape loneliness, provide comfort, smother uncomfortable feelings); are a manifestation of a sense of entitlement, grandiosity, or anger; express a wish to remain infantile and be taken care of; or are an acting out of negative beliefs, such as "I'm not enough" or "I don't deserve anything" (and consequently stripping the money from one's life).

Know Where They Come From. Admitting that compulsive shopping or thrill spending isn't something that's just happening in your life, over which you have no control, but is rather the result of certain psychological dynamics within you, and learning to recognize and name those dynamics will help you begin to overcome the problem. Psychotherapy may also help, particularly if the shopping or spending is truly compulsive and resulting in impoverishment or deep indebtedness. Daily meditation will help—*daily*, not hit or miss. So, in some cases, will a regular program of exercise.

Make a Spending Plan. A Spending Plan isn't a budget—it is a *plan*. It is not an absolute, it is merely a set of guidelines to point you in the direction you wish to go. Do you want a blazer and some shirts and slacks or would you prefer a formal suit? Should you buy a video camera or new speakers? Do you wish to spend the money flying to Spain or renting a cottage in the Hamptons?

Make at least some kind of plan for your spending each month. Be sure to include spending—on a sensible level—for entertainment, clothes, and other categories that enhance your life, unless you have a history of being excessive in any of those areas. In that case, plan to spend in that category only every other month, and in the months that you do, minimize the amount you allocate to it.

Dealing with Difficult Emotions. Everyone has these feelings; no one likes them. Some people ride them out, others try to change them. There are an infinite number of ways to change them, from working out in a gym to asking a friend to go dancing with you to building a model ship or catching a movie. Draw up a list of non-spending ways you could change your mood for the better *before* the difficult emotions come. You might not feel capable of thinking of other ways or motivated to do so if you're already in the difficult state. It is easier to refer to such a list at that point than to try to create one, and easier to undertake an action for relief when it has already been preplanned. Many people find that making such a list also has a prophylactic effect. Somewhere between fifteen and twenty actions is a good number to put down.

Free Pleasuring. There are many ways you can give yourself pleasure—genuine pleasure—that cost little or even nothing. To prove this to yourself, and make a blueprint, sit down with a pad. Across the top write, "One way I could pleasure myself that's free or nearly free is . . ." Below the heading, put down the first thing that comes to mind, maybe something like "Play a game of chess with my husband" or "Go outside and throw a ball for the dog for half an hour." Then put down the next thing that comes to mind, maybe "Take a bubble bath" or "Go swimming." Then the next thing, such as "Play the guitar for an hour" or "See a smooshy, romantic movie [or a kick-ass action film]." Then the next thing. . . . List only activities you would *truly* enjoy doing, not that you think you ought to or could scrape by with.

With a little thought, you'll be able to come up with twenty to thirty possibilities. Work one, two, preferably three of them into your schedule each week. Regular partaking of inexpensive or cost-free, but *real,* pleasure helps weaken your drive to find excitement or relief—which is experienced as pleasure—through shopping or spending. It offers you pleasure without damage and begins accustoming you to the knowledge that you can experience pleasure, and quite a bit of it, in ways nearly too many to count that cost little or nothing at all.

Seeing What's There Already. Compulsive shoppers and thrill spenders end up with a lot of stuff: clothes, kitchenware, knickknacks, tools, beauty items, most anything you can think of. Don Aslett's excellent book *Clutter's Last Stand* is very effective at helping people lighten and clear out their lives. It can also help compulsive shoppers and thrill spenders to see—truly *see,* perhaps for the first time in their lives—the physical reality of what they have been doing, the impact it has had upon their environment if nothing else, and through that, gain some recognition of the spending for what it is, and though *that,* even an amelioration of it.

Practices for:
Being Out of Work

Being out of work is unpleasant. It is stressful, disorienting, and depressing. It can also make some of the practices in this book harder to follow. Not impossible, if you are willing to put forth additional effort, and think about them with care, but harder. The goal when you are out of work is twofold: first, to take charge of your financial condition, and second, to return to work as soon as possible.

Reconceive Your Situation. You are not really unemployed—you are *self-employed.* This is an important perspective. Your work in this business you own, in your self-employment, is to find a job for you. And you need to go about that work as you would any other, for any other employer. You need to show up each day, five days a week, and put in five or six hours each day: answering ads, making cold calls, canvassing friends and associates for leads, sending out letters, making appointments, seeing head hunters, executive search firms, placement agencies, and the like. Richard Bolles's book *What Color Is Your Parachute?* can help you in this. Remember: You're not unemployed, you are self-employed—in finding work for yourself.

Take Charge of Your Financial Condition. You want to keep your finances as strong as you can during this period and minimize damage to them. So generate income. Since you've limited your day's work at finding a job to five or six hours, you have another hour or two in which could do something else, something that could bring in money, anything from high-level consulting to baby-sitting. Sit down with a pad and list fifty ways you could bring in money, along with the amount each action could bring in. You might have to take less per hour during this period than would be necessary to meet your basic needs humanely if you were doing it full-time, but any income is better than none at this point—so as long as you keep putting in your daily five or six hours looking for full-time work.

Next, use a Spending Record as well as a Spending Plan. We've already discussed the plan. The *record* is a sheet of paper with the same categories as the plan, but which you use simply to *track* what you spend, with no other purpose. Record your spending each day, total the amounts in each category at the end of each week, then do a grand total at the end of the month. The record gives you a clear picture of where your money is actually going, which helps you make intelligent choices. Further, the awareness that results from simply *keeping* the record, with no conscious effort to cut spending, often reduces spending by 5 to 10 percent.

Avoid New Debt, Especially Unsecured. Try to avoid new debt during this period. The debt will only put you under pressure later, eating up great chunks of what you'll be making when you *are* working again. Generate as much income you can in the manner discussed above, reduce expenses, defer purchases and services, barter when possible, use your savings, liquidate an asset. Nearly anything is better than new debt at this time.

If you *must* borrow, use home equity. If that's not possible, secure the loan with some other kind of collateral. If you must incur unsecured debt, go first to relatives and friends, unless your relationships with them are already strained over money. Offer to pay them a point above what money-market funds are paying in interest. That can take the sting out of this kind of borrowing, for both sides. If you must take a commercial unsecured loan, seek out the lowest interest rate possible, the longest term you can get (to keep the monthly payment as low as possible for now), and no penalty for prepayment.

Finally, remember that when your self-employed workday is over, it is over—just as it would be if you were working for someone else. You need time off from this work of looking for a job to relax and rest every bit as much as you would from any other work. Take that time. Meditate. Exercise. Play.

Practice for:

Anorectic Spending

Anorectic spending is an inability or an impaired ability to spend money on yourself, or for pleasure. Anorectic spending usually originates in a poverty mentality, a perception of the world as threatening with a consequent clinging to money as a defense, fear that once begun such spending would go out of control, or the feeling that it's not proper to spend on yourself or that you doesn't deserve spending on.

A Formula for Fun. This is a potent—and I hope enjoyable—way to begin learning how to spend on yourself, which you will have to do if you are ever truly going to make peace with money. It has five parts.

1. Sit with a pad and a calculator. Figure out how much money you have in cash that is liquid. This includes money lying about the house, in your wallet, in a piggy bank, or in a drawer; it includes money in a savings account or money-market fund; and it includes money in a certificate of deposit (even though that isn't liquid in the strict sense, it is in a larger one). Come up with a total.
2. Divide the total in half.
3. Multiply that number by 5 percent. The formula is:

$$\text{Total Cash Available} \div 2 = \text{Half}$$
$$\text{Half} \times 5\% = \text{Result}$$

For example:

$$\$500 \div 2 = \$250$$
$$\$250 \times 5\% = \$12.50$$

Or:

$$\$7{,}250 \div 2 = \$3{,}625$$
$$\$3{,}625 \times 5\% = \$181.25$$

4. Over the next ten days, spend the result on yourself (in the examples above, $12.50 or $181.25). Spend it on something frivolous, pleasurable, or aesthetic, and non-needed. Spend it on something you would like but which you would never ordinarily dream of buying or doing, Spend it and enjoy it: It's what you're *supposed* to do, what you *need* to do. It is an important part of your making peace with money.

5. Repeat this act every three months over the coming year.

Practices for:

Excessive Giving

Some people give too much. Nearly always the individuals and causes to whom they give are deserving. But there are tens of millions of deserving people in the world, and tens of thousands of deserving causes. Reflecting on that for even a few moments, it becomes clear that none of us can possibly give to all of them, even in tiny amounts.

When does giving become excessive? We can't set an objective mark, but this much can be said—if you are giving to the point where you find it difficult to meet your basic expenses, or are carrying ongoing unsecured debt, or have no savings or investments, or are beginning to resent the giving you do or feel deprived or oppressed by it, or sometimes feel overwhelmed in the face of such great need, then you are almost certainly giving excessively.

Some people do so out of a conviction that good people ought to help others, some in the hope of receiving love in return, some because they can't *express* love any other way, some in order to control, not let go, or build their ego, some out of guilt or through fear that they will somehow be punished if they don't, and still others to make amends for some transgression, real or imagined.

Your first task, if you think you might be an excessive giver, is to recognize that no matter how limited your personal field of giving might be in comparison to the larger world—all the deserving people, all the worthy causes—it is probably still too large. Or, if it isn't, that you almost certainly give in amounts you cannot actually afford.

Know the Numbers, Really Know Them. Keep a Spending Record for six months. Pay close attention to the categories that are consistently low. Compare them with the amount in your giving category, no matter to whom you are giving. You will almost certainly discover that your categories involving personal care, life enhancement, and pleasure, are all quite low—even anorectic—while your giving is disproportionately high. Impress this upon your consciousness. *See* what you are doing, the self-hurt you are inflicting. Understand that you need to stop if you are to make peace with money. Stopping doesn't mean that you cease to give; it means that you cease to give excessively.

Invest and Give. First, balance your spending; that is, make sure you are spending humanely in each category that contributes to your sense of well-being. Then, limit your giving each month to an amount no greater than the amount you are putting into savings or investments that month. If you have truly brutalized yourself with excessive giving, you might need to limit yourself to giving only half the amount you are putting into savings or investments, even a quarter. These, of course, are top limits. Giving less than these limits, or even nothing at all, may be appropriate until you are confident that you have healed from this malady.

Practice:

Service and Community

This practice is a general one, rather than addressed to a particular circumstance. Isolation is difficult for everyone, and *on* everyone. It is easier to make constructive changes in our lives, and more effective, when we are part of a community, and *feel* part of it. The kind of community—secular, spiritual—matters less than that we are a member of it. It can be practically anything: the neighborhood or town in which you live, a professional association, an amateur sports league, a church, temple, or sangha, a recovery program, an underwater dive group, a bridge club. Being a member of more than one community is fine, though most of us will be more active in a given one than in the other or others.

Giving service to a community, or to particular people within it, has a powerful positive impact on your life. Service—from being treasurer of your computer club to refereeing in your child's Little League or reading to bedridden hospital patients—connects you with other human beings. It provides you with support, helps proof you against loneliness, and lowers vulnerability to depression; it lifts self-esteem, expands happiness, and gives a sense of worth and usefulness; it helps you live in the present rather than in the past or future, and is a context in which you can be known, valued, and appreciated.

If you are not connected with a community already, seek out one or two that are appropriate for you and establish yourself within them. If you are established in a community, strengthen your connection to it, and if not already doing some kind service within it, find how and where you can, and do so. The service needn't be momentous or greatly time consuming. It just needs to be service.

Practices for:

Self-Employment

Being self-employed poses problems not encountered by people who hold jobs. Self-employed people, for example, are subject to federal self-employment tax, have to make estimated tax payments every three months, need to market their services or goods on an ongoing basis, may have to buy inventory or raw materials, and may have to rent office space. They aren't given paid vacations, holidays, or medical insurance. They may have to hire assistants or full-time employees. Some work in isolation, others must supervise employees.

None of that, however, negates any of the practices and concepts in the previous twelve chapters; in fact, it may make some of them even more important. What it definitely does do, though, is require the individual to adopt some additional practices, which are irrelevant to people who have jobs.

Separate Business Money from Personal Money. Business money needs to be kept apart from personal money. Otherwise, confusion results, clarity fades, and money becomes messy, at best. You should have two sets of checking and savings or money-market accounts: one set strictly for the business, the other strictly for your personal life. Pay all business expenses out of the business checking account, keeping excess business funds or operating capital in the business savings account until needed. Do not pay any personal expenses with business money. Do not pay any business expenses with personal money. Separating business money from personal money this way will strengthen your self-employment considerably.

Deposit All Revenues into Your Business Account. Whenever you are paid for your self-employment activity, deposit the money directly into your business savings account or money-market fund. At the beginning of each month, transfer whatever amount you need to cover the month's business expenses into your business checking account.

Pay Yourself a Salary. Each month, or every two weeks, pay yourself. Pay yourself out of your business checking account. Write one check for your net salary, to deposit into your personal checking account, and another for the amount of tax that would be withheld from your gross salary if you were working for someone else, to deposit into a tax holding account. (The latter would include federal, state, and local taxes, plus another 7.5 percent for the part of your self-employment tax that is above what jobholders pay for Social Security). For example, if you estimate that you'll owe 40 percent of your gross income in combined tax liabilities after all deductions, and you want a net income of $2,500 per month, you would write yourself a net salary check for $2,500 (to deposit into your personal checking account), and a "withholding" check for $1,665 (to deposit into a personal savings or money-market account that you use *only* for storing tax monies until they are due).

Handling your money in this fashion helps you regularize your income. Even if you make $500 one month and $15,000 the next—which kind of erratic income is not unusual among certain kinds of self-employed people, such as performers or writers—you will still have a steady, predictable cash flow in your *personal* life. The business money may wax and wane, but your own "salary" stays the same each month.

Don't Touch the Money in Your Tax Account. It isn't yours. It's the government's. Treat it as if it doesn't exist, as if you worked for a corporation and the corporation had deducted that money from your check for tax withholding. If that were the case, you would never see the money. Don't see it here either. The quickest and most common way self-employed people get into debt is to live on the gross, treating all the money they receive as if it were completely theirs, putting nothing away for taxes and therefore having nothing with which to pay the government when those finally come due.

If Your Art (or Other Self-Employment Activity) Can't Support You, You Have to Support It. There's no way around this. It's fine to desire, or even hunger, to spend your days practicing your art or at some other activity you love, but if that activity can't bring you in enough money to meet your needs in a humane way, then you will have to devote however much time is necessary to doing something else, too, if you ever wish to make peace with money; something that *will* bring that money in: either working for someone else or in some other form of self-employment.

Your Self-Employment Activity Is a Business, No Matter What the Activity Is. You need to treat your self-employment activity like a business—even if it is the practice of an art—because it *is* a business. And if you don't treat it accordingly, then, like any other business that is neglected, poorly managed, and not understood, it will go under; and you will no longer be able to engage in it, and will probably have to go work for someone else. Undertake the practice "The Yellow Brick Road," from Chapter Three, specifically for your self-employment activity. Doing this will help you succeed at the activity, or if you are already succeeding at it, will strengthen it.

Take Holidays and Vacations. Treat yourself *at least* as well as any other employer would treat you. Take weekends off, just like other people do; holidays, too. Take vacations: two weeks, three weeks, more. Self-employed people, including those who own their own businesses, often work harder and put in more hours than other people do. That's all right. They work for themselves because that's what they *want* to do. Still, the work does take a toll. If you are self-employed, you *need* time off, even more than people with jobs do.

Be Aware of the Need to Generate Revenue. People who work for others don't have to wonder where their next check will come from: All they have to do is show up, do their job competently, and it will be there, regular as clockwork. Self-employed people have a steady need to find new projects, new clients. Some, such as accountants and psychotherapists, may have a core group of clients on whom they can more or less depend, and others, such as contractors or writers, may work on a single project for as long as a year or more. But even in these cases, clients will leave and projects end. When you are self-employed, it is important to keep always in mind your steady need to generate revenue. For those whose self-employment is marketing driven, as with most entrepreneurs, that awareness is generally present. Those whose self-employment is activity or talent driven—composers, painters, for example—often don't realize that, generally, they need to spend one to three hours once a week (more if appropriate) in formal marketing. That usually means calling or writing in search of new business.

Practices for:

Unequal Incomes in a Marraige or Partnership

Like self-employed people, people who live with a partner or family also face dynamics not encountered by others, people who live alone, when they are making peace with money. While the basic practices and concepts remain the same for both, there are additional practices to consider when you live with a partner.

Use Three Spending Plans. In any marriage or partnership, there are three sets of expenses: mine, yours, and the house's. The house's expenses are those we have in common, that are necessary to us as a couple, such as rent or the mortgage payment, and children's maintenance, or that benefit us both, such as a vacation or season tickets to the opera. What is helpful to any couple, and needed when the partners' incomes are unequal, are three Spending Plans—one for you, one for me, and one for the house.

Apportioning Expenses. How do we apportion household expenses fairly between us when there is a discrepancy in our incomes? Ideally we would each still pay 50 percent of our shared expenses, and in some cases that is what actually or eventually happens. But in others, it is neither reasonable nor possible. Following the three principles below will enable you to divide up your common expenses successfully.

1. Do the apportioning within the framework of this entire book, with knowledge and understanding of all its concepts and practices. Do it out of a commitment to making peace with money and do it with respect and regard for your partner.

2. Acknowledge any *legitimate* discrepancy between your incomes—one that results from the realities of life rather than underearning or one partner's distaste for working. For example: You are a medical doctor, your partner is a professor of English literature. You earn four times the income he does and can. Here, it is reasonable for you to pay a greater share of the household expenses than he; perhaps even as high as 80 percent, especially of those that are lifestyle choices such as vacations or dining out. (In some categories, it may be reasonable for you to pay 100 percent.) Of course, the reverse is true, too.

3. Factor into your plan the work that either of you does around the house that is necessary to daily living: cooking, cleaning, childwatching, lawn-mowing, house maintenance, and the like. *Factor it in as a cash contribution.* Assign a value to it by calculating how much you would have to pay someone else to perform those serv-

ices. That work, including child care, is the joint responsibility of both partners.

Personal Money, Shared Money. Both partners will be happier and there will be more harmony in the relationship when there are three separate checking accounts and three separate savings accounts—one set for each partner and one set for the house. The house's accounts are held jointly by both partners, with all shared expenses paid directly out of them. This arrangement makes clear what is the household's money and what is not, provides both partners with a sense of privacy and independence, and helps each gain a more accurate vision of his or her real circumstances.

Conferences. After you've established a household Spending Plan, schedule regular conferences with your partner in which you can sit down together to discuss everything pertinent to the household's finances and to make any decisions required. After taking care of the household's needs, you should each be free to discuss anything you would like to about your own personal finances and ask for feedback. For the first few months, hold such a meeting once a week, later on use whatever schedule keeps things running smoothly.

Live and Let Live. Finally, live and let live. Live your own life as you choose, and let your partner, your grown children, and everyone else you know live theirs as they choose—or for reasons beyond our ken, perhaps as they must. We need to attend to the beam in our own eye;

the mote in theirs is their business. Your making peace with money depends only on you. Their making peace with money, if they wish to or are ever to do so, depends only on them. We cannot ever be certain we know what is best for other people. Therefore, be kind to yourself, and to everyone else: Live, and let live.[‡]

Practices for:

De-Evilizing Money

It always surprises me to discover anew how many people think money is dirty, evil, and corrupting, that it is impossible for anyone who makes a lot of it to be an ethical or decent human being. It always surprises me to discover anew that traces of this belief still linger within *me*.

Actually, that money is evil is much more common a view than not, I think, even if some who hold it are only dimly aware that they do and in others it is only lightly held. This is not surprising: The scriptures of every major religion warn and even rail against many of money's manifestations. Our own social consciences and sensibilities sometimes make it difficult for us to use our money comfortably when others have so much less than we do, are suffering and dying around the

---

[‡]A full chapter on handling money when living with a partner or in a family appears in *Earn What You Deserve: How to Stop Underearning & Start Thriving.* You may find it helpful even if you are not an underearner.

world because of lack. And finally, we fear the power of money. We are afraid of the harm we might to do ourselves and others if we were to become truly powerful through having money, if the restraints on us were to be eliminated, if we were able to indulge ourselves in nearly any way we wanted. We are assailed steadily by examples of celebrities, film stars, athletes, politicians, celebrated artists, business giants, and others with the power that comes from money destroying themselves or damaging themselves almost beyond repair.

It's likely that by now, at this point in the book, whatever belief you may have had in the idea that money is evil, that to have it is wrong, unfair, or sinful, has been at least diminished some. Actively working with the practices and concepts in the preceding chapters will weaken it further. To help you rid yourself of it completely, here are a few practices that address the problem head-on.

Look for Yourself. No scripture from any religion condemns or warns against money *itself.* What they do condemn and warn against are certain kinds of *engagement* with money, and the increasing temptations and freedom to act on those temptations that accompany money in increasing amounts. No one ever said that money is the root of all evil. The biblical passage, in the Book of Timothy, reads, "The *love* of money is the root of all evil." And the word "love" is used there in the sense of lust or covetousness. Buddhism, which is the religion most often regarded as opposed to money and possessions, with its classic images of barefoot monks with shaven heads and begging bowls, is *not* opposed to these. It simply cautions against attachment to them. The Thai Buddhist monk and prominent social critic Sulak Sivaraska, in his book *Seeds of Peace: A Buddhist Vision for Renewing Society* writes: "Many people think that Buddhism regards poverty as a desirable quality. They equate poverty with the Buddhist virtues of simplicity and non-indulgence. But poverty, as such, was in no way praised or encouraged by the Buddha. What he regarded as important was how one gained one's wealth and how one used it. The Buddha taught not to be attached to wealth, for this creates craving and suffering."

Whatever your religious heritage or spiritual practice, look for yourself. Search out the passages on money and wealth in the scriptures of your own faith or discipline, find them in the words of its saints, sages, and holy men and women. Read them, hear what they say. It is not money that corrupts, but the *love* of money; not money, but the *attachment* to money; not money, but the *enslavement* to money; not money, but the *craving* for it. Look for yourself.

Truly Understand That Money Is Neutral. That money is anything but neutral is a belief, not a fact—a perception, like any other. You may want to return to chapter 9 again briefly, "Perception," while reflecting on this. I cited this passage from Lewis H. Lapham earlier in the book, in the chapter on money, but it is appropriate to repeat here. Taken

> from Lapham's work *Money and Class in America*, it is as concise
> and clear a statement on money's real nature as one is likely to find:

> Money is like fire, an element as little troubled by moral-
> izing as earth, air and water. Men can employ it as a tool
> or they can dance around it as if it were the incarnation
> of a god. Money votes socialist or monarchist, finds a
> profit in pornography or translations from the Bible,
> commissions Rembrandt and underwrites the technology
> of Auschwitz. It acquires its meaning from the uses to
> which it is put.

You can buy cocaine with money or feed a child. Without it, you
can't buy the cocaine; but neither can you feed a child.

On a pad, list the names of five people or organizations whom you
think are doing a lot of good in the world and using money to accomplish that. On a separate page for each, write out five good things that
each is doing with the money. Below that, write out five basically neutral
things that each *could* do with the money instead, if he or she or it chose
to. And finally, below that, write out five hurtful or destructive things
that each could do with the money instead, if he or she or it chose to.

Now reverse the process. List five people or organizations you
think are doing harm or evil with the money they have. On a separate page for each, write out five harmful or evil things each is doing
with the money. Below that, write out five basically neutral things

that each could do with the money. Then five good, people-helping, planet-helping things each could do with the money if he or she or it chose to.

Money, and having it, is neither good nor bad.

Taking Stock. How many needy infants and children are you sponsoring through Save the Children? How much money do you give to the Nature Conservancy or the World Wildlife Fund? How much did you donate this year to help find a cure for Alzheimer's disease or breast cancer, to find cheaper, safer, renewable forms of energy, to support a shelter for the homeless? How much did you give to personal friends who were truly in need through no fault of their own or to specialized causes or charities to which you might be personally attached, such as the hospice movement, AIDS home care, Associated Black Charities, or the National Organization for Women?

Ask this question of yourself for real, not just rhetorically. Take some time. Sit with your checkbook register. Search back through it for the past twelve months. Make note of any donations you made, help and support you gave. Comb your memory, too, for cash donations or contributions. Add up the total figure. What does it come to? Not much, probably. Because if you have viewed money as evil and corrupting, and the people who have it as evil and corrupted, then you have probably done an effective job of keeping it away from yourself. And if you don't have money, there just isn't much to give, no matter how worthy or needful the recipient.

What if you could afford to double the amount of money you gave last year, triple it, quadruple it—or even increase it by a factor of ten or more? You would be able to do much more good for these organizations and people. No one says you would have to do that or even that you ought to. But you could, if you wished to. People with money can usually do a great deal more good than those without it, can help a great many others.

This Would be Possible. Sit with a pad again. List ten good and beneficial things you could do for yourself and for others if you had more money. Not indulgences of appetite, such as buying a closetful of Armani suits, but truly good and beneficial things, like taking fine medical and dental care of yourself, visiting your grown children who live in other parts of the country, going off on a trekking vacation in Nepal, contributing to the support of a spiritual organization you appreciate, or even endowing a chair in religious studies at a small college. . . .

You might be asking, List good and beneficial things I could do for *myself* as well as others? Yes. You are as fundamentally worthy and deserving of as much good and care as any other person on this planet. The Thai Buddhist monk Sulak Sivaraska also wrote, "A praiseworthy Buddhist layperson seeks wealth rightfully and uses it for the good and happiness of herself and others." The same can be said of *any* praiseworthy layperson: Christian, Jewish, Muslim, secular, or anything else.

Go on. Write out the list of ten good, beneficial things you could do for yourself and others if you had more money. After you have finished, look at it. What do you think, are those reasonable things for someone to do with money?

You're Better Than You Might Fear. Your character is just fine, exactly as it is. Odds are that you think about such things: about life, your being, your character. And odds are that you find yourself more wanting and judge yourself more harshly than you find and judge other people, or than they would find and judge you. Listen—if you doubled your income next year, you could rise to the moral challenge. You could. I know it. You do, too, if you stop to think about it. If you tripled your income, you could still maintain your integrity. You are too conscious, and have come too far, for that not to be the case.

Now on the other hand, if you were to win a million dollars in the lottery next week, or two, or three, or five, or even ten, there might be a problem. There might be a problem for me, too, in that circumstance3. But there is a way to handle even that, or a similar problem on a reduced scale, such as tripling your income. Here's how.

Upon learning that you are going to get the money: First, intensify your engagement with whatever philosophy, religion, or spiritual practice guides you—right away. Second, begin doing good works, by personal labor as well as with money. Third, *immediately* set up a network of half a dozen people—ranging from friends with money who live well with it to spiritual or moral advisers and teachers whose genuineness and authenticity you know by personal experience, such as a meditation teacher, a psychotherapist, or a cleric—who are willing to serve as guides for you, as checkpoints, as agents of balance and clarity. Use this network on a regular basis for as long as is necessary or helpful. Do that, and you will be all right.

Making peace with money is a living process. Work with this book. Integrate its material into your life on a daily basis. Undertake its practices. Absorb its concepts. If you do, you *will* make peace with money. May you know happiness and pleasure as you do.

And in closing . . .

It is said that soon after his enlightenment, the Buddha passed a man on the road who was struck by the extraordinary radiance and peacefulness of his presence. The man stopped and asked, "My friend, what are you? Are you a celestial being or a god?"

"No," said the Buddha.

"Well, then, are you some kind of magician or wizard?"

Again the Buddha answered, "No."

"Are you a man?"

"No," said the Buddha.

"Well, my friend, what then are you?"

The Buddha replied, "I am awake."

Be well

For Further Reading

This isn't, and can't be, a definitive list: Different readers have different backgrounds and needs. I have picked these books because I believe they will be of the most help to the most people. The titles are placed where they are because they relate primarily to that theme, but several overlap into others as well.

One: DEBT

Feinberg, Andrew. *Downsize Your Debt.* New York: Penguin Books, 1993.
Intelligent and knowledgeable. Feinberg is less concerned with eliminating unsecured debt than with dealing with it in a less damaging way. He also addresses subjects such as prepaying mortgages and the perks offered by different credit cards.
Lawrence, Judy. *The Money Tracker.* Chicago: Dearborn Financial Publishing, 1996.
A little portable and painless way to keep track of daily expenses. It contains helpful self-diagnostic quizzes, too, and some sound money-management strategies.
Leonard, Robin. *Money Troubles: Legal Strategies to Cope with Your Debts.* 5th ed.
Berkeley, Calif.: Nolo Press, 1997. Legal strategies for coping with debts of various kinds, from student loans to alimony. Leonard is an attorney. Good short-term, nuts-and-bolts material.
Mundis, Jerrold. *How to Get Out of Debt, Stay Out of Debt & Live Prosperously.* New York: Bantam Books, 1988. A complete and detailed program for doing precisely what the title says. If you read only one book from this list, make it this one. Obviously I can't help but be biased here, but still, even if someone else had written the book, I'd recommend it just as strongly.

Two: EARNING

Cohen, Herb. *You Can Negotiate Anything*. New York: Lyle Stuart, 1980. Easy,
   delightful to read, potent. Cohen is not only a master negotiator but has been
   likened by some to a thoughtful philosopher, insightful rabbi, and brilliant Zen
   master as well. With some justification.
Kelley, Robert E. *How to Be a Star at Work: Nine Breakthrough Strategies You Need*.
   New York: Times Books, 1998. Sound and practical. Kelley teaches at Carnegie
   Mellon University's business school and consults for major corporations. He provides concrete, effective guidance that will help people at any stage of their career
   stand out, possibly vividly, from their peers.
Mundis, Jerrold. *Earn What You Deserve: How to Stop Underearning & Start
   Thriving*. New York: Bantam Books, 1995. To underearn is repeatedly to gain
   less money than you need on which to live humanely despite your desire and
   best efforts to do otherwise. Here is a comprehensive program that enables the
   reader to stop underearning, win freedom from fear of economic insecurity, and
   transform money from a cause of anxiety into something that enhances life.

Three: VISION

Bolles, Richard Nelson. *What Color Is Your Parachute?* Berkeley, Calif.: Ten Speed
   Press, 1998. (Updated every year.) A practical manual for job-hunters and
   career-changers. This book has been *the* definitive work on the subject for more
   than twenty-five years. The exercises take time and thought, but are worth the
   effort. A fine tool.
Sher, Barbara, and Barbara Smith. *I Could Do Anything If I Only Knew What It Was:
   How to Discover What You Really Want and How to Get It*. New York: Delacorte,
   1994. Sher, a psychologist and career counselor, presents practical and realistic
   ways to ferret out what it is that one genuinely wants to do. Pleasant anecdotes,
   useful techniques.
Sinetar, Marsha. *Do What You Love, the Money Will Follow: Discovering Your Right
   Livelihood*. Mahwah, N.J.: Paulist Press, 1987. Insightful, useful. Unfortunately

the title has become a catch phrase over the past decade, with millions of people tossing it around as if that were all there was to know about it, without ever having read the book. Just up and quitting your job and deciding you're going to make a living as a flutist (or whatever) because that's what you love to do isn't going to work. There's much more to it than that. But if you want to make the transition, Sinetar lays out a careful plan that, if followed, will help you.

Four: WORK

Fox, Matthew. *The Reinvention of Work: A New Vision of Livelihood for Our Time.* New York: HarperSanFrancisco, 1995. Fox, a former Catholic priest, sees widespread malaise in our current attitude toward work and proposes a new spiritual foundation for work, rooted in the unity of all things. Not greatly helpful in making practical decisions, but worthwhile for anyone trying to rethink his or her relationship to work, trying to translate personal values into work he or she can feel better about.

Toms, Justine, and Michael Toms. *True Work: The Sacred Dimension of Earning a Living.* New York: Bell Tower, 1998. Small, warm, helpful. Intended to assist people in transforming their work from something enervating into a source of pleasure and refreshment. Co-founders of the National Public Radio show "New Dimensions," the authors draw on their own lives as well as on the experience and wisdom of the many laborers in the realm of consciousness they have interviewed over the years: Joseph Campbell, R. Buckminster Fuller, the Dalai Lama, Thomas Moore, Alice Walker, Jon Kabat-Zinn, Marsha Sinetar, and others.

Whitmyer, Claude, ed. *Mindfulness and Meaningful Work: Explorations in Right Livelihood.* Berkeley, Calif.: Parallax Press, 1994. A wonderful, rich book. Edited by the director of the graduate business program at the California Institute of Integral Studies in San Francisco, it offers thirty-five essays on different aspects of mindfulness and meaningful work by writers and thinkers such as Thich Nhat Hanh, Joanna Macy, Sam Keen, Marsha Sinetar, Rick Fields, Michael Phillips,

Gary Snyder, Shunryu Suzuki, and E. F. Schumacher. Slow mining of this book will yield much value.

Five: MONEY

Needleman, Jacob. *Money and the Meaning of Life.* New York: Doubleday, 1991. Needleman, a philosopher and professor of comparative religion, contends that the primary problem with money is not that we take it too seriously, but that we don't take it seriously *enough.* Man, he says, is unlikely to be successful in a spiritual quest unless he can deal effectively with the fundamental issue of money, which has come to contain practically the whole of human activity. Insightful, wise.

Phillips, Michael. *The Seven Laws of Money.* Abridgement edition by the author, from his original 1974 book. Boston: Shambhala, 1997. A seminal work, the first to look at money clearly, unemotionally, and offer an effective, practical approach to it based solidly on humanistic values. Nothing has been lost in the abridgement; if anything, the book has become more lucid. Good, reliable.

Schor, Juliet B. *The Overspent American: Upscaling, Downshifting, and the New Consumer.* New York: Basic Books, 1998. This is an important book. Schor, a leisure economist and Harvard University professor, analyzes the crisis that has overtaken middle-class and upper-middle-class America—a culture in which spending has become the ultimate social act. Blaming neither consumers' lack of discipline nor powerful and pervasive advertising for the problem, the conclusions she draws are original and compelling; they include the concepts of competitive spending and the lives of television-series characters becoming absorbed into community referent groups. This is not a self-help book, but its insights are potentially as valuable as those in most of the other titles here in helping a reader bring about personal change.

Six: Flow

Aslett, Don. *Clutter's Last Stand.* Cincinnati, Ohio: Writers Digest Books, 1984. A marvelous book that should be read once a year for at least five consecutive years. It's about getting rid of all the *stuff* that fills up your life—junk, things, life debris. This book is freedom, and a means through which to invite in the new and finer.

Boundy, Donna. *When Money Is the Drug.* Woodstock, N.Y.: Maverick Media Resources, 1997. Reissue. (Originally published by HarperCollins, 1993.) Innovative, shrewd. Boundy names and explores a handful of strikingly common disorders about money. She understands how to have a healthy relationship with it.

Dolan, Ken, and Daria Dolan. *Smart Money: How to Be Your Own Financial Manager.* New York: Berkley Books, 1990. Personal banking, home-buying, insurance, taxes, retirement plans, and similar topics. Each is covered in a single chapter presented in the form of common questions with short, simple answers. Inclusive, reliable.

Seven: Generosity

Hyde, Lewis. *The Gift: Imagination and the Erotic Life of Property.* New York: Vintage Books, 1983. An original, perceptive analysis of the relationship between gift-giving and the creative act. Ranging comfortably across history, anthropology, folktales, psychology, and other fields, Hyde spends the first part of his book examining gift-giving cultures, gifting rituals and acts in commodity cultures, and finally usury. In the second part, he turns to Walt Whitman and Ezra Pound to study the idea of "gift" in and from the modern artist.

Katakis, Michael, ed., and Russell Chatham (Illustrator). *Sacred Trusts: Essays on Stewardship and Responsibility.* San Francisco: Mercury House, 1993. Thirty essays by writers like Frederick Turner, Gerald Vizenor, Mary Catherine Bateson, Bill McKibben, and Wendell Berry on the concept of natural stewardship, on loving and caring for the land and its life. Spirit is deep-felt here, fundamental. Many of the works are powerful, some stunning.

Salzberg, Sharon. *Lovingkindness: The Revolutionary Art of Happiness.* Boston: Shambhala, 1997. *Metta*—lovingkindness, unlimited friendliness—is a form of meditation that opens the heart. One begins by directing *metta* towards oneself; only after that is mastered does one start expanding outward. *Metta* is a 2,500-year-old practice. Salzberg, a deeply experienced mediator and one of the founders of the Insight Meditation Society in Barre, Massachusetts, nearly a quarter of a century ago, and herself a person of open heart, is a renowned teacher of this discipline.

Eight: GRACE

Chödrön, Pema. *When Things Fall Apart.* Boston: Shambhala, 1997. How to use painful emotions to cultivate wisdom, compassion (for oneself and others), and courage. Chödrön is Abbot of Gampo Abbey in Nova Scotia, the first Tibetan Buddhist monastery for Westerners in North America. A clear presentation of a powerful set of concepts and techniques.

Kurtz, Ernest, and Katherine Ketcham. *The Spirituality of Imperfection: Storytelling and the Journey to Wholeness.* New York: Bantam Books, 1992. To deny one's essential imperfection is to deny one's humanity, even one's self—and therefore to suffer. Interweaving tales from several spiritual traditions into the text, the authors write for people "who seek meaning in the absurd, peace within the chaos, light within the darkness, joy within the suffering," without denying the reality and even necessity of those, for people "who suffer from what the philosopher-psychologist William James called 'torn-to-pieces-hood.'" Intelligent, compelling, deeply empathetic.

Moran, Victoria. *Shelter for the Spirit: Create Your Own Haven in a Hectic World.* New York: HarperCollins, 1997. Graceful, pleasant. The book instructs gently, and effectively, on how to transform one's home into a place of peace and comfort, into what Thomas Moore, in his forward, calls "deep home," which can balm a troubled soul or enchant an ordinary life.

Powell, John, S. J. *Happiness Is an Inside Job.* Valencia, Calif.: Tabor Publishing, 1989. Powell, a spiritual teacher, asserts that happiness is within the reach of everyone, but that our reach for it must be inward, not outward, if ever we are truly to have it. He presents a clear, psychologically and spiritually sound ten-point program for doing that. His own personal religious (as opposed to spiritual) orientation is minimal and unobtrusive here.

Nine: PERCEPTION

de Bono, Edward. *Lateral Thinking: Creativity Step by Step.* Reissue. New York: Harper Collins, 1990. A groundbreaking book when first published thirty years ago, and still sound. Defining our classical, logical way of thinking, perceiving, and problem solving as vertical, de Bono links what he calls lateral thinking to the experience of insight, creativity, and humor, and provides techniques for fostering and strengthening lateral thinking. Challenging to read, but rewarding for those who elect to work with it.

von Oech, Roger. *A Whack on the Side of the Head: How You Can be More Creative.* Revised edition. New York: Warner Books, 1990. This is indeed a whack on the side of the head, and one that can jar loose a great number of possibilities. The book is accessible and clearly structured, the style easy and entertaining. Effective ways to knock down mental barriers and strike off mental shackles.

Ten: ENLIGHTENMENT

Anderson, Bob. *Stretching.* Bolinas, Calif.: Shelter Publications, 1980. If you choose to do no other kind of physical activity, at least stretch: you'll like it, it will keep you limber and flexible, and it will relax you, strengthen you, and help protect you from injuries. This helpful, well-executed book covers everything from daily stretches to lower back work, routines for people over fifty, others to do while sitting or watching television, others for strength development, and still others with which to warm up for various common sports and activities.

Aurelius, Marcus. *The Meditations*. Translated by Maxwell Staniforth. New York: Penguin Books, 1964. This is simply brilliant: psychologically, philosophically, spiritually. And often beautiful, too. Aurelius, a Roman emperor in the later second century C.E., and philosopher, never intended these musings on life and death for publication. He did them in his private journals, for himself. But fortunately, they were saved. My own copy of this work is tattered, thumbed, and much highlighted.

Bailey, Covert. *Smart Exercise: Burning Fat, Getting Fit*. New York: Houghton Mifflin, 1994. Bailey is friendly, confident, and very knowledgeable. An expert in fitness, he offers a clear and comprehensive guide to how muscles and metabolism work and how we can work with them, through exercise and training, to get and stay lean, healthy, and with a continuing physical sense of well-being.

Burns, David D., M.D. *Feeling Good: The New Mood Therapy*. New York: William Morrow, 1980. A fine exposition of cognitive psychology, which concerns itself with dysfunctional attitudes and perceptions that result in self-crippling depression and anxiety; offers effective techniques for reworking these into realistic and beneficial ones.

de Mello, Anthony S. J. *One Minute Wisdom*. New York: Image Books, 1985. Unfortunate title; superb anthology. Small parable/lessons drawn from the mystical traditions of East and West. The Master in these little tales is not one but many: a Hindu guru, a Zen roshi, a Taoist sage, a Jewish rabbi, a Christian monk, and a Sufi mystic. Anything by de Mello, an East Indian Jesuit and spiritual director, is worth reading.

Nhat Hanh, Thich. *The Miracle of Mindfulness*. Revised edition. Boston: Beacon Press, 1975. Simple, beautiful, lucid treatment of mindfulness, a form of meditation. Nhat Hanh is a contemporary Vietnamese Zen master. His works are elegant and of great value.

Smith, Huston. *The World's Religions*. Revised edition. New York: HarperSanFrancisco, 1991. A good and accessible introduction to the world's major religions: Hinduism, Buddhism, Taoism, Islam, Judaism, and Christianity, with a chapter on primal religions as well. Smith is learned, engaged, and unbiased, and writes well. An excellent starting point for any investigation.

Eleven: WEALTH

Bogle, John C. *Bogle on Mutual Funds.* New York: Dell, 1994. A clear, complete, no-nonsense guide to investing in mutual funds—from money-market funds to stock, bond, real-estate, and other funds. As comprehensible to beginners as to experienced investors. Excellent.

Buffett, Mary, and David Clark. *Buffettology.* New York: Rawson Associates, 1997. Warren Buffett is the most successful investor in American history, having made more than $20 billion—starting with almost nothing—and still going strong today. Here, his former daughter-in-law and co-author of this book provides a full insider's analysis of his techniques and strategies. Invaluable for long-term investors.

Clason, George S. *The Richest Man in Babylon.* New York: Hawthorn Books, 1955. A slim volume on personal finance presented in the style of parables. Clear, comprehensive treatment of basic principles. Effective and useful.

Tobias, Andrew. *The Only Investment Guide You'll Ever Need.* Revised edition. New York: Bantam, 1983. Amusingly written and sound, devoted mostly to down-to-earth investment strategies, but with some good comments on dealing with money in general.

Twelve: ABUNDANCE

Dominguez, Joe, and Vicki Robin. *Your Money or Your Life: Transforming Your Relationship with Money and Achieving Financial Independence.* New York: Viking-Penguin, 1992. The ultimate frugal-living, life-downsizing, priority-reorganizing book. The authors hold that we drain life force in trying to earn more simply so we can consume more. They present a nine-step program that involves accounting for every penny spent, avoiding every expense that can be avoided, and putting all savings into Treasury bonds until one can live off the interest. Most readers will never follow all the book's prescriptions, and probably shouldn't, but there is valuable and useful material here for everyone.

St. James, Elaine. *Simplify Your Life*. New York: Hyperion, 1994. A guide to slowing down and finding peace of mind. Practical ways to reduce the need for money, space, and material things in general, and to create a simpler, yet elegant, life. A good tool.

Stanley, Thomas J., and William D. Danko. *The Millionaire Next Door*. Atlanta, GA: Longstreet Press, 1996. There are many millionaires in the country today— a great many. You probably know some, without even knowing that you do. Most don't live flashily and 80 percent are self-made, didn't inherit any of their wealth. This excellent, comprehensive study of who the millionaires really are, how they live, and how they got that way will surprise most people. Revelatory.

Wakefield, Dan. *Creating from the Spirit: A Path to Creative Power in Art and Life*. New York: Ballantine, 1996. A wonderful book—wise, literate, humane; also insightful and passionate. Wakefield, a novelist, journalist, and screenwriter, knows the creative life deeply and knows it firsthand. Through discursive explorations, exercises, and interviews—not just with other writers and artists but with scientists, CEOs, chefs, athletes, and others as well—he offers a generous and effective means through which anyone, by means of innate, awakened creativity, can make the experience of life more abundant.

Acknowledgments

· ·

Every reasonable effort has been made to trace ownership and when necessary obtain permission for each selection included. The author apologizes if any work has been used without appropriate permission and would be glad to be told of such. Grateful acknowledgment is made to the following publishers, authors, and translators for permission to reprint from their work:

"i thank You God for most this amazing," copyright 1950, © 1978, 1991 by the Trustees for the E. E. Cummings Trust, reprinted from *Complete Poems: 1904–1962* by E. E. Cummings, edited by George J. Firmage. Copyright © 1979 by George James Firmage. Used by permission of Liveright Publishing Corporation.

"Play all the symphonies you like," version by Thomas Merton, reprinted from *The Way of Chuang Tzu*. Copyright © 1965 by the Abbey of Gethsemani, Inc. Used by permission of New Directions Publishing Corp.

Excerpts from *Taking Flight* by Anthony de Mello, copyright © 1988 by Gujarat Sahitya Prakesh; from *One Minute Wisdom* by Anthony del Mello, S. J., copyright © 1985 by Anthony de Mello, S. J.; and from *Heart of the Enlightened* by Anthony de Mello, copyright © 1989 by the Center for Spiritual Exchange. Used by permission of Doubleday, a division of Random House, Inc.

Excerpts from *Tao Te Ching,* a new English version with foreword and notes by Stephen Mitchell, translation copyright © 1988 by Stephen Mitchell; from *The Gospel According to Jesus* by Stephen Mitchell, copyright © 1991 by Stephen Mitchell; and from *The Enlightened Heart* edited by Stephen Mitchell, copyright © 1989 by Stephen Mitchell. Reprinted by permission of HarperCollins Publishers, Inc.

"The Golden Tent Spikes," "A Good Model," "A Story on the Way," "The Right Treatment," "Theory and Practice of Knowing People," "The Secret of the Seed," "Another Long Program," "The Hakim Knows Everything," and "The Teacher, a Gardener," reprinted from *Oriental Stories as Tools in Psychotherapy* by Nossrat Peseschkian. Copyright © 1986 Springer-Verlag Berlin Heidelberg. Used by permission of Springer-Verlag Berlin Heidelberg and by permission of Nossrat Peseschkian, MD, Ph.D.

"Zazen on Ching-t'ing Mountain" by Li Po, translated by Sam Hamill. Used by permission of the translator from his *Crossing the Yellow River: Three Hundred Poems from the Chinese,* BOA Editions 2000.

"The ecstatic meditation ended," and "A long cry at midnight near the mosque," by Rumi, translated by Coleman Barks, reprinted from *One-Handed Basket Weaving* by Coleman Barks, copyright © 1991 by Coleman Barks, and *Rumi: We are Three* by Coleman Barks, copyright © 1988 by Coleman Barks, Used by permission of the author.

Two poems, each beginning "In the autumn," by Izumi Shikibu, translated by Jane Hirshfield with Mariko Aratrani, reprinted from *The Ink Dark Moon* by Jane Hirshfield with Mariko Aratrani. Translation copyright © 1988 by Jane Hirshfield. Used by permission of Vintage Books, a division of Random House, Inc.

Acknowledgments

"I was alone on a sunny shore," by Edith Södergran, translated by Stina Katcha-dourian, reprinted from *Love and Solitude* by Edith Södergran, translated by Stina Katchadourian. Translation copyright © 1992 by Stina Katchadourian. Used by permission of the translator.

St. Paul's "Though I speak with the tongue of men and angels," Marcus Aurelius's "At daybreak, when you loathe the idea of leaving your bed," and "There is one type of person, who, whenever he does a kind," reprinted from *Two Suns Rising* by Jonathan Star. Copyright © 1991 by Jonathan Star. Used by permission of the author.

"Out of mist, God's," reprinted from *New and Selected Poems, 1923–1975,* copyright © 1975 by Robert Penn Warren. Used by permission of William Morris Agency, Inc. on behalf of the author.

"An Eye for an Eye," "The Two Brothers," "The Milk Cow," and "The Miser," reprinted from *Stories for Telling* by William White, copyright © 1986 Augsburg Publishing House. Used by permission of Augsburg Fortress.

"The Peasant in Heaven," "The Elves: Third Tale," "The Old Beggar Women," "The Ungrateful Son," "Simelei Mountain," and "The Gifts of the Little Folk," reprinted from *The Complete Fairy Tales of the Brothers Grimm* by Jack Zipes, translator, translation copyright © 1987 by Jack Zipes. Used by permission of Bantam Books, a division of Random House, Inc.